"THE PARABLES OF PEANUTS is filled with wonderful quotes and is a real delight to read from beginning to end. I could not possibly be more pleased." —CHARLES M. SCHULZ

"Altogether a sane, balanced, deeply serious book buttressed with those delightful cartoons."
—Publishers Weekly

"Probably the liveliest-reading and best illustrated theology being published." —Christian Herald

"Here are the major themes of Christian faith seen from the uniquely sane, down-to-earth Peanuts perspective, in a book that's funny, warm, and just plain wonderful!" —Cokesbury

"Only a fine line separates the cute from the brilliant, the scavenger and the true eclectic poet. Short crosses that line. . . . And he succeeds in making theology enjoyable."
—The Christian Century

The Parables
of
PEANUTS

Robert L. Short

FAWCETT CREST • NEW YORK

THE PARABLES OF PEANUTS

THIS BOOK CONTAINS THE COMPLETE TEXT OF THE ORIGINAL HARDCOVER EDITION.

Published by Fawcett Crest Books, a unit of CBS Publications, the Consumer Publishing Division of CBS Inc., by arrangement with Harper & Row, Publishers, Inc.

Text copyright © 1968 by Robert L. Short

ISBN: 0-449-23677-3

Scripture quotations, unless otherwise noted, are from **The Holy Bible, Revised Standard Version.** New Testament Section, copyright © 1946, and Old Testament Section, copyright © 1952, by Division of Christian Education of the National Council of the Churches of Christ in the United States of America. Reprinted by permission. The quotations noted NEB are from **The New English Bible, New Testament.** Copyright © The Delegates of the Oxford University Press and the Syndics of the Cambridge University Press 1961. Reprinted by permission.

Drawing by Joseph Hirsch (page 16) courtesy of Bantam Books, Inc.

Lines (page 17) from **Death of a Salesman** by Arthur Miller copyright 1949 by Arthur Miller. Reprinted by permission of The Viking Press, Inc., and Ashley Famous Agency, Inc.

Segment of the lyric to "Love Me With All Your Heart" by Sunny Skylar, Mario Rigual and Carlos Rigual (page 205) copyright © 1961 by Editorial Mexicana de Musica Internacional S.A.; copyright © 1961 by Peer International Corporation. Used by permission.

Lines (page 249) from "Choose Something Like a Star" from **Complete Poems of Robert Frost** copyright 1949 by Holt, Rinehart and Winston, Inc. Reprinted by permission of Holt, Rinehart and Winston, Inc.

Lines (page 268) from "For the Time Being" by W. H. Auden from **The Collected Poetry of W. H. Auden** copyright 1945 by W. H. Auden. Reprinted by permission of Random House, Inc.

Selections from **Ethics** by Dietrich Bonhoeffer reprinted by permission of The Macmillan Company and SCM Press, Ltd. Copyright © SCM Press, Ltd., 1955.

Lines (page 291) from **A Day in the Death of Joe Egg** by Peter Nichols copyright © 1967 by Peter Nichols. Reprinted by permission of Grove Press and of Faber and Faber Ltd.

Lines (page 180) from "Lord of the Dance" by Sydney Carter from **Risk—New Hymns for a New Day,** Vol. II, No. 3. Reprinted by permission of Sydney Carter.

Selections from **The Complete Poems and Plays** by T. S. Eliot reprinted by permission of Harcourt, Brace & World, Inc. and of Faber and Faber Ltd.

Peanuts cover design and **Peanuts** cartoons as arranged in this book copyright © 1968 by United Feature Syndicate, Inc.

Printed in the United States of America

14 13 12 11 10 9 8 7 6 5

For My Own Sweet Ellen Kay
. . . of whom Professor Barth must have been thinking when he wrote, "If there is a way of bringing man to repentance, it is the way of the woman who refuses to let herself be corrupted and made disobedient by his disobedience, but who in spite of his disobedience maintains her place in the order all the more firmly. . . ."

Contents

Preface

Since 1964, when *The Gospel According to Peanuts* was first published, I have been invited by amazingly divergent groups from all over the country to come and bring my *Peanuts* color slides and to speak on the theological implications I see in Charles M. Schulz's phenomenally popular comic strip, *Peanuts*. I have gone. Actually, since that time I have been so busy "un-shelling" *Peanuts* for people that I've scarcely found time to crack a book in working toward the doctorate in theology and literature I had been pursuing at the University of Chicago.

But this kind of circuit-riding from airport to airport has furnished me with the rare opportunity of a close-up inspection of the very age and body, the form and pressure, of American Christianity today. And in reporting back on what my general impression has been, I must first confess that I've always identified more closely with Linus than with any of the other *Peanuts* characters. (Linus is the little boy with the blanket, obviously the most insecure of the *Peanuts*.) For my travels and opportunities to meet

talk with countless members of countless churches have more
and more often brought to mind the following little scene:

And of course I am here thinking of "flabby" in the "spiritual"
sense, or more specifically in the Kierkegaardian sense, the kind
of sleepy flabbiness no President's Physical Fitness Program will
be able to work off, but the flabbiness of those who

> remain pitiful half-men, forgetting (what surely needs to be re-
> membered in every sermon in Christendom) that not only thieves
> and murderers and whoremongers but also flabby and effeminate
> persons cannot enter into the kingdom of heaven—ah, when
> some day the reckoning shall be made of the countless multitude
> of the human race, there will be found a greater number under
> the rubric "The Flabby," than under all these rubrics taken to-
> gether: "Thieves," "Robbers," "Murderers."[1]

But no one should understand from the above cartoon or
quotation that I feel that American churchmen are flabby as
far as activity is concerned. The genius of American business has
apparently spilled over into the busy-ness of American Christendom. We are once again building the Kingdom of God in
America, just as we did in the last century; the Age of Martha
is once more upon us. This is not to disparage Martha (Lk.

10:38–42), except to say that on stopping some of the mode day Marthas long enough to ask Mary-like questions, I find the usually follows an embarrassing silence or else a hopeless confusion of tongues. Whatever precise ideas and goals there may have been at one time, seem to be lost now in a great flurry of activity.

And so it is that much of the current "Christian activism" seems to be a smokescreen for shallowness, for lack of roots, for the activist to hide the fact that he hasn't the foggiest notion of what he's about. He is, as he likes to say, "the man for others." And this is as it should be. But many are the activists today who, when scratched only superficially, reveal only the vaguest notion of what it means to be "for" anyone.

I confess that after *The Gospel According to Peanuts* was published I was anxious also to "leave the elementary doctrines of Christ and go on to maturity." But I have become increasingly persuaded that the religious situation in the United States today demands from all of us a much harder and more rigid examination of the foundations of the Christian faith before we go much higher in building the modern-day theological Tower of Babel we seem so determined to embark on. I offer one rather typical example of what I mean by our "flabbiness"—and as God is my witness, I ot lie: One senior at a very fashionable and well-known New ngland girls' college asked me: "Would you mind going over that 'sin' business again? Our teachers here in the Religion Department have never mentioned it." I cried and laughed most of the rest of the evening.

So emphasis on the "basics" is what I feel called to press for in this book—the basics, along with a much greater emphasis on the "positive" aspects of the Christian faith. For it is easy enough for anyone to see that Schulz has "penned down" the *problem* that all of us face in one way or another. But what is not so easy to discern is the *answer*, which any description of a problem must somehow imply. "After all," said Camus of art, "even the work that negates still affirms something and does homage to the wretched and magnificent life that is ours."[2] I further feel that this is definitely not the occasion only to "hint-and-run" at what I want to say, as perhaps I have done in the past. I now want to become, as far as I am able, clear and explicit. For, as Karl Barth once said about a somewhat similar theological task, "Someone has to do it."

Dropping the names of Barth and Camus at this point, brings up something else I should like to say: The reader will find in this book a veritable host of witnesses, not only in the *Peanuts* characters, but also in other friends of mine of long standing. Therefore, before anyone gets the idea that I think "Charlie Brown" is really a pseudonym for "Karli Barth," or that Linus is only a thinly disguised Kierkegaard, or that Schroeder is actually a miniature Dietrich Bonhoeffer, I want to say that I have brought these and other saints along primarily for two reasons: First, Charles Schulz himself is certainly no mean theologian and I want to try to show how frequently the same thoughts expressed in *Peanuts* will appear not only in the Bible, but also in such seemingly unlikely places as Barth's massive *Church Dogmatics* or Bonhoeffer's *Ethics* or Camus' *Myth of Sisyphus*, etc. Secondly, I bring along these others simply as a means of introducing them to readers who, like so many of the college students I have spoken to, may be interested in further investigations along the theological lines found in this book. I believe my own favorites will be readily apparent from the ways they have been quoted. Indeed, it is even difficult for me to try to tell my wife how much I love without dragging one of the great doctors of the Church into the picture—as in the dedication of this book. But withal I hope these names will add authority to my own weak words.

And now I would like to add a personal word of thanks to the friends who have helped in putting together this rather unusual book—a sort of modern-day "illuminated manuscript," in which the "perfect praise," instead of rolling from the mouths of the saints on printed ribbons, now comes from out of the mouths of babes and sucklings on inscribed balloons. Dr. Tadashi Akaishi, of Harper & Row, my editor from the beginning and good friend to the end, I humbly thank you, sir. Your expertise is surpassed only by your warmth of spirit. Mr. James Hennessy of the United Features Syndicate, many, many thanks to a gentleman I count myself most fortunate in knowing and working with. New-found friends Charles (Sparky) and Joyce Schulz, the finest and most generous two people anyone could ever hope to know, what can I possibly say to you that could express my gratitude and affection? In cases like this I always have to rely on someone much better spoken than I:

> But if the while I think on thee, dear friends,
> All losses are restored and sorrows end.

ROBERT L. SHORT

1 Of Parables and Peanuts

Jesus said, "With what can we compare the kingdom of God, or what parable shall we use for it?"   —MARK 4:30

How do we speak . . . in a "secular" way about "God"?
—DIETRICH BONHOEFFER,
Letter from Tegel Prison, Berlin, 1944[1]

Where are the modern parables to fit the New Age? One rarely hears them from the pulpit, though one occasionally reads them in the newspapers, which seem sometimes to have usurped the function of the pulpit.—PIERRE BERTON, The Comfortable Pew[2]

I preach in these cartoons, and I reserve the same rights to say what I want to say as the minister in the pulpit.
—CHARLES M. SCHULZ, creator of Peanuts[3]

When two seemingly disparate elements are imaginatively poised, put in apposition in new and unique ways, startling discoveries often result. . . . Learning, the educational process, has long been associated only with the glum. We speak of the "serious" student. Our time presents a unique opportunity for learning by means of humor—a perceptive or incisive joke can be more meaningful than platitudes lying between two covers.
—MARSHALL MCLUHAN and QUENTIN FIORE[4]

"What is the use of a book," thought Alice, "without pictures or conversations?"
—LEWIS CARROLL, Alice's Adventures in Wonderland[5]

Conversation takes place when one party has something new and interesting to say to the other. . . . One must say something engaging and original, something with an element of mystery. The Church must sound strange to the world if it is not to be dull.
—KARL BARTH[6]

sing to the Lord a new song; sing to the Lord, all the earth!
—PSALM 96:1

A good laugh is a mighty good thing, and rather too scarce a good thing; the more's the pity. . . . And the man that has anything bountifully laughable about him, be sure there is more in that man than you perhaps think for. —MELVILLE, *Moby Dick*[7]

A man may go into one field and say his prayer and be aware of God, or he may be in Church and be aware of God, but if he is more aware of Him because he is in a quiet place, that is his own deficiency and not due to God. . . . He knows God rightly who knows Him everywhere. —MEISTER ECKHART, 1260–1327[8]

What I am going to tell you has something to do with how sometimes it's necessary to go a long distance out of the way in order to come back a short distance correctly.
—EDWARD ALBEE, *The Zoo Story.*[9]

. . . and a little child shall lead them. —ISAIAH 11:6

"JESUS CHRIST IS the same yesterday, today, and for ever" (Heb. 13:8, NEB). Who cares? Who knows what this means? Who even listens to this kind of thing any more?

The Church, like Charlie Brown, is not used to having someone listen to what it says. Occasionally, again like Charlie Brown, is surprised, but this also is unusual. This is too bad for the Church because the Church lives in order that others might listen and hear—*really* hear. This is what the Church is, the *Ekklesia*, those called of God to tell of God in word and deed. Everything it does—*absolutely everything*—is done for this purpose, "for edification" (Rom. 15:2; 1 Cor. 14:26). Then what should the Church do if only few seem to be listening? Turn up the volume? Resort to more and louder direct appeals, the "Lucy approach"? "So you don't believe me, eh, Charlie Brown?" she says to him in one cartoon. "Well, let's see . . . How can I put it so you do? I suppose I should make it simple, clear and direct . . . BELIEVE ME!!" she shouts at him at the top of her "fussbudget champion" voice. But Charlie Brown is only flipped over by the force of her shriek. He does not believe.

Why is this? Why is it that so often the message of the Church falls on deaf ears? We will want to say more about this problem later, but primarily it exists because all men show up in the world spiritually deaf. They cannot hear, even if they should want to. This is why Christ could say, even to people eager to believe in him, "Why do you not understand my language? It is because my revelation is beyond your grasp. Your father is the devil and you choose to carry out your father's desires. . . . He who has God for his father listens to the words of God. You are not God's children; that is why you do not listen" (Jn. 8:43, 44, 47, NEB). This means then that it is no good trying to shout into man's spiritual ears when it is these very ears that have been closed from the beginning in the first place. "You can knock forever on a deaf man's door" (Kazantzakis).[10] These ears first must be opened, and always from the outside.

The natural man, man just as "human nature" originally and naturally is in this world, is what the New Testament calls a "strong man" (cf. 1 Cor. 1:27). Basically, he feels he has the answer to all of life's problems; hence his "strength." Life is simply a matter of applying this answer to the various problems as they arise. And since the answer that all men originally take for granted is never the answer of Christianity, Christianity knows that this false faith we originate with must first fail us before we any chance of accepting Christianity's answer. One must come around to asking a basic question before there can ever be a change in basic answers. But far too often the Church cheapens its answer by making it aggressively available for "strong men" before they are even aware that they need it. This tendency of the Church to "answer before it is asked" is what the New Testament calls "feeding your pearls to pigs: they will only trample on them, and turn and tear you to pieces" (Mt. 7:6, NEB) —like this:

There is an apocryphal *Peanuts* cartoon that I have seen on several college campuses in which the first panel shows Schroeder holding a sign that says, "Christ is the Answer!" In the final panel, Snoopy is holding a sign that says, "What is the question?" This rather stupid Schroeder-like lack of tact on the part of the Church is no small problem because, as Kierkegaard could say, "A direct attack only strengthens a person in his illusion, and at the same time embitters him. There is nothing that requires such gentle handling as an illusion, if one wishes to dispel it."[11] Bonhoeffer could be even more explicit:

> Every attempt to impose the gospel by force, to run after people and proselytize them, to use our own resources to arrange the

salvation of other people, is both futile and dangerous. It is futile because the swine do not recognize the pearls that are cast before them, and dangerous because it profanes the word of forgiveness. . . . Worse still, we shall only meet with the blind rage of hardened and darkened hearts, and that will be useless and harmful. Our easy trafficking with the word of cheap grace simply bores the world to disgust, so that in the end it turns against those who try to force on it what it does not want.[12]

In the following cartoon, Snoopy does a good job of playing the role of this kind of "aggressive evangelist," the "mountain lion" type, which Bonhoeffer just described above. We'll let Linus be "the strong man":

hen "direct attacks" on strong men only produce this kind of sult, especially when attacked by the Church—the community of "the weak" (1 Cor. 1:27)—how can the Church best approach them? The answer to this question has been given to the Church by Christ himself when he said: "No one can enter a strong man's house and plunder his goods, unless he first binds the strong man; then indeed he may plunder his house" (Mk. 3:27).

Today the same question still arises that was put to Christ: "Why do you speak to them in parables?" (Mt. 13:10). For, as the New Testament makes clear, "All this Jesus said to the crowds in parables; indeed he said nothing to them without a parable" (Mt. 13:34); and, "With many such parables he would give [the crowds] his message, so far as they were able to receive it. He never spoke to them except in parables; but privately to his disciples he explained everything" (Mk. 4:33, 34, NEB). C. H. Dodd calls the parables "the most characteristic element in the teaching of Jesus."[13] But why did he speak to them in parables? Why did Christ choose an artistic, indirect, parabolic, generally puzzling means of expression, rather than launching immediately into a forceful, no-nonsense "direct attack"? The answer is obvious: the people he spoke to were basically "strong men," men of this world, just as all men of all times basically are. And "no one can enter a strong man's house and plunder his goods, unless he first binds the strong man." Art-Parable—even in its simplest form, as in the parables of Christ—*binds* men. This is why the New Testament can speak of the crowds as being "*spellbound* by his teaching" (Mk. 11:18, NEB). For Art-Parable does bind us with its spell, its attractiveness. Ask any woman. She will tell you that women instinctively know how to use beauty and mystery to fascinate, bind, and "catch" a man—especially a "strong man." Likewise Art-Parable can catch a strong man's conscience. "The play's the thing/Wherein I'll catch the conscience of the King" (Shakespeare). Art-Parable is a baited hook; a "tender trap"; a "calculated trap for meditation" (Denis de Rougemont);[14] "a lie that makes us realize the truth" (Picasso);[15] it is reality's "soft-sell" that uses this approach precisely because it is confronted with the hard hearts of men; it uses the strategy of St. Paul, who said, "I have become all things to all men, that I might all means save some" (1 Cor. 9:22); "I always try to meet every-one half-way . . . so that they may be saved" (1 Cor. 10:33, NEB). The method of Art-Parable, be the artist Christian or non-Christian, is to take seriously the New Testament admonition to "Behave wisely towards those outside your own number; use the present opportunity to the full . . . . Study how best to talk with each person you meet" (Col. 4:5–6, NEB). This is why experts on the parables of Jesus can point out that his parables were primarily addressed to "non-believers" and "critics" (the "strong men"), rather than to believers or to "sinners"—those desperate and weak enough really to want and need this message in no uncertain terms.[16] Both Art-Parable and the kingdom of heaven use

tactics of infiltration: "The kingdom of heaven is like leaven which a woman took and *hid* in three measures of meal, till it was all leavened" (Mt. 13:33). The word "art" is never mentioned in the Bible. But the biblical concept that is virtually the same, with all of the different forms, techniques, and devices we commonly associate with art, is "parable." For both are the strategy in communication that first *binds* the strong man in order to enter his house; both realize a direct, frontal assault will avail nothing. Art-Parable is the strategy of "wounding from behind" (Kierkegaard). (See cartoon above.)

> No, an illusion can never be destroyed directly. . . . it must be done indirectly, not by one who vociferously proclaims himself an extraordinary Christian, but by one who, better instructed, is ready to . . . approach from behind the person who is under an illusion. . . . One must . . . have resignation enough to be one who is far behind him—otherwise one will certainly not get the man out of his illusion, a thing which is difficult enough in any case.[17]

This does not mean of course that there is not an equally valid time and place for a very direct and clear proclamation of the Church's message; but the Church must first capture the attention, open the ears, of those whom it would address. "The communication of Christianity must ultimately end in 'bearing witness' . . . . For truth, from the Christian point of view, does not lie in the subject (as Socrates understood it) but in a revelation which must be proclaimed" (Kierkegaard).[18] Thus Christ could say, "Till now I have been using figures of speech; a time is coming when I shall no longer use figures, but tell you of the Father in plain words" (Jn. 16:25, NEB). In all eternity it is impossible for the Church to compel a person to accept an opinion, a conviction, a belief. But one thing it can do: it can compel him to *take notice*. And binding in such a way that one is *forced* to take notice is precisely what Art-Parable does.

But is this true of all art? It is true of anything worthy enough to be called "art." As a working definition, we can say that "Art-Parable is that creation of man with no practical use except to communicate meaning indirectly through forms that capture one's attention." This is the kind of definition that could easily

help wear someone out, but it is also why all art is parable,
vice versa.

Charles Schulz's famous comic strip, *Peanuts*, certainly meets this
definition of Art-Parable. But since this cannot be said of all
comic strips, we need to distinguish between "art" and "entertainment." All art involves "entertainment" of sorts, but not all
entertainment is art. Mere entertainment leads us away from
reality; indeed it can even be considered an escape from reality.
Entertainment wants to live our lives for us. We are simply caught
up in a dream and left there. Hence it is possible to have "TV
addicts" as well as drug addicts and alcoholics. Art, on the other
hand, can also entertain us, but it goes further. It leads us through
its dream back to a reality that perhaps we had not seen before or
to a reality that we now see in a new light. It helps us to see our
lives as they really are and frequently provides suggestions as to how
those lives can better be faced and accepted without the constant
need for escape. Art-Parable then always has "something to say";
and for this reason it will always be more significant for mankind
than mere entertainment ever could be.

This extra dimension of Art-Parable no doubt accounts for
much of the phenomenal popularity of *Peanuts*. For in addition

being consistently well drawn and funny and entertaining, it
is easy to see that this important "plus factor" is also there. Not
only can we see it, but we know that Schulz intends for it to be
there. "In a sense, anyone can learn to draw, but having something to say makes the difference," he says in regard to the strip's
success.[19] ("There's no sense in doing a lot of barking if you
don't really have anything to say," is the way Snoopy has expressed this idea.) As one interviewer has put it: "Schulz ap-
proaches his work with a high regard for its importance. He refuses to think of cartooning as merely an exercise in providing
amusement. Of course, the strips must amuse, but, Schulz con-
tends, 'I look upon the comic strip as being an art form.' "[20] "I am
giving you a little bit extra, and this is what raises the strip's
quality, I hope," as he has said on another occasion.[21] As an
example of how high "the lowly comic strip" can rise on the
scale of artistic expression, let us use a graphic illustration. Prom-
inent American painter Joseph Hirsch once created some now
famous drawings for Arthur Miller's modern classic, *Death of a
Salesman*. The most famous of these drawings, a strongly ex-
pressive picture of the play's protagonist, Willy Loman, is here
reproduced:

Notice how this picture compares with the pictures of Lucy and
Linus and Charlie Brown on pages 76, 238, 251 respectively.
But the comparison does not stop simply with the design of the

pictures. For Charlie Brown, the protagonist of *Peanuts*, is also
kind of Willy "Low-man," a comic-strip counterpart to the man
who is reduced to the lowest levels of human suffering. Indeed,
much of what is said of Willy Loman in the play, could just as
well be said of Charlie Brown:

> I don't say he's a great man. Willy Loman never made a lot of
> money. His name was never in the paper. He's not the finest
> character that ever lived. But he's a human being, and a terrible
> thing is happening to him. So attention must be paid. He's not
> to be allowed to fall in his grave like an old dog. Attention,
> attention, must finally be paid to such a person. You called him
> crazy—. . . . But you don't have to be very smart to know what
> his trouble is. The man is exhausted. . . . A small man can be
> just as exhausted as a great man.[22]

Pathos is still pathos, even though it often appears in the context of comedy and can even be found in the "comics" section
of the daily newspaper. And just because this kind of material
can be found in such a popular and palatable medium as the
comics, the comics often are capable of effectively saying more to
more people. The popular arts are important precisely because
they are popular. (In the United States alone the comics are read
by more than 100 million people every day.) It is to Schulz's credit
then that he has taken such a popular entertainment medium and
raised it to the level of art. For everything we have a right to
expect from art is there. Therefore, in considering *Peanuts* as a
significant body of art, we should not be put off by the fact it
remains hilariously funny and is enjoyed by almost everyone. This
is exactly the same audience that Jesus wanted to attract—"everyone." Hence we have his parables, or "word-pictures," as the
New Testament word for "parables" can be translated. The
parables, then, in a very valid way, can be thought of as the
cartoons of the Bible. And *Peanuts*, more than any other strip
we know of, is "the Bible" among cartoons. There is little doubt
that someday in the future, when we are browsing among the
literary classics that have had wide appeal for young and old,
literary scholars and pure pleasure seekers—titles such as *Moby
Dick, Gulliver's Travels, Huckleberry Finn*—we shall also find
The Collected Cartoons of Charles Schulz. But in speaking of

ssics," with the dusty meaning this word can sometimes have,
et me quickly add that the last thing we want to do in this
book is to decrease one jot of the sheer enjoyment and entertainment value that comes to anyone from *Peanuts*. Long may this
enjoyment live and increase! For our part, we simply want to
show how the strip *also* can be seen as a work of art, and hence
can be read and appreciated on other levels as well, especially on
the level of the "preaching" Schulz has admitted doing:

> If you do not say anything in a cartoon, you might as well not
> draw it at all. Humor which does not say anything is worthless
> humor. So I contend that a cartoonist must be given a chance to
> do his own preaching.[23]

There is, however, a sense in which Schulz could hardly avoid
preaching even if he should want to, given the basic recipe he
has chosen for *Peanuts:* take a few small children; render them
honestly in the way that children really think and act; put into
their midst one small, "peculiar" dog; and stir this mixture into
the framework of spare simplicity and high comedy. It seems to
me that with these ingredients (the strip "is full of ingredients,"
as Linus says about a box of cocoa-mix) one will necessarily concoct a strip that not only will speak eloquently about man and his
problem, but also a strip that at least will be highly suggestive of
the answer to that problem. The hallmarks of *Peanuts* are its
simplicity and its honesty about life; and these are precisely the
hallmarks of the parables of Jesus. "The parables are pictures
from life as it *is*, pictures that mean something. For life as it *is*
means something. And the one who does not understand life
as it is cannot understand its meaning" (Barth).[24] All of the
greatest theologians of the Church's history have finally found
it necessary to speak in a very simple, parabolic form. How does
Blaise Pascal, for instance, the famous French existentialist theologian, talk about the fundamental origin of "man's inhumanity
to man"? Does he write a tome? No, but he almost draws a
cartoon:

> *Mine, thine*—"This dog is mine," said those poor children; "that
> is my place under the sun." Here is the beginning and the image
> of the usurpation of all the earth.[25]

But if you have difficulty image-ing Pascal's image, here it is another form:

In the world of the popular arts, *Peanuts* then is like the "Du form of address" of German. This word means "you," but this is not just any old "you." It is used only in very special cases: to address very close friends, little children, dogs, or God. And these are the same few elements that the most basic aspects of life have been reduced to in the parables of *Peanuts*. The very fact that Schulz has limited the little world of *Peanuts* to such micro scope and proportions, tends to make the strip a kind of cosmic comic: it is forced to play on the basic themes of life in depth, since it cannot range widely over the world's surface. When all the world is reduced to one neighborhood of only a few little children, this leaves only the vertical dimension for an artist of great imagination to work in—he can go as deep as the abyss of man's heart or as high as the Kingdom of God.

Karl Barth once said that "any Christian who wishes to live responsibly must read two things: the Bible and the daily newspaper—and never one without the other!"[26] As a matter of fact, anyone who is interested in learning to understand "life as it is" should read these two things. But for its part, the Church cannot simply be content with reading the newspaper. For the Church

…alled out and set apart from the world only to go back into the world, to go "to the uttermost parts of the earth" to proclaim its gospel. And "uttermost parts" certainly includes the daily newspaper. This is why in his *Journals*, Kierkegaard could make the following entry, entitled, "Why I make use of this newspaper":

> Sermons should not be preached in churches. It harms Christianity in a high degree and alters its very nature, that it is brought into an artistic remoteness from reality, instead of being heard in the midst of real life. . . . For all this talk about quiet, about quiet places and quiet hours, as the right element for Christianity is absurd. So then sermons should not be preached in churches but in the street, in the midst of life, of the reality, of daily life, weekday life. Nevertheless . . . I lack physical strength. To me is allotted to speak with the individual, to converse, and then to use the pen. Nevertheless I desired to attain an approximation to preaching in the street, or to bring Christianity . . . into the midst of life's reality and into conflict with its various interests. And to that end I resolved to use this newspaper.[27]

At this point Kierkegaard launched a journalistic attack on the flabby "Christendom" of his time, an attack so furious that it eventually cost him his life. Charles Schulz is another man so concerned that Christianity enter "into the midst of life's reality" that he has found himself preaching in the streets—literally. He talks about the experience this way:

> In our St. Paul (Minn.) Bible class we young people used to feel that we should make some sort of public stand for Christ, so we commenced holding outdoor testimony meetings at the Union Gospel Mission downtown. It was rather difficult for me, yet I felt driven to stand up at these meetings and say something. So, with the streetcars going by, I stepped out on the sidewalk and managed some way to make my statement for the Lord. By the time we held our third such meeting I had been elected president of the group, and it was my responsibility to give the main sermon. So I found myself that night standing on the sidewalk preaching, without having any real ability for this sort of thing. Right in the middle of my sermon I happened to glance over to my left, and there were three of my golfing buddies, staring at me in complete surprise. They did not even know that I attended

church. But we survived this, too, and it was good for
think all Christians should have to go out and do some preac-
ing like that.[28]

Schulz, however, like Kierkegaard, finally resolved to use the
newspaper by way of getting his message into the streets; for as
he says, "It's much better to be a good cartoonist than a terrible
minister."[29] But, as we have seen, he still considers himself a
minister even though a cartoonist. Or, as he has said on another
occasion, "If we are all members of the priesthood, why cannot
a cartoonist preach in the same manner as a minister, or anyone
else?"[30] At the same time he recognizes that in working "for the
secular press through a newspaper syndicate I must exercise care
in the way I go about expressing things. I have a message that I
want to present, but I would rather bend a little to put over a
point than to have the whole strip dropped because it is too
obvious."[31] This then is his answer—to "bend a little," a *parabolic* expression of his faith. For this is literally what a parable is
—a *bending*, a curved or roundabout or less than obvious way of
getting to "a point." And this bending can constantly be seen in
Peanuts. Both the parables of Jesus and the parables of *Peanuts*,
to use Bonhoeffer's famous phrase, "speak in a 'secular' way about
God." For one thing, they bring the explanations for the Christian

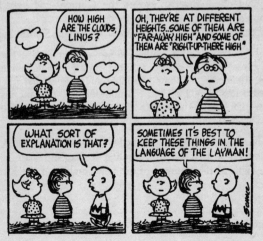

out of the metaphysical clouds and on down to earth. In s regard, all parabolic expressions of faith are strictly in keeping with the spirit of the Bible. For "the Biblical authors themselves . . . far from speaking a celestial language, spoke in many earthly languages," says Barth.[32] (See cartoon above.)

Anyone who does his reading with the Bible in one hand and the daily newspaper in the other cannot be far from the Kingdom of God. And especially if he is a fan of *Peanuts* is he on the right track, as *Peanuts* is such a happy combination of these two elements: the proclamation of God's love for the world, and the world as it really is. "*Peanuts* must be recognized as the timeliest part of any newspaper," opines theologian Theodore Gill, "and that's because *Peanuts* is true."[33] Peanuts is literally "fresh every morning" and as contemporary as today's newspaper. Likewise the Church should constantly be concerned to find and create new parables to fit our time. Jeremias, one of the foremost authorities on the parables, can tell us: "It becomes clear that Jesus was never tired of expressing the central ideas of his message in constantly changing images."[34] But "the men in the pulpit," says Pierre Berton, "seem content to retell the ancient stories, so many of which make no impact on a modern congregation."[35] "No one puts new wine into old wineskins," said Christ (Mk. 2:22). "No one," that is, except the Church—the very people who should know better!

In talking about how he became a Christian, Schulz has said:

> I joined the Army after mother's death and then when I returned from three years of service I found myself very lonesome, so I finally attended . . . church one night and noticed that the church needed a new sign. I said to the minister . . . "Let me make you a new sign." This helped to draw me in and I became more interested.[36]

Schulz has been making much needed "new signs" for the Church ever since. Woe betide the Church if it does not learn to interpret the signs of the times or to use new parables of the Kingdom!

2 Interpreting the Signs of the Times

Now [that] we've had examples of [cartoons] where I did intend exactly your interpretation, I'm glad you finally used one like this. Because this would be a perfect example of one where I didn't intend this message—not that I don't agree with your interpretation. And I even agree with your right to be able to read this into it. Because this is what makes me so happy, that you are able to use the strip in this way. This delights me no end.

—CHARLES SCHULZ TO ROBERT SHORT,
KPIX-TV, San Francisco, February 1966

If an image displays the universal pattern, it will display it at all levels and in all circumstances, whether the poet was or could have been conscious of these possible applications or not. It has happened even to me in writing a novel, to resolve a problem of human relationships in a manner which was recognised by a priest of my acquaintance as symbolising the right . . . relationship between the soul and God. I protested that I had no such ambitious idea in mind: but, when once the significance of what I had written was pointed out to me, I had to recognise that what the priest said was true . . . I had unwittingly stumbled upon a universal image. The meaning that another person had "read into" that image was the real meaning: and as soon as I was shown it, I accepted it. . . . I am here to admit that I did not see the full meaning of what I was writing: I am here to admit that, when the full meaning was "read into" it, I was ready to accept and acknowledge that meaning for the real meaning.

—DOROTHY SAYERS[1]

…eat works . . . always mean more than they are conscious of
…aying. . . . Myths are made for the imagination to breathe life
into them.
—CAMUS[2]

When a woman makes an altar cloth, so far as she is able, she
makes every flower as lovely as the graceful flowers of the field,
as far as she is able, every star as sparkling as the glistening stars
of the night. She withholds nothing, but uses the most precious
things she possesses. . . . But when the cloth is finished and put
to its sacred use: then she is deeply distressed if someone should
make the mistake of looking at her art, instead of at the meaning
of the cloth; or make the mistake of looking at a defect, instead
of at the meaning of the cloth. For she could not work the sacred
meaning into the cloth itself, nor could she sew it on the cloth
as though it were one more ornament. This meaning really lies in
the beholder and in the beholder's understanding . . . . it was a
trespass against God, an insulting misunderstanding of the poor
needlewoman, when someone looked wrongly and saw only what
was there. . . .
—KIERKEGAARD[3]

Nobody, I think, ought to read poetry, or look at pictures or
statues, who cannot find a great deal more in them than the poet
or artist has actually expressed.
—HAWTHORNE[4]

[Christians] shall certainly continue to read the best . . . of what
our time provides, but we must tirelessly criticize it according to
our own principles, and not merely according to the principles
admitted by the writers and by the critics who discuss it in the
public press.
—T. S. ELIOT[5]

ART-PARABLE CAN BE thought of as a kind of sugar-coated pill, as
a treat that contains a treatment, as a means of bringing people
to swallow—by appealing to more superficial desires—medicine that
is deeply needed. As this is true of all Art-Parable, it is true of
the "parabolic art" of Charles Schulz no less than of the "artistic
parables" of Christ. One interviewer wrote of Schulz: "Most of
the 90 million readers who chuckle over the troubles of Charlie
Brown do not suspect that they are getting a disguised dose of

theology or psychology with their laughs. But they buy it cause it is so unobtrusive and so acceptable to their experience for Schulz "does confess that the theological vitamins are injected intentionally."[6]

Ingmar Bergman, the brilliant Swedish film writer and director, has described his relationship to his audiences by saying, "At first you give the audience a pill that tastes good. And then you give them some more pills with vitamins, but with some poison too. Very slowly you give them stronger and stronger doses."[7] By "poison" Bergman means a potent ingredient that has the power of healing ultimately, but is not so easy to swallow. The same kind of "bitter pills" are found among the parabolic sayings of Jesus. For instance, when Christ spoke of himself as "the bread which came down from heaven," and that "whoever eats this bread shall live for ever," we are told that "many of his disciples on hearing it exclaimed, 'This is more than we can stomach! Why listen to such words?'" (Jn. 6:58, 60, NEB). But obviously not all of his parables contained doses so difficult to swallow.

We need to be clear at this point that from the Christian perspective the medicine of Art-Parable is never simply a treatment the self-righteous Christian administers to the non-Christian. The Christian is in need of the healing powers of Art-Parable as much as anyone—its powers to instruct, to judge, and to confound the countless complacencies Christians so easily and often slip into. The Christian knows that his basic task of "edifying" others is never best accomplished unless he himself be edified. Also, it should be clear that we are not talking only about Art-Parable that could be called "religious" or "Christian," that deals explicitly with God or religious subjects. As De Rougemont has said, "every . . . work, even when its subject is secular, implies a theology—whether the author knows it or not."[8] Therefore, since all works of art contain some amount of medicine to be administered, it is possible to characterize the different types of Art-Parable on the basis of the different types of doses they can contain·in one admixture or another. Generally speaking, there are three types, moving in the direction of what Bergman calls "stronger and stronger doses." But in speaking of these types of doses, we will use the metaphor of "glass" and the ways in which

Parable helps us to see (as glass can) deeper and deeper into ality. For "where there is no vision, the people perish" (Prov. 29:18, KJV).

1. THE LENS

Art-Parable that is like a lens is the least threatening to us. Of the three types it is the most "direct." Its purpose is to show us by word or example and to bring into sharp focus. Some of the parables of Christ were lenses in this respect; they were in no sense puzzling to those who heard them, but were used to project brief examples or illustrations meant to influence and clarify. For instance, the parable of the Good Samaritan is in no way meant to threaten or to confuse its hearers, but rather to encourage action and to illustrate. At its conclusion Christ could simply say, "Go now and do likewise" (Lk. 10:37). This is literally the Art-Parable of "show and tell." Christ could even preface one such parable by saying, "Every one who . . . hears my words and does them, I will show you what he is like" (Lk. 6:47). There is no great mystery here, but we are simply given a kind of "audio-visual" presentation to help us understand. But as Marshall McLuhan has shown and told us in our own time, we should never underestimate the power of "show and tell":

This is the type of Art-Parable that teaches; and what is taught is often more told than shown, more spoken than implied. But what is spoken is spoken so that the "lesson" comes across in a very gentle, painless way. This method is close to being propaganda; but at some point propaganda stops being indirect and becomes plainly blunt. Art-Parable, on the other hand, is never so completely plain; what is said is always spoken "artfully." For example, although the following cartoon appeared in 1966 during some of the most intense United States Vietnamese involvement, probably very few readers associated the cartoon with that war. And even after having said this we are still not completely sure of the artist's intentions. Nevertheless, a good word is spoken:

chulz has said that "as a comic-strip artist, I feel called upon
be uplifting and decent."[9] This is as it should be. For as T. S.
Eliot has confessed, "I incline to come to the alarming conclusion that it is just the literature that we read for 'amusement,' or
'purely for pleasure' that may have the greatest and least expected influence on us. It is the literature which we read with the
least effort that can have the easiest and most insidious influence
upon us."[10] But we also can be most easily *uplifted* and *sensitized*
by Art-Parable that is like a lens and that teaches us by example.
The lens can be used to project a picture from which we can
just as easily and unconsciously draw positive inspiration. This
is the kind of art Kazantzakis was writing of when he said,
"Art is . . . a magic incantation. Obscure homicidal forces lurk
in our entrails, deadly impulses to kill, destroy, hate, dishonor.
Then art appears with its sweet piping and delivers us."[11] This is
an approach that we consistently find in *Peanuts*:

2. THE MIRROR

In the famous "closet scene" of Shakespeare's *Hamlet*, Hamlet
says to his mother, the Queen:

Hamlet: Come, come, and sit you down. You shall not budge,/

You go not till I set you up a glass/ Where you m
    see the inmost part of you.
Queen: O Hamlet, speak no more./ Thou turn'st mine eyes into
    my very soul,/ And there I see such black and grained
    spots/ As will not leave their tinct.[12]

What Hamlet actually forced his mother to look at was not a
"glass" (mirror), but a small picture of his murdered father, in
which his mother began to see herself implicated in that murder.

This is the kind of mirror Art-Parable often can be, and also
why we frequently do not like what we see or hear in art. But, as
Chekhov could say, "Don't blame the mirror if your mug is
crooked." The classic Old Testament parable of this type is the
story the prophet Nathan told David. In the story, a certain rich
man slaughters the single little lamb of a very poor man, rather
than giving one of his own many sheep to a wayfarer. At the end
of the story, David is outraged: "As the Lord lives, the man who
has done this deserves to die." And Nathan says to David, "You
are the man" (2 Sam. 12:5, 7). Art-Parable that is like a mirror
completely binds and enthralls us with its fascination and ingenuity until, as the "exciting tale" progresses, we begin to realize
that it is our own lives and values that are here being threatened,
as they are the very material out of which the story is made. It
works like this:

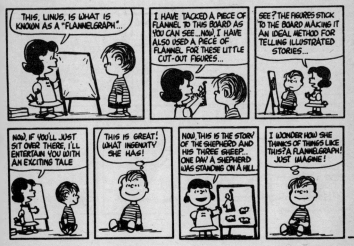

Many of the parables of Jesus were mirrors in this sense. Even his arch foes would stand rapt in complete attention listening to his parable until, at the parable's conclusion, "they began to look for a way to arrest him, for they saw that the parable was aimed at them" (Mk. 12:12, NEB). This type of parable, then, has a reflection or backlash in which the person at whom it is aimed not only can see who he has been, but also can get a *feeling* for the kind of person he must be. In the following cartoon, we'll again let Linus play the part of David:

The analogies of this mirror-like type of Art-Parable can "hit home" with deadly accuracy. Schulz tells us, "Not long ago I had Linus' blanket-hating grandmother come to his house for a visit. She tried to get him to give up his propensity for the blanket; so he threw up to her the fact that she was drinking 32 cups of coffee a day!"[13] And what was Linus' comment about all this?— "She didn't like the comparison." Christ frequently used this kind of discomforting comparison in his parables. He could say, for instance:

> The man who can be trusted in little things can be trusted also in great; and the man who is dishonest in little things is dishonest also in great things. If, then, you have not proved trustworthy with the wealth of this world, who will trust you with the wealth that is real? (Lk. 16:10, 11, NEB)

reason why the Church should always be concerned with the
ility of Art-Parable to mirror, is that it not only mirrors us as
individuals, but also can accurately reflect the image, the tone,
the thinking, the disposition, the peculiar vocabulary of the entire
age in which the Church must work. This is the ability of Art-
Parable "to hold . . . the mirror up to Nature—to show Virtue
her own feature, scorn her own image, and the very age and body
of the time his form and pressure" (Shakespeare). Of course, the
ability to do this comes from the unusual sensitivity of the artist;
he is a kind of cultural and spiritual seismograph who can feel and
record forces at work in this world that lesser men would never
notice if the artist did not draw their attention to them. "The
artist, whether his medium is verbal, pictorial, plastic, or musical,
is the man equipped with radar to penetrate the cultural fogs
of the age. Like the canaries that used to be taken down the
mines or the white rabbits that once were carried aboard sub-
marines, this race of mankind knows, before the rest, when the
air is becoming poisonous and exhausted," says Kenneth Hamilton.[14] Schroeder is the real artist of the *Peanuts* patch, a sort of
"miniature Leonard Bernstein" as "Peppermint" Patty calls him.
As such, he is certainly able to "tune in on" the characteristic
sounds of the age. He also shows us, in the following cartoon,
what an accurate index of the times art—or pseudo-art—can be:

3. THROUGH A GLASS DARKLY

Jesus, just as Art-Parable, often had the annoying tendency to raise more questions than he answered. Thus many of his parables began with the question, "What do you think?" On one occasion in his ministry, when "three big boys were chasing him," this is what he did:

> One day . . . the chief priests and the scribes with the elders came up and said to him, "Tell us by what authority you do these things, or who it is that gave you this authority." He answered them, "I also will ask you a question; now tell me, Was the baptism of John from heaven or from men?" And they discussed it with one another, saying, "If we say, 'From heaven,' he will say, 'Why did you not believe him?' But if we say, 'From men,' all the people will stone us; for they are convinced that John was a prophet." So they answered that they did not know whence it was. And Jesus said to them, "Neither will I tell you by what authority I do these things." (Lk. 20:1–8)

The type of Art-Parable that is most unsettling to us is not the Art-Parable that shows us more clearly, as through a lens, a way we may go; nor the type that holds up a mirror before us so that we may turn from that image to move in a new and better direction; but it is the Art-Parable that is deeply puzzling, that cuts

understanding out from under us so that initially we do not
ow which way to go. Many of the parables of Jesus were designed to do just this: not to give an easy answer, but to provoke
an altogether new kind of question. This is why Christ could say
to his disciples when they asked him about the parables, "To
you it has been given to know the secrets of the kingdom of God;
but for others they are in parables, so that seeing they may not see,
and hearing they may not understand" (Lk. 8:10). And yet, even
though Christ could intentionally *hide* the mysteries of the Kingdom in this way, "nothing is hid that shall not be made manifest,
nor anything secret that shall not be known and come to light"
(Lk. 8:17). What is propounded here is the kind of mystery or
"dark saying" that riddles us in our attempts to unriddle it; in our
attempts to untangle the knot we become more and more deeply
entangled ourselves; in our desire to find where truth is hid,
though it were hid indeed within the center, we ourselves are
confounded. This kind of Art-Parable, then, acts as an emotional
and intellectual catalyst. Just because of its mystery, secrets begin
to be brought to light, secrets about ourselves and others. With
this kind of mystery as a "conversation piece," discussion is called
forth, discussion not only between ourselves and others, but also
discussion *within* ourselves. We are *forced* to come to some conclusion about what this riddle means. And our interpretation of
such a mystery will often reveal more about us than it does about
the riddle itself. Thus, the more practical among us will always
have little use for this type of Art-Parable as it simply never
seems to "win any ball games," never seems to come to any
clear-cut conclusions. But this type of Art-Parable plays another
game; and the name of that game is "making manifest" the hearts
and minds of men:

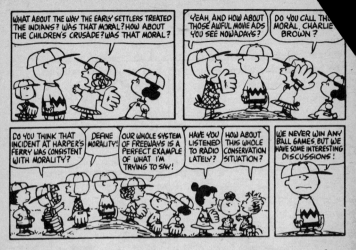

"Take care, then, how you listen," said Christ; "for the man who has will be given more, and the man who has not will forfeit even what he thinks he has" (Lk. 8:18, NEB). That is to say, for those "who have been granted to know the secrets of the Kingdom," the parables will not only make sense but will be edifying as well. But for those to whom these secrets have not been given, the only way they can possibly understand is to forfeit the misunderstanding they now have. In one series of *Peanuts* strips, Lucy becomes furious with the outrageously happy dancing of Snoopy. She simply does not understand how anyone can be so happy. Day after day she tries to discourage him. "Stupid dog!" she yells at him. "You'll be sorry, Snoopy! My great-grandmother says if you're too happy today, something bad will happen to you tomorrow!" But no bad hap happens to the happy dog. "Are you trying to make a fool out of my great-grandmother?" she shouts. Try as she may, she cannot understand. Being simultaneously attracted and repelled by Snoopy's happiness, her ambivalence resembles the attitude Herod had for John the Baptist: "He liked to listen to him, although the listening left him greatly perplexed" (Mk. 6:20, NEB). "Nothing seems to disturb him," concludes Lucy in utter discouragement. Finally, there is only way to understand Christ, the mystery that he was, the mysteries that he taught, and the happiness that he offered:

Now we want to turn from types to interpretation of Art-Parable.

At the end of a flight to Chicago, the stewardess told her passengers good-by over the intercom by saying, "Have a pleasant stay in Chicago and all points beyond." "Good theologian, that girl!" I immediately thought to myself, silently congratulating us both for our great wisdom. "She knows that all points beyond." Quite obviously, though, it is possible to see any and everything as a kind of parabolic expression or sign or symbol for something else. God can be thought of as the great artist with all creation as his "creation" in the same sense that a finite artist produces a "creation." The Bible is filled with this idea. "Everything," says the New Testament, "when once the light has shown it up, is illumined, and everything thus illumined is all light" (Eph. 5:13, NEB). To the mind not darkened by sin, says St. Paul, it is true that "ever since the creation of the world [God's] invisible nature, namely, his eternal power and deity, has been clearly perceived in the things that have been made" (Rom. 1:20). Great literature

has also testified that "all points beyond": "All visible obj[ects],
man," says Ahab in Melville's *Moby Dick*, "are but as pasteboa[rd]
masks. But in each event . . . some unknown but still reasoning
thing puts forth the mouldings of its features from behind the
unreasoning mask. If a man will strike, strike through the mask!"[15]
Luther was fond of saying that "if God once spoke through
Balaam's ass, he can speak through anything, whether stone, stick,
thunder or what not."[16] "We proclaim the incorruptible of which
all corruptible is only a parable" (Barth).[17] So then if it is true
that "The heavens are telling the glory of God; and the firmament
proclaims his handiwork" (Ps. 19:1), how much more of that
glory can we expect to see in the work of an artist like Charles
Schulz, who has told us that it is his intention to give us an
"actual word," to "preach in these cartoons," as he has expressed
it.

"There is not so poor a creature," said John Donne, "but may be
thy glass to see God in."[18] But of course the last thing most men
want to see is God or "the truth," as Christ spoke of himself.
Therefore, if anyone comes to us and tells us that *truth* can be
seen in a certain work of art, we can all too easily dodge what

be seen there by resorting to the "genetic fallacy," the fallacy logic that attempts to avoid the truth by criticizing the source through which that truth has come. In aesthetics this is called the "intentional fallacy" and it avoids the work of art itself by examining the intentions of the artist. For instance, Lucy is of the opinion that "Indian summer" is a device whereby "the Indians would trick the approaching cavalry into thinking the weather was nice while in reality it was about to snow." She gets into an argument with Charlie Brown about this, and in the following cartoon we can get a good picture of how both the intentional and genetic fallacies work:

One reason why we should never finally try to judge the meaning of a work of art on the basis of the artist's intention is: Who knows what these intentions are? Apparently, artists themselves have difficulty knowing this. Plato's Socrates can tell us:

> I went to the poets; tragic, dithyrambic, and all sorts . . . . I took them some of the most elaborate passages in their own writings, and asked what was the meaning of them . . . . Will you believe me? . . . there is hardly a person present who would not have talked better about their poetry than they did themselves. Then I knew that not by wisdom do poets write poetry, but by a sort of genius and inspiration.[19]

Schulz himself has said of his strip, "There is lots of mean[ing] but I can't explain it."[20] But the question is not whether he ca[n] not or *will* not explain his work; for he obviously should not. This is not his job. As an artist he has said to us what he has to say through his art. The rest, by the very nature of what Art-Parable is, is up to us. Or, as Christ himself could say of interpreting the signs of the times:

> You hypocrites! You know how to interpret the appearance of earth and sky; but why do you not know how to interpret the present time? . . . why do you not judge for yourselves what is right? (Lk. 12:56, 57)

But in case you would *still* rather not judge for yourself, but get the word straight from the horse's mouth, Schulz has this to say: "I don't discuss [my strip] with anybody."[21] Therefore, be careful in saying you understand the intentions of any artist. This kind of understanding can be embarrassing:

How then are we to judge the meaning of Art-Parable? First of all, we should never lose sight of what is under consideration, the work itself, and always be completely true to it. Any interpretation of the work must "suit" or "fit" the work. As much as possible,

...eces of the puzzle should be in place and accounted for in ...herent way. Second, since all Art-Parable has something to ...y, we must give it adequate opportunity to speak for itself and, for our parts, really listen.

My own experience with *Peanuts* has taught me that the problem of seeing *not enough* in Art-Parable is far greater than the problem of seeing too much. Too often I have said, to my later great embarrassment, "A very funny cartoon, but certainly no theological implications here." We have been like those on the left hand of Christ who asked him, "Lord, when was it that we saw you hungry or thirsty or a stranger or naked or ill or in prison, and did nothing for you?" Christ's answer was, "anything you did not do for one of these, however humble, you did not do for me" (Mt. 25:44, 45, NEB). We just as well could ask him, "When did we see you in a film and did not listen to you or in a novel and did not learn from you? When did we see you in a painting and did not grieve with you or in a cartoon and did not laugh with you?" And as far as "the intentions of the artist" are concerned, no doubt it was never the intention of the hungry, thirsty, naked, ill or in prison to furnish anyone with some kind of "Christ-figure." And yet he was there.

We are called, then, to "judge for ourselves." Art-Parable, like Christ, "always brings everything back to the individual, for that is where the battle must be fought" (Kierkegaard).[22] "Who do you say I am?" they both ask us. We are called to a decision about *meaning*, not so much about the *artist's* meaning—again, how can anyone ever be sure of this?—but about the meaning the work has for us. "A great poem," says novelist Dorothy Sayers, in words applicable to all Art-Parable, "is not the perquisite of scholars and critics and historians: it is yours and mine—our freehold and our possession; and what it truly means to us is a real part of its true and eternal meaning."[23] Or, as W. K. Wimsatt has put it, "The poem is not the critic's own and not the author's (it is detached from the author at birth and goes about the world beyond his power to intend about it or control it). The poem belongs to the public."[24]

Where does the critic, then, or the interpreter, fit into all of this? First of all, his job is to forget about taking apart the

artist himself and, second, to avoid criticism in the nega
sense—"destructive criticism," to use Lucy's language. The cri
who engages in these types of criticism may well wonder why no
one ever listens to him. No one has described "author dissection"
better than Nietzsche or "destructive criticism" better than
Schulz:

> Something good and true may be done, in action, poetry or music;
> but the hollow culture of the day will look beyond the work and
> ask the history of the author. If the author has already created
> something, our historian will set out clearly the past and the
> probable future course of his development . . . . he will wisely
> sum up the author and give him general advice for his future
> path . . . . The historical training of our critics prevents their hav-
> ing an influence in the true sense—an influence on life and
> action.[25]

If the critic is to have an influence on life and action, the approach to his task must be overwhelmingly positive, and this is
because he himself has been positively overwhelmed. He is a man
who has been *astonished* by the work at hand and simply wishes
to share this astonishment. His job is not unlike that of the
minister's in the pulpit, who stands between his congregation

the Bible not to dazzle his congregation with his oratory or exceptional knowledge of biblical criticism, but simply to share the excitement that comes to him from this book. Nor does he demand agreement with his views, for he fully admits these views to be his. But he simply steps aside and asks that you look for yourself, come to conclusions of your own, and—hopefully—come to share in the same excitement also.

Christ was himself not only "the one mediator between God and men" (1 Tim. 2:5), and the "explainer" of the scriptures for the disciples (Lk. 24:32), but he also could be considered more of an *interpreter* than a *creator* of Art-Parable. For he also "explained" his parables to the disciples (Mk. 4:34). Furthermore, many of his parables were not even his own "creations," but were actually stories and material that he had gathered from earlier folklore or from life as he saw it around him. This material he simply used and interpreted for his own purposes.

However, the people of Christ's time were not so cleverly sophisticated in questions of literary criticism as every college sophomore is today. Otherwise, we could easily imagine the following passage in the gospels: "Then the literary critics and doctors of aesthetics came to him and said, 'Are you not reading into Rabbi So-and-So's parable far more than he intended? Is your interpretation of his story actually what he wanted to say? Are you not, rather, using the story for your own purposes, rather than allowing the work to speak for itself? Certainly your use of the story in this way ignores one of the ancient maxims of our fathers: Art for art's sake!'" This kind of criticism can certainly be made: Christianity is absolutely shameless in its desire to "take every thought captive to obey Christ" (2 Cor. 10:5). This is because its central concern is to "proclaim the message, press it home on all occasions, convenient or inconvenient, use argument, reproof, and appeal" (2 Tim. 4:2, NEB). To do this, Christianity will literally stop at nothing, including objections from "the literary critics and doctors of aesthetics." The Church "must be engaged in conversation with the contemporary world, whatever the means of dialogue" (Barth).[26] As St. Paul could put it:

Some, indeed, proclaim Christ in a jealous and quarrelsome spirit;

others proclaim him in true goodwill . . . the others, moved
personal rivalry, present Christ from mixed motives . . . . Wha
does it matter? One way or another, in pretence or in sincerity,
Christ is set forth, and for that I rejoice. (Phil. 1:15–18, NEB)

Every day in my newspaper I receive a valentine from Charles
Schulz. We know it is his intention to enclose valentines in his
cartoons, as he has so often told us. But did he intend to send
the exact valentine I see there? What does it matter? One way
or another, Christ is set forth, and for that I rejoice!

One thing more: both the parables of Peanuts and the parables
of the New Testament are best not seen as *allegories*—that form
of Art-Parable that attributes special significance to every last
detail. Just as New Testament scholars can tell us "that most of

parables have each of them one main point and only one,"[27] has also been observed that in *Peanuts* "each strip is usually a lesson, complete in itself."[28] Also, allegories use a quite consistent symbolism; and this certainly is not always true of *Peanuts*. Although there are symbols that can be seen in the strip, Schulz is no slave to any intricately devised symbolic scheme that will solve all of the world's problems in a single cartoon. Such a cartoon would probably look like this:

Schulz has said that he believes his characters "should be as inconsistent as most of us unfortunately are."[29] His characters are best seen then, I think, as a small repertory company of actors, the same type of company that Shakespeare wrote and acted for, in which "one man in his time plays many parts." Schulz has even compared himself to a "playwright" with a small "cast of characters"[30]—a cast of characters who must frequently change roles, if on this tiny stage it is really possible to see "all the world." I believe it is wrong, then, to expect too much consistency from them. Or, as one of his characters, Lucy, could put it in a writing assignment for her teacher:

I will not talk in class.
I will not talk in class.

I will not talk in class.
On the other hand, who knows what I'll do?

Nor is it fair, I think, to expect to see "profound theological implications" in everything that comes off Schulz's drawing board. What we might expect, however, has probably been best expressed by Schulz himself:

> The thing which you must try to do is to develop a change of pace so that your ideas are not too heavily weighted along certain lines. I like to have a simple idea one day and then go for something profound the next. . . . When a person has to turn out something funny every day of every month of every year, and this goes on year after year, you obviously have to draw upon every thought which comes to your mind! Everything that you know becomes part of this comic strip! Of course, I do have an interest in spiritual things. I do like to study the Bible. It is fun to throw in some of these items now and then.[31]

"To have great poets, there must be great audiences, too," said Whitman. Thus if Charlie Schulz's job, like Charlie Brown's, is to stand on the pitcher's mound and, always changing the pace, to "throw them in," the job of "catching" is up to us.

3 Savior?!—Who Needs a Savior?

The one observation on which the strip initially was based is something which I recall from the seventh grade, when to my horror I saw two girls after class go over to another girl and say, "We're going to have a party this week and we're going to invite all the other girls, but we're not going to invite you." Now this girl was just crushed by this statement! It would have crushed me, but I was just like Charlie Brown—I knew I didn't have a ghost of a chance being invited anyway. . . . But this is one of the basic themes of Peanuts which is the cruelty that exists among these children.
—CHARLES SCHULZ[1]

Man is very far gone from original righteousness, and is of his own nature inclined to evil, so that the flesh lusteth always contrary to the Spirit . . . in every person born into this world. . . . And this infection of nature doth remain, yea in them that are regenerated. —THE BOOK OF COMMON PRAYER[2]

The people who are most discouraged and made despondent by the barbarity and stupidity of human behavior . . . are those who . . . cling to an optimistic belief in the civilizing influence of progress and enlightenment. To them, the appalling outburst of bestial ferocity in the Totalitarian States, and the obstinate selfishness and stupid greed of Capitalist Society, are not merely shocking and alarming. For them, these things are the utter negation of everything in which they have believed. It is as though the bottom had dropped out of their universe. The whole thing looks like a denial of reason, and they feel as if they and the world had gone mad together. Now for the Christian this is not so. He is as deeply shocked and grieved as anybody else, but he is not astonished. He has never thought very highly of human nature left to itself. He has been accustomed to the idea that there is a deep interior dislocation in the very center of human

46

personality, and that you can never, as they say, "make peop[le] good by an Act of Parliament". . . . The delusion of the mechani[cal] cal perfectability of mankind through a combined process of scientific knowledge and unconscious evolution has been responsible for a great deal of heartbreak. It is, at bottom, far more pessimistic than Christian pessimism, because, if science and progress break down, there is nothing to fall back on. Humanism is self-contained—it provides for man no resources outside himself.
—DOROTHY SAYERS, 1949[3]

Saddest of all is the disappointment one feels over the conduct of mankind in general. Younger people may feel little surprise; but, then, they have never known times of calm and reason. Things appeared rather differently to us when [you and I] were young. We believed the brutality of former times had been eliminated forever and had yielded to an age of reason and stability. . . . Now it becomes clear that our only hope . . . . is a slender hope, for our faith in human nature has been so severely shaken. . . . Let us hope posterity will have more than a smile of pity for our last hope—provided there is any posterity.
—ALBERT EINSTEIN, 1952,
in a Letter to the Queen Mother of Belgium[4]

There is a familiar old maxim which assures us that Man is the noblest work of God. Who found that out?   —MARK TWAIN[5]

I believe, and hold it as the fundamental article of Christianity, that I am a fallen creature; that I am of myself capable of moral evil, but not of myself capable of moral good, and that an evil ground existed in my will, previously to any given act, or assignable moment of time, in my consciousness. I am born a child of wrath.
—COLERIDGE[6]

There's no one who causes more trouble in this world than humans. They drive me crazy. I get so mad when I think about humans that I could scream!
—SNOOPY

To you is born this day . . . a Savior, who is Christ the Lord.
—LUKE 2:11

ON OCTOBER 1, 1950, Charlie Brown was first introduced to the world, through nine newspapers. In his very first cartoon, Schulz

...an at the beginning in the same way the New Testament ...egins— by setting the stage for all that is to come. When the drama of the New Testament opens, we are given a clear picture of all men and their predicament at the time "when the kindness and generosity of God our Saviour dawned upon the world":

> For at one time we ourselves in our folly and obstinacy were all astray. We were slaves to passions and pleasures of every kind. Our days were passed in malice and envy; we were odious ourselves and we hated one another. (Tit. 3:4, 5, NEB)

This is not a commentary on one little boy or on little boys in general, but on men. As if to be sure we understand this, Schulz gives us no relief in his second strip: Patty is walking down the street sweetly reciting the verse, "Little girls are made of sugar and spice and everything nice . . ." In the third panel she spots a much smaller *Peanut* and slaps him across the face. "That's what little girls are made of!" she concludes in the final panel. In the beginning, then, we know what little boys *and* little girls are made of.

The central "message" of the New Testament is: "God was in Christ reconciling the world to himself" (2 Cor. 5:19). This statement takes for granted the belief that the world—*all* the world—needs to be "reconciled." The idea that Christ was "in-

word for "man") a very simple "whatever you do" type of command. But Adam—out of sheer spiritual laziness, his natural tendency to spiritual inertia and slumber, his "sinfulness"—proceeds to break or let go of the command; he proceeds "to sin." As a result, God says to Adam:

> Because you . . . have eaten of the tree of which I commanded you, "You shall not eat of it," cursed is the ground because of you; in toil you shall eat of it all the days of your life. (Gen. 3:17)

So, then, substituting in the following cartoon a bright red balloon for the traditionally bright red apple, we can see another parable of how man was originally destined to proceed for the rest of his life in darkness down the same tracks—tracks leading away from home:

As Catholic theologian W. J. McGucken has said (speaking of lost balloons): "Unless this fact of the 'Fall of Man'—or, if you will, the dogma of original sin—be admitted, Christianity simply collapses like a pricked balloon. . . . For without the Fall, there would be no need of the Incarnation and Redemption, the two cardinal points of Christian belief."[12] Spiritually understood, man differs from the animals only by having a "heart" with passion enough for infinite commitment, for "taking a stand." But man's upright posture points only to the *possibility* of his becoming God-committed. For when man comes into the world and distinguishes himself from the animals by standing upright, he is still only a little higher than the beasts; he is still, as they are, a child of the world; the foundation for his life is still based upon the world itself; he is infinitely committed—but only to the finite. And thus, as novelist Taylor Caldwell can put it, "To ignore the pervading evil of mankind is to ignore the powerful force that has always motivated it from the moment humanity stood upright and became conscious of itself."[13]

"As indicated by the coming of Christianity into the world after a foregoing preparation," says Kierkegaard, "the invariable law is this: *No one starts by being a Christian, everyone becomes*

such in the fullness of time . . . if he does become such."[14] Our basic problem, then, belongs to our origin, our "start" in life. We are all off to a false start, running altogether in the wrong direction. This is why Christ's first command to all who would follow him is always—"Repent!" Turn around! Go the other way! You're running in the wrong direction! No one comes into life believing the Gospel, but only believing in a false gospel. Therefore, previous to all true belief, a true repentance is required. Christ's entire ministry began with this assumption: everyone is running in the wrong direction, attempting to avoid "the big problem." Thus, at the very beginning of his ministry, "Jesus came into Galilee proclaiming the Gospel of God: 'The time has come; the kingdom of God is upon you; repent, and believe the Gospel'" (Mk. 1:14–15, NEB). It was Christ's "distinct philosophy," then, that the best way for us all to solve our problems is to turn around and face *him*—head on.

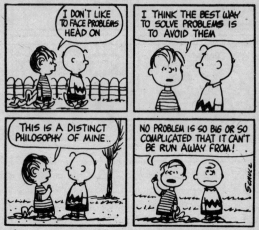

"What if everyone was like you?" Charlie Brown asks Linus. "What if everyone in the whole world suddenly decided to run away from his problems?" Says Linus: "Well, at least we'd all be running in the same direction." This is true; and it is also why Christ could say, "Unless you repent, you will all of you come to the same end" (Lk. 13:3, 5, NEB).

Because, then, of what the doctrine of original sin says about everyone, it will scarcely ever be popular with anyone. Even the Church frequently attempts to flatter itself and to win friends and influence people by watering down Christ's bedrock teaching of man's basic and innate depravity. If Christ had wanted to be more popular, he should have done the same. Apparently, however, Christ was not interested in sacrificing truth to win popularity contests: "The world . . . hates me because I testify of it that its works are evil" (Jn. 7:7). Therefore, any confrontation between the world and Christ will inevitably look like this:

Thus man is blinded to his own sin (or "crabbiness") by sin itself. Or, as Luther could put it, "The ultimate proof of the sinner is that he does not know his own sin."[15] Indeed, it was because of this basic spiritual blindness that Christ's contemporaries could not understand his most *direct* teachings—much less his parables. Because of sin, even his clearest teachings became —and still become—"parabolic" and incomprehensible:

That is why I speak to them in parables; for they look without seeing, and listen without hearing or understanding. There is a prophecy of Isaiah which is being fulfilled for them: ". . . this people has grown gross at heart; their ears are dull, and their

eyes are closed. Otherwise, their eyes might see, their ears hear, and their heart understand, and then they might turn again, and I would heal them." (Mt. 13:13, 15, NEB)

And so, as Pascal could say, "There are only two kinds of men: the righteous who believe themselves sinners; the rest, sinners, who believe themselves righteous."[16] As we have already seen, Lucy has a tendency to think of herself as one of the righteous ones. We are grateful to her for playing this role, because self-delusion can produce some hilarious comedy. And "if a man imagines himself to be somebody, when he is nothing, he is deluding himself" (Gal. 6:3, NEB).

But this is hardly a childish fancy. Man's self-delusion is extremely tough and durable from the moment he becomes a man. "The imagination of man's heart is evil from his youth," the Old Testament quotes God as saying (Gen. 8:21). Originally *hollow*-hearted, man is also originally *hard*-hearted. The hard layers surrounding man's empty heart are thick indeed—they "go down deep . . . layer after layer after layer!" And this is why "the un-redeemed mind of man, split off from the mind of the Creator, denies its Origin, denies itself" (Barth).[17]

For this reason far more than an ordinary mirror or a truthful friend is required if one is ever really to see oneself. What is finally required? The Psalmist puts it this way:

> For the inward mind and heart of a man are deep! But God will shoot his arrow at them; they will be wounded suddenly. (64:6, 7)

Even from their youth, all men and women "are like white-washed tombs, which outwardly appear beautiful, but within are full of dead men's bones and all uncleanness" (Mt. 23:27); but God himself "will break down the wall that you have daubed with whitewash, and bring it down to the ground, so that its foundation will be laid bare" (Ezek. 13:14).

Schulz has said of Lucy that "perhaps if you scratched deeper you'd find she's even worse than she seems."[18] But our intention is not to equate sin with Lucy-like villainy or "crabbiness," although sin often does show up as such. "Sin" is no more or no less than this: worshiping anything that is *not* God; "sinfulness" is our *tendency*—which we never fully escape—to do just this; and "origin-al sin" points to our origins in life wherein all of us are "sinful sinners"—that is, with the tendency to continue in this way, we begin our lives by "serving the creature rather than the Creator" (Rom. 1:25). The largest thing in the world

is the heart of man, for it is capable of containing God himself. But man's originally empty heart is only infinitely desolate and anxious. Therefore, even from our earliest days, little experience is required for us to know that deep within our inmost selves something is dreadfully wrong and woefully lacking. As St. Augustine could put it in his famous prayer: "Thou hast formed us for Thyself, and our hearts are restless till they find rest in Thee."[19] Or, as another famous North African, St. Camus, could say: "Beginning to think is beginning to be undermined. Society has but little connection with such beginnings. The worm is in man's heart. That is where it must be sought."[20]

We do not require great education of the mind to understand that here is no real and lasting satisfaction; that our pleasures are only vanity; that our evils are infinite. (Pascal)[21]

Schulz tells us that at one time early in his career he attempted to illustrate the entire Old Testament book of Ecclesiastes with cartoon figures, but later scrapped the effort as he "didn't know what to do with it." Nevertheless, the major themes of Ecclesiastes still constantly reappear in *Peanuts*. For instance, Ecclesiastes begins by lamenting the family of man's ancient "charter,"

from which there seems to be no escape and in which man seems to be beaten before he begins. In this sense no generation is different from any other: the "vanity" or hollowness of man's life is inherited from generation to generation in the same sense that men beget men and not angels. ("That's always been the trouble with our family," says Linus. "We have too much heredity.")

> Vanity of vanities, says the Preacher, vanity of vanities! All is vanity. What does man gain by all the toil at which he toils under the sun? A generation goes, and a generation comes, but the earth remains for ever. (Eccles. 1:2–4)

A deep yearning is everywhere present: the yearning for a new breakthrough into the imprisonment formed by man's age-old inability to change himself or his world radically for the better:

> The sun rises and the sun goes down, and hastens to the place where it rises. . . . What has been is what will be, and what has been done is what will be done; and there is nothing new under the sun. Is there a thing of which it is said, "See, this is new"? It has been already, in the ages before us. (Eccles. 1:5, 9–10)

I said to myself, "I have acquired great wisdom . . . and my mind has had great experience of wisdom and knowledge." And I applied my mind to know wisdom and to know madness and folly. I perceived that this also is but a striving after wind. For in much wisdom is much vexation, and he who increases knowledge increases sorrow. (Eccles. 1:16–18)

We here break off and limit ourselves to the first chapter of Ecclesiastes, as Schulz—very much like Dante—could easily furnish us with tour guides who could help us to see the entire book as a sort of divine comedy.

One of the purposes of Art-Parable is, as Shakespeare could put it, "to hold the mirror up to nature." Schulz is a master in this regard, especially in holding the mirror up to human nature. This job is made easier for him by the fact that he deals exclusively with small children—and deals with them honestly. If one man is a microcosm, "a little world," a child is—in several ways—an even more clearly defined and concentrated microcosm. One of these ways is the clearer view we can obtain from children of the primitive, unadulterated evil in man. Evil is literally "unadulterated" in children as children lack the adult's sophisticated ability to mask and disguise evil. By "evil" we mean "sin." And although man's basic alienation from God does not always manifest itself in the form of "sins" (behavior such as envy, hatred, jealousy, anger, etc.), the Christian learns to recognize a close connection between man's *being* alienated and his *acting* alienated. A person who is fundamentally miserable will tend to act miserable and make life miserable for others sooner than a person who is fundamentally whole and happy. "Sins" are usually, to borrow a phrase from Linus, "only a manifestation of a deeper problem." (For this reason, only he who is without sin should throw stones at the Church's venerable teaching of man's basic—or original—sinfulness.) In Art-Parable, then, as well as in "real life," sin is most often dramatized by "sins." This is why, as one magazine article could say of Schulz, "There is no doubt that Schulz, a fervent Bible reader, is aware of original sin. He owns up to making his Peanuts mean because he believes that kids are born mean. But by making his characters cruel on occasion, he has also made them believable."[22] Cruelty, like crabgrass, runs rampant throughout the Peanuts patch, so much so that there is no need to cite particular examples. Rather, it should be sufficient to say that in the Christian's view of things, including Schulz's, the games people play as children do not essentially change by the time they are adults:

"Fancy thinking the Beast was something you could hunt and kill!" says the "Beast" in one of the children of *Lord of the Flies*, a novel dramatizing the heart of darkness in man and particularly in children. "You knew, didn't you? I'm part of you? Close, close, close! I'm the reason why it's no go? Why things are what

they are?"[23] Likewise the Christian has learned to understand the root of evil to be in man's heart, not elsewhere. The Christian is one who has met the enemy and it is he—the Christian. Thence he knows that "the heart of the sons of men is full of evil, and madness is in their heart while they live" (Eccles. 9:3, KJV). Schulz also has indicated, in word and cartoon, where he feels the source of each generation's problems is to be found. He has said, for instance: "I don't think all the terrible things young people end up doing should be blamed on their parents. Some kids just do dumb things, no matter what their parents were like."[24] Schulz has also expressed this thought in the cartoon above.

"Our generation has been given the works," laments Lucy in another cartoon. "All of the world's problems are being shoved at us!" "What do you think we should do?" asks Linus. Replies Lucy with clenched teeth and fist, "*Stick the next generation!*" In thinking of sin, says Barth,

> We may all be inclined to think of man's countless foolish and selfish intentions, his twisted and mischievous words and deeds. From all these sin can be known, as a tree can be known from its fruits. Yet these outward signs are not sin itself, the wages of which are death. Sin is not confined to the evil things we *do*. It is the evil within us, the evil which we *are*. Shall we call it our pride or our laziness, or shall we call it the deceit of our life? Let us call it for once the great defiance which turns us again and again into the enemies of God and of our fellowmen, even of our own selves.[25]

This is why doing battle with "sins" rather than sin is to miss the mark and to achieve nothing. The misdirected struggle against "sins" is what Bonhoeffer calls "moral fanaticism":

> The fanatic imagines that his moral purity will prove a match for the power of evil, but like a bull he goes for the red rag instead of the man who carries it, grows weary and succumbs. He becomes entangled with non-essentials and falls into the trap set by the superior ingenuity of his adversary.[26]

St. Augustine tells us that the glorious virtues of good pagans are only "splendid vices." This means that all good works, charities, deeds, however magnificent they may be and from whatever high-minded motives, are like cities built on sand as far

as the workman himself is concerned, unless they are built on what the New Testament calls *the* foundation stone—a stone that is nevertheless not a part of the original equipment of any of us. Therefore "let each take care how he builds. There can be no other foundation beyond . . . Jesus Christ himself" (1 Cor. 3:11, NEB). "Whatever does not proceed from faith is sin" (Rom. 14:23), is another New Testament expression of this thought. Or, as Luther could put it with characteristic bluntness: "If a man were not first a believer and a Christian, all his work would amount to nothing at all and would be freely wicked and damnable sins."[27] This means not so much that "faith without works

is dead," as it means that "works without faith are dead." And if our works are "sin," or are done from the basis of any other foundation than Christ himself, regardless of how good or great they may seem to be, they will finally be incapable of overcoming that depression or "death" which is the inevitable wage or payment or accompaniment of our sin. (See cartoon above.)

For the Christian, then, "it is not enough to live a moral, honest life" (Donne);[28] it is not enough to be a man of strong personality or character. The Christian sees that "the morality of modern civilized man has turned out to be a terribly thin covering of ice over a sea of primitive barbarity" (Barth);[29] the Christian knows that "from lust men have founded and extracted excellent rules of policy, morality, and justice; but in reality this vile root of man . . . is only covered, it is not taken away" (Pascal).[30] But when the Church drops its preoccupation with "sins" or works or morality, and begins again to concentrate on its own proper concern—sin, man's basic estrangement from God—this change is upsetting to the state, to secular society and to the moral, honest man. Why? Because these three have learned to use the Church's moral concerns as a guarantor of their own interests, and now the Church has turned to other matters—matters that they have never fully understood anyway. This is why in periods of history where the Church has clearly addressed its Gospel to sin, as in the first century of its existence, the state—however "democratic"—has looked upon the Church with deep suspicion and mistrust. But when the Church is feeble enough to substitute "the law" for its Gospel, it is hypocritically received with open arms by the state as the state's little brother and welcome ally, a force to "regulate congregations and keep people in order." Thus the Church's tendency toward legalism or what Nietzsche called a "slave morality," is used by the state in this way:

It has often been protested that the Church's doctrine of man's basic sinfulness is unnecessarily harsh and pessimistic in its view of man; that the Church should not allow its "mind to become so darkened with mistrust that it loses its ability to believe in people." But the Church is finally far more optimistic about man—all men—than any other point of view ever could be. The Church simply does not believe that man is God, nor that man is—in and of himself—good. The Church believes that "no one does good, not even one" (Rom. 3:12), that "no one is good but God alone" (Mk. 10:18); but that nevertheless God loves all men infinitely. The difficulty at this point, as C. S. Lewis has observed, is that "no sooner do we believe that God loves us than there is an impulse to believe that he does so, not because He is Love, but because we are intrinsically lovable."[31] God loves man out of His own freedom and election and not because He ever owes man anything. And when man loves man, unless this love is based on the supremely *realistic* view of man furnished only by God's revelation in Christ of who man actually is, man's "love" for man will quickly degenerate into unconcealed hate and the utmost pessimism. This is why Bonhoeffer could say:

Contempt for man and idolization of man are close neighbors. . . . there is also an honestly intended philanthropism which amounts to the same thing as contempt for mankind. It consists in judging man according to his latent values, according to his underlying soundness, reasonableness and goodness. This kind of philanthropism will generally arise in peaceful times . . . . with forced indulgence evil is interpreted as good. Baseness is overlooked and the reprehensible is excused. . . . One's love is directed to a picture of man of one's own making, a picture which scarcely preserves any resemblance with the reality. And consequently one

finishes once again by despising the real man whom God has loved and whose nature He has taken upon Himself. It is only through God's being made man that it is possible to know the real man and not to despise him.[32]

To say that God is God, and man is not God; to say that "God is in heaven, and you upon earth" (Eccles. 5:2), is not to despise man but simply not to worship him or place one's absolute trust in him. This is why the Old Testament can advise us: "Put not your trust in princes, in a son of man, in whom there is no help" (Ps. 146:3); and why the New Testament can say: "But Jesus did not trust himself to them, because he knew all men and needed no one to bear witness of man; for he himself knew what was in man" (Jn. 2:24, 25). A naïve trust in the basic trustworthiness of man has probably caused more wrenching heartache for humanity as a whole than any other single misplacement of faith. "It is a Christian theological intuition, confirmed by all of historical experience," wrote Catholic theologian John Courtney Murray, "that man lives both his personal and his social life always more or less close to the brink of barbarism."[33] The assassination of President John F. Kennedy, in broad daylight on the streets of Dallas, furnishes an ironic example of misplaced trust in man. Two days later, as Kennedy was being

officially eulogized in Washington, one of the eulogists began by saying "The only thing we learn from history is that we do not learn." Literally within minutes of the moment Supreme Court Justice Warren spoke these words, history was indeed repeating itself: Kennedy's apparent assassin was himself assassinated in broad daylight on the streets of Dallas. As T. S. Eliot has put it:

> We do not know very much of the future
> Except that from generation to generation
> The same things happen again and again.
> Men learn little from others' experience.[34]

No doubt this is true—especially when we consider how little we learn from our own experience:

Jesus did not instruct his Church to trust in men, but rather to "beware of men." If Christ had sent his disciples into the world only as sheep ministering to sheep, why send them at all? It was a radical change in the deepest nature of man the disciples were commissioned to seek to bring about: "Behold, I send you out as sheep in the midst of wolves" (Mt. 10:16, 17). And thus St. Paul could say, "if any one is in Christ, he is a new creature" (2 Cor. 5:17).

Just as *Peanuts* appears in the context of the daily newspaper, the Gospel was meant to be proclaimed in the midst of the real world and to the real world. The real world is a world of sin, as any daily newspaper would almost seem to shout at us. "Most newspaper headlines," says Robert McAfee Brown, "are more effective examples of man's sin writ large than any book on theology ever could be."[35] Therefore, if the Gospel is to be heard by the real world in a meaningful way, it must never let itself be beguiled by "the thin covering of ice" that exists over the human situation in the form of superficial human advancements. If there is ever to be any advance in the *real* human situation, that situation must first be faced in all honesty for what it honestly and truly and always is. "This generation's deepest need," said Fosdick in words applicable to every generation, "is not these dithyrambic songs about inevitable progress, but a fresh sense of personal and social sin."[36]

The real difference in the believer who follows Christ and has mortified his will and died after the old man in Christ, is that he is more clearly aware than other men of the rebelliousness and perennial pride of the flesh, he is conscious of his sloth and self-indulgence and knows that his arrogance must be eradicated.[37]

The Christian knows, like Bonhoeffer in the above statement, that he has been given an insight into and understanding of human nature that is not given to "the natural man." We say "given" because this insight is only made certain in God's revelation in Christ. We confess with Pascal "that so soon as the Christian religion reveals the principle that human nature is corrupt and fallen from God, that opens my eyes to see everywhere the mark of this truth."[38] But however obvious to anyone "this truth" might seem to be, it is only made known through Christ. Furthermore, the Christian's understanding of his fellow man is only the *beginning* of his witness; he must never stop here. For the Christian witnesses to the beginning *and* the end, to One wholly other than himself, to One who can do more than simply understand, to One who can also help—or pity. "Pity," by definition, comes from one much greater than ourselves, one who can understand *and* help, otherwise blind will lead blind and both will fall into a pit (Lk. 6:39). And so, as the New Testament can tell us: "And Jesus in pity touched their eyes, and immediately they received their sight and followed him" (Mt. 20:34).

When Bonhoeffer said, "I don't think it is Christian to want to get to the New Testament too soon and too directly,"[39] he was simply saying that no doctor in his right mind would attempt to cure a patient without first carefully diagnosing the malady; that "you cannot and must not speak the last word before you have spoken the next to last"; that "if the Church refuses to face the stern reality of sin, it will gain no credence when it talks of forgiveness."[40] Nuclear physicist J. Robert Oppenheimer was getting at the same point when he said, "When we deny the evil in ourselves, we dehumanize ourselves, and we deprive ourselves not only of our own destiny but of any possibility of dealing with the evil in others."[41] Christ also had some observations about "dealing with the evil of others." He suggests that anyone who wants to be a reformer will have a hard life unless he or she first begins at the beginning with an honest eye for the real nature of the problem and where it lies. Then, perhaps, they will be able to help:

> Why do you look at the speck of sawdust in your brother's eye, with never a thought for the great plank in your own? How can you say to your brother, "My dear brother, let me take the speck out of your eye," when you are blind to the plank in your own?

You hypocrite! First take the plank out of your own eye, and then you will see clearly to take the speck out of your brother's. (Lk. 6:41–42, NEB)

Everyone who has a little experience knows at heart that this is a rotten world. But just as it is the done thing in a prison to keep a stiff upper lip . . . as it is in consequence the custom in prisons to tease and torment the man who lets it be seen that he is suffering, so with mankind in the world. In general, anyone who wants to understand human life as a whole would do best to study the criminal world—this is the really reliable analogy.[42]

Alas for Kierkegaard's day, when it was necessary to have everyone study the gloomy world of crime in order that they might "understand human life as a whole." In our day we are much luckier: we have all mankind (including some eternity) hilariously bounded in the nutshell of the little world of *Peanuts*; for here also is a "really reliable analogy."

4 *Where Your Blanket Is, There Will Your Heart Be Also*

The devil took him to a very high mountain, and showed him all the kingdoms of the world and the glory of them; and he said to him, "All these I will give you, if you will fall down and worship me." Then Jesus said to him, "Begone, Satan! for it is written, 'You shall worship the Lord your God and him only shall you serve.'" Then the devil left him, and behold, angels came and ministered to him. —MATTHEW 4:8–11

The Church . . . has not proclaimed often and clearly enough her message of the one God who has revealed Himself for all times in Jesus Christ and who suffers no other gods beside Himself. —BONHOEFFER[1]

God designed the human machine to run on Himself. He Himself is the fuel our spirits were designed to burn, or the food our spirits were designed to feed on. There isn't any other. —C. S. LEWIS[2]

As for the rich in this world, charge them not to be haughty, nor to set their hopes on uncertain riches but on God who richly furnishes us with everything to enjoy . . . . thus laying up for themselves a good foundation for the future, so that they may take hold of the life which is life indeed.—1 TIMOTHY 6:17, 19

ALL MEN SEEK ONE THING in the present moment and one thing from the future. Pascal put it this way:

> All men seek happiness. This is without exception. Whatever different means they employ, they all tend to this end. The cause of some going to war, and of others avoiding it, is the same desire in both. . . . The will never takes the least step but to this object. This is the motive of every action of every man, even those who hang themselves.[3]

The Christian faith knows that at all times all men basically desire to be outrageously happy and that they cannot wish to be otherwise. Christianity acknowledges this basic motive, approves of it, and itself wishes for all men the fullest possible happiness now and forever. For this very reason Christ came into the world: "I came that they may have life, and have it abundantly" (Jn. 10:10); for this very reason Christ spoke all that he said: "These things I have spoken to you, that my joy may be in you, and that your joy may be full" (Jn. 15:11). An essential part of the good news Christianity wants to make clear about the Kingdom of outrageous happiness sought by all men, is that "It is your Father's good pleasure to give you the kingdom" (Lk. 12:32). "We are working with you for your own happiness" (2

Cor. 1:24, NEB), St. Paul could say, thus summing up precisely
what he was attempting to accomplish. "I repeat: God is not
against us, he is for us . . . . the Savior is no kill-joy" (Barth).[4]

Christ's message, then, took for granted and accepted the fact
that all men, "without exception," seek to "find" or "save" their
own lives—seek to find the greatest possible happiness for themselves. To ask a man to do otherwise is to ask him not to be a
man. No change is asked for here. What *does* need to be changed,
however, is the way or place in which this happiness is found.
Christianity is "the way [that] leads toward possession of what
you have sought for in the wrong place" (T. S. Eliot).[5] Christianity does not condemn the "self-love" that seeks happiness for
itself; but it does claim that no other "object" of devotion, other
than God himself, is capable of giving man the happiness he
seeks and that God would have him find. And since man is
easily capable of making even *himself* an object of devotion,
Christ could say: "Whoever would save his life will lose it, and
whoever loses his life for my sake will find it" (Mt. 16:25). Thus
the self must first learn to love itself properly, by giving its ultimate devotion to God alone. As Kierkegaard could put it:

> The command reads thus, "You shall love your neighbor as your-
> self," but properly understood, it also says . . . "You shall love
> yourself in the right way." If anyone, therefore, refuses to learn
> from Christianity how to love himself in the right way, he can-
> not love his neighbor either. He can perhaps cling to one or
> more men "through thick and thin," as it is called, but this is,
> by no means, loving one's neighbor. To love oneself in the right
> way and to love one's neighbor correspond perfectly to one another;
> fundamentally they are one and the same thing.[6]

In the meantime, the originally empty men of this world trust
in the world itself to love them and furnish them with the fulfillment they seek. Indeed they *must* trust in the world, or some
aspect of it, for originally the world is all they know. Where else
can they turn for help? "It is natural for the mind to believe,
and for the will to love; so that, for want of true objects, they
must attach themselves to false" (Pascal).[7] And so it is that
when God begins putting the squeeze on spiritual infants to
"become a man" and "give up childish ways" (1 Cor. 13:11), the

child's first evasive action is to stop "drifting along" with the world in general and to make a well-considered decision about which "stand" to take in order to reap the most returns. It works like this:

And thus our vague *idolatry*, our worship of "the world in general," is forced into the more well-defined shape of a particular *idol*. When God begins to press in on us, "like a weaver I [roll] up my life" (Is. 38:12) and "foul sin gather[s] head" (Shakespeare). Our lives deepen and become more concentrated by developing a "ruling passion" (Pascal), an "ultimate concern" (Tillich), a "joy above the rest" (Shakespeare), "some sort of cause" (Lucy). What Lucy has failed to notice in the above cartoon is that Linus *already* has taken a stand and "associated himself with a cause"—his blanket. It is his blanket that gives hope and meaning to his life and around which his life is centered. "What are we really devoted to? That is the question," says Bonhoeffer;[8] and one look at Linus will clearly show what *he* is devoted to. "I can't live without that blanket," he says. "I can't face life unarmed." Schulz himself has said that Linus' blanket "is a symbol of things we cling to";[9] and in this sense, none of us are without "blankets":

"Our hearts have room only for one all-embracing devotion," said Bonhoeffer, "and we can only cleave to one Lord."[10] All of us, then, have our one security blanket, our Lord, our faith, our god, or that which we do not question but "take seriously without any reservation" (Tillich). "Who ain't a slave? Tell me that," asks Melville in *Moby Dick*, weighing the nature of things —as he says—"in the scales of the New Testament."[11] And the New Testament fully agrees: "You know well enough that . . . you are slaves of the master whom you obey; and this is true whether you serve sin, with death as its result; or obedience,

with righteousness as its result" (Rom. 6:16, NEB). This is also why Christ could tell us that "No one can serve two masters; for either he will hate the one and love the other, or he will be devoted to the one and despise the other. You cannot serve God and mammon" (Mt. 6:24). Obviously, then, the question is not *whether* we shall have a god to serve and worship, but *which* god we shall worship. From the biblical point of view, "the Lord is greater than all gods" (Ex. 18:11); "the Lord is the true God" (Jer. 10:10). "There are countless places of refuge," said Kafka; "there is only one place of salvation."[12] In Christianity's view of things, Christ is *the place* of salvation. All other ways, all other places, are mere unsatisfactory refuges ultimately, and for this reason there is finally little that really matters to distinguish them—as in the cartoon above.

The cause of so much trouble between people today lies far deeper than misunderstandings between liberals and conservatives, or even between "blockheads" and "dumbbells." Differences between all false gods are insignificant when compared to the infinite distinction between God and *anything* which is not God. Barth puts it this way:

> The world is worshipped and served . . . quite apart from its creator. . . . Contradictions within the deified world—Nature and Civilization, Materialism and Idealism, Capitalism and Socialism, Secularism and Ecclesiasticism, Imperialism and Democracy —are not so serious as they give themselves out to be. Such contradictions are contradictions within the world, and there is for them no paradox, no negation, no eternity.[13]

"I began as a child," comedian Bill Cosby tells us. This is also true of all of us in a spiritual sense. All of us begin our lives as spiritual children and victims of "misdirected faith," a phrase Schulz has used to characterize Charlie Brown.[14] In this sense, then, Charlie Brown is a "born loser" because he is "born lost." For Charlie Brown, more than the other Peanuts, is constantly made aware of the futility that inevitably arises in having one's first-rate concerns attached to only second-rate causes. More than anything else, Charlie Brown wants "to win." It doesn't matter whether it is winning a game or a friend or one of his struggles with his unco-operative kites; he just wants to win—*anything*.

In the first eighteen years of his existence, we can recall his actually having "won" only once. And in this strip we are reminded not so much of the futility of *losing*, as we are again shown the futility of *winning the wrong thing*. For the Second Commandment, like all biblical commandments, is only a commentary on the First:

1. You shall have no other gods besides me.
2. You shall not make for yourself a graven image, or any likeness of anything . . . you shall not bow down to them or serve them; for I the Lord your God am a jealous God. . . . (Ex. 20:3–4)

This does not mean that God has anything against "winning," as such. It just means that most of us live our lives primarily attempting to win the wrong contests:

You know (do you not?) that at the sports all the runners run the race, though only one wins the prize. Like them, run to win! But . . . they do it to win a fading wreath; we, a wreath that never fades. (1 Cor. 9:24–25, NEB)

Fading wreaths and trophies are also God's good gifts to his children, as is everything else in all creation. But the creation, or any part thereof, becomes demonic, disappointing, and harshly cruel to us whenever we place it *first* in our lives, whenever we "worship and serve the creature rather than the Creator" (Rom. 1:25). Not unless "the first" (God) is put first in our lives can anything else give us any real satisfaction. "Lo! naught contents thee, who content'st not Me" (Francis Thompson).[15] This is why Christ could tell us to "seek ye first the kingdom of God, and his righteousness; and all these things shall be added unto you" (Mt. 6:33, KJV). To be "a Charlie Brown," then, means to hope in the wrong things for the happiness we seek. "I thought having a baby sister would change my whole life, but it hasn't," he sadly tells Linus soon after Sally's arrival. "People still hate me. Nobody *really* likes me. I get just as depressed as I always did." "Poor Charlie Brown," observes Linus. "Of all the Charlie Browns in the world, he's the Charlie Brownest!" The Christian is simply a man who has "let God be God," to use Luther's phrase. His relationship to everything else is a secondary relationship, to "hang loose," to "have . . . as though [he] had none" (1 Cor. 7:29). For, as Kierkegaard has pointed out, "every Christian has had his earthly Messiah."[16] And the Christian has learned from sad experience that pursuing false gods and false messiahs not only entangles *him* hopelessly, but also that running after strange gods often brings misery to those around him:

> The word of the Lord came to me: "Son of man, you dwell in the midst of a rebellious house. . . . I will spread my net over [the prince who is among them], and he shall be taken in my snare. . . . And I will scatter toward every wind all who are round about him, his helpers and all his troops. . . ." (Ezek. 12:1, 13–14)

"For all is vanity and a striving after wind" (Eccles. 2:17). Putting our final trust in *anything* other than God himself is "vanity" and futility:

> I saw that . . . the race is not to the swift, nor the battle to the strong, nor bread to the wise, nor riches to the intelligent, nor favor to the men of skill; but time and chance happen to them all. For man does not know his time. Like fish which are taken in an evil net, and like birds which are caught in a snare, so the sons of men are snared at an evil time, when it suddenly falls upon them. (Eccles. 9:11–12)

What of Iago's advice to "put money in thy purse"? Is this also vanity and a striving after wind?

> Do not toil to acquire wealth; be wise enough to desist. When your eyes light on it, it is gone; for suddenly it takes to itself wings, flying like an eagle toward heaven. (Prov. 23:4, 5)

Like this:

Then he said to the people, "Beware! Be on your guard against greed of every kind, for even when a man has more than enough, his wealth does not give him life." (Lk. 12:15, NEB)

At this point, Jesus "told them a parable." But we will use a modern one:

However, we should be careful not to leave the impression that idolatry consists only in the worship of *things*. It can be far more subtle and sophisticated than that. It can just as easily exist as the worship and service of ideas, philosophies, notions, speculations, abstractions of any sort. For this reason the New Testament can again tell us to

Be on your guard; do not let your minds be captured by hollow and delusive speculations, based on traditions of man-made teach-

ing and centred on the rudimentary notions of the world and
not on Christ. For it is in Christ that the complete being of the
Godhead dwells embodied. . . . (Col. 2:8–9, NEB)

But Lucy's philosophies seem to have little staying power as she,
like history, changes them regularly. She did hit on one, however, that seemed to be better thought out than many of the
others. She tells Charlie Brown: "I have a profound philosophy
that has stood the test of time difficult as it may be for the lay-
man to understand. I have a philosophy that has been refined
in the fires of hardship and struggle: 'Live and let live!' "

But we should not overlook that final refuge for those who
have sought happiness in place after place and have been disappointed time after time. This is the refuge of stoic renuncia-
tion, of "not expecting too much," of "learning to live with one's
despair." T. S. Eliot has described man and wife with this malady by saying:

> They may remember
> The vision they have had, but they cease to regret it,
> Maintain themselves by the common routine,
> Learn to avoid excessive expectation,
> Become tolerant of themselves and others,

Giving and taking, in the usual actions
What there is to give and take.

Two people who know they do not understand each other,
Breeding children whom they do not understand
And who will never understand them.[17]

Schulz, on the other hand, has described a little boy with this illness in this way:

"Sometimes when I get up in the morning," says Snoopy, "I feel very peculiar. I feel like I've just got to bite a cat! I feel like if I don't bite a cat before sundown, I'll go crazy!! But then I just take a deep breath and forget about it. That's what is known," he adds sarcastically, "as real *maturity!*" Maturity? Perhaps a psychiatrist might call this frame of mind "maturity" or "adjustment." In the New Testament, however, it is known as being "dead even while [one] lives" (1 Tim. 5:6).

Christianity believes it is literally true that, in the words of the popular song, *You're nobody 'til somebody loves you!* But this poses a problem. For if all of us remain nobodies 'til somebody loves us, how then can there ever come to be "a somebody" in the first place? If all of us begin as nobodies, where will we ever find the somebody to love us and to get this trans-

formation started? Christianity proclaims the good news of how a *real Someone* from the outside has broken into this closed and vicious circle of nobodies, has *loved* all of these nobodies, and hence has created other "real somebodies." It proclaims "the God who makes the dead live and summons things that are not yet in existence as if they already were" (Rom. 4:17, NEB); it is the proclamation of a people who "once . . . were no people but now . . . are God's people" (1 Pet. 2:10). Furthermore, Christianity not only affirms that this *real Someone* has *started* this process of creating somebodies out of nobodies, but it also believes that apart from an active relationship to this *real Someone*, all of us either remain or return to being nobodies. If, then, we only look to our brothers and sisters to love us so that we may become "real somebodies," and in this way worship *them* as gods, we are doomed to disappointment. For our brothers and sisters, in and of themselves, are only nobodies too, as we all are. Thus disappointed we will, as Eliot says, "maintain ourselves by the common routine." That is, we will hang on all the more desperately to our shaky little securities, concluding that the whole world has been programed in a lousy way and is only one large sour grape anyway.

5 *The Heart Is a Slave*

You may believe that smoking is bad for your health and nevertheless be a heavy smoker. And this holds true for all evil impulses that poison life. I do not need to emphasize my respect and appreciation for every possible effort in the direction of truth and knowledge. But I do not believe that the lack of moral and aesthetic values can be counterbalanced by purely intellectual effort. —ALBERT EINSTEIN[1]

When we ask the Bible what it has to offer, it answers by putting to us the fact of election. What we call religion and culture may be available to everybody, but the belief, simple and comprehensive, which is offered in the Bible, is not available to everybody: not at any time nor in any respect can any who will, reach out and take it. —KARL BARTH[2]

What other dungeon is so dark as one's own heart! What jailer so inexorable as one's self! —HAWTHORNE[3]

So it depends not upon man's will or exertion, but upon God's mercy. For [God] . . . has mercy upon whomever he wills, and he hardens the heart of whomever he wills. —ROMANS 9:16, 18

If the heart is devoted to the mirage of the world, to the creature instead of the Creator, the disciple is lost. . . . However urgently Jesus may call us, his call fails to find access to our hearts. Our hearts are closed, for they have already been given to another. —BONHOEFFER[4]

Once there was a time when I thought I could give up thumbsucking. Now I doubt if I ever could. I'm hooked! —LINUS

Sᴛ. Pᴀᴜʟ ᴛᴇʟʟs his "brothers in the faith" at Colossae to

> put to death those parts of you which belong to the earth . . .
> which is nothing less than idolatry. . . . Stop lying to one another,
> now that you have discarded the old nature with its deeds and
> have put on the new nature. . . . (Col. 3:5, 9–10, NEB)

But Paul knew, just as Linus knows, that the basic problem is
not one of "lying to one another." The problem of lying to
one another is only a derivative from the more fundamental
problem of "discarding the old nature":

"Perhaps I shall come away with you," Zorba's boss said to him.
"I'm free."

   Zorba shook his head. "No, you're not free," he said. "The

string you're tied to is perhaps longer than other people's. That's all. You're on a long piece of string, boss; you come and go, and think you're free, but you never cut the string in two. And when people don't cut that string . . ."

"I'll cut it some day!" I said defiantly, because Zorba's words had touched an open wound in me and hurt.

"It's difficult, boss, very difficult. You need a touch of folly to do that; folly, d'you see? You have to risk everything! But you've got such a strong head, it'll always get the better of you. A man's head is like a grocer; it keeps accounts: I've paid so much and earned so much and that means a profit of this much or a loss of that much! The head's a careful little shopkeeper; it never risks all it has, always keeps something in reserve. It never breaks the string. Ah no! . . . If the string slips out of its grasp, the head, poor devil, is lost, finished! But if a man doesn't break the string, tell me, what flavor is left in life? The flavor of camomile, weak camomile tea! Nothing like rum—that makes you see life inside out!"[5]

Or, to use the words of Linus, life will only have the flavor of a thumb—"a good thumb, but not a great thumb!" Later, however, he complains: "I think I'm losing my flavor."

It is the nature of man's heart *to love, to give itself* totally and completely—"with all its heart." The heart of man is like a dog in its slavish devotion to its real and true and ultimate master. Even though its master be unbelievably cruel, man's dog of a heart will cling to its true love, its true master, its "god," to the very end. The heart's basic devotion is blind; it can see no other master. Its adherence is like that of the apostles when Jesus asked them if they would "also go away? Simon Peter answered him, 'Lord, to whom shall we go? You have the words of eternal life . . .'" (Jn. 6:68). The heart *cannot* choose another master because choice is always made on the basis of an ultimate criterion or standard that is trusted without reservation; and the heart's basic master is also the heart's ultimate criterion or standard that is so trusted. Everything else is judged in relation to this *one master* that the heart could never seriously judge or question without admitting its own god's total failure and defeat. "Oh, 'Great Pumpkin,' you've let me down again!" screams Linus at another one of the false gods in *Peanuts*. "I'll never

believe in you again! Never! (Pause) Don't listen to me . . . I don't know what I'm saying!" This, then, is the meaning behind Christ's question: "How can Satan cast out Satan?" (Mk. 3:23). How can the heart of the "natural man," originally *in love* with the world itself, or some part thereof, be expected to overthrow its own true, first love and love another? It *cannot.* Man's heart is a virtual slave; it "belongs" to what it truly loves (Rom. 7:4). For instance, if a person should happen to be what the New Testament calls a "lover of self" (2 Tim. 3:2), how can this self possibly stop being itself and become another?

In the first place, why *should* Satan cast out Satan? How can we expect any radically new changes or "resolutions" to occur within a person if they feel no *need* for such changes. Man is basically inclined to "like himself just the way he is." As long as his heart's desire, his god, is serving him well, why should he—or she—change? (See next cartoon.)

Luther can tell us that no man is "sinner" by nature, but that he must "become" one. That is, the original basis for one's life is never *thought* to be a false foundation until it "becomes"— or proves to be—such by its total collapse from under the duped

idolator. But this collapse must be total. Man will cling to whatever false foundation he has built his life on until there is absolutely no ground left for him to stand (or lie) on. He has to stand this ground; this is a man's god we are talking about: it is the very foundation of his life and without it he is "lost, finished!" For "the worldly man," then, nothing less than the most devastating earthquake of the spirit will shake him from his foundation. Until that time, he will stubbornly hold his ground—in one way or another:

"How stubborn you are, heathen still at heart and deaf to the truth! You always fight against the Holy Spirit. Like fathers, like sons" (Acts 7:51, NEB). This is why asking a man to abandon his god before this god has utterly abandoned him—no, that's just not possible. Forget it!

"I'm not guilty, it's a misunderstanding. And if it comes to that, how can any man be called guilty? We are all simply men here, one as much as the other . . . . (yes,) that's how all guilty men talk" (Kafka).[6] Thus men will cling to the central belief of their lives—whether belief in their own righteousness or belief in the future or whatever—until this belief has completely failed them and there is no hope left in it. "Roy, I need some good advice," says Peppermint Patty. "What do you do when something you've counted on doesn't happen? This thing I really believed was going to happen, didn't happen. What do I do?" Says Roy, "Well, you could admit you were wrong." Says Peppermint Patty, "Besides that, I mean."

Man's total commitment to his god, to whatever gives meaning to his life, also accounts for the defensiveness he has for this god—especially if it is a weak one, as all false gods ultimately are. With our blankets securely in our grasp, we may behave

as brave men and women. With Camus, we can see people "getting killed for the ideas or illusions that give them a reason for living (what is called a reason for living is also an excellent reason for dying). I therefore conclude that the meaning of life is the most urgent of questions."[7] For a Charlie Brown-type, whose life generally has no meaning, this *is* the most urgent question. But for a Lucy-type, who is "sure of herself" (as Schulz has described Lucy), the first concern is to let nothing threaten this certainty, especially if it's a bit shaky to begin with:

Thus the stubbornness and depth of man's idolatry makes any basic *self*-improvement in him virtually impossible. "For the mind that is set on the flesh is hostile to God; it does not submit to God's law, indeed it cannot" (Rom. 8:7). And even though man's inability to change himself radically for the better is a central tenet of the Christian *belief*, it would often seem "There needs no ghost, my lord, come from the grave to tell us this" (Hamlet). Observation and reason tell us this. Albert Einstein, a personification of reason in our time, could observe: "Things always remain essentially the same. Nations continue to fall into the same trap, because atavistic drives are more powerful than

reason or acquired convictions."[8] On another occasion the famous scientist could say: "The real problem is in the hearts of men. . . . It is easier to change the nature of plutonium than man's evil spirit."[9] The Church fully agrees. Faith in God through Christ and faith in human nature are two totally different faiths. This is why Herbert Butterfield can tell us that "it is essential not to have faith in human nature. Such faith is a recent heresy and a very disastrous one."[10] Disastrous? Just ask Charlie Brown!

"She's always going to do that, you know. He's never going to get to kick that football" (Schulz).[11] But we are not just discussing Lucy's nature; we are talking about *all* human nature. Even Charlie Brown is a slave—a slave to his wishy-washiness.

"Next year I'm going to be a changed person!" he tells Lucy. "That's a laugh, Charlie Brown!" she says. "I mean it!" he replies. "I'm going to be strong and firm!" "Forget it," she says as she walks off. "You'll always be wishy-washy!" "Why can't I change just a little bit?" he asks himself. "*I'll be wishy one day and washy the next!*" he shouts. Charlie Brown's hope is that he will not need to "change," or to relinquish any false gods, but that "tomorrow" will change things for him. This is why, as he can tell us, his favorite day has "always been . . . tomorrow. No matter what today was like, there is still *tomorrow!* In the meantime, I have my problems!" he says. In the meantime, he never changes and thus remains consistently "doomed":

We will always attempt to escape from the painfully deep revolution we need *inside* ourselves *now*, by holding out for a favorable change in *future outward* circumstances. "If you have some problem in your life, do you believe you should try to solve it right away or think about it for awhile?" Linus asks Charlie Brown. "Oh, think about it," he tells Linus, "by all means. I believe you should think about it for awhile." "To give yourself time to do the right thing about the problem?" Linus asks. "No," replies Charlie Brown, "to give it time to go away!" The Christian, on the other hand, has learned to expect only despair in looking first to what "tomorrow" may bring. Instead he finds fulfillment in every present moment (as well as hope for the future) by trusting in God in every present moment. "Set your mind on God's kingdom and his justice before everything else, and all the rest will come to you as well. So do not be anxious about tomorrow; tomorrow will look after itself" (Mt. 6:33–34, NEB).

But setting one's mind on God's kingdom is precisely the change in man that is next to impossible. "Change your mind!" Charlie Brown shouts over and over at Patty. "Change your mind, I say!!! It's almost impossible to get people to change their minds these days!" he says, walking away with no changes made. For in "these days" or in olden days, there is no change in mind-changing. John Donne put it this way:

> Men and women call one another inconstant, and accuse one another of having changed their minds, when, God knows, they have but changed the object of their eye, and seen a better white or red. An old man loves not the same sports that he did when he was young, nor a sick man the same meats that he did when he was well: But these men have not changed their minds; The old man hath changed his fancy, and the sick man his taste; neither his mind.[12]

Immediate, superficial circumstances change for all of us every day; but the change that *really* matters is rare indeed. Said Kierkegaard:

> The majority of men do never really manage in their whole life to be more than they were in childhood and youth, namely, immediacy with the addition of a little dose of self-reflection.

No, despair verily is not something which appears only in the young, something out of which one grows as a matter of course .... though people are foolish enough to think so.[13]

We can always "try harder." But trying harder is usually only a last-ditch effort to avoid facing the real problem, the more fundamental problem that from the beginning we have embarked upon the altogether wrong path in pursuit of false gods. To turn back now would mean renouncing everything we have staked our lives on thus far. Therefore we will go on—and try harder! This is the kind of effort T. S. Eliot calls "a necessary move/ In an unnecessary action,/ Not for the good it will do/ But that nothing may be left undone/ On the margin of the impossible"[14]:

An awareness of the radical character of the problem goes hand in hand with an awareness of the radical character of the remedy. So long as one assumes that odd bits of tinkering with one's character-structure may do the job, or that with a little more effort, a little more enlightenment, and a firm faith in man's goodness, everything will somehow turn out all right, awareness of the need for faith in God's redemptive power will not arise. Hence rejection of the uncomfortable notion that man is caught in a dilemma which he cannot solve by means of his own energy and ingenuity is explicable in terms of his intense need to hang onto the illusion of self-sufficiency. The refusal to admit how deeply wrong he is, and how much he needs help, is symptomatic of the basic problem. If he were able to repent, and to admit (as Alcoholics Anonymous do) that only some divine power "greater than himself" can save him, he would already be in a condition of humility, moral realism and readiness for faith. (David E. Roberts)[15]

The heart's slavish and dogged devotion to its idol is what fathers of the Church have called "the bondage of the will." This bondage becomes most painfully apparent in our lives when we earnestly feel the need of changing but cannot; when we are attracted to another value that for one reason or another conflicts with the desires of our true god—that value nearest and dearest to us. But our true god lies so deeply inside us that often we are not even consciously aware of its presence or of what it actually is. Therefore when conflict arises between a god we are not conscious of and some other value that appears, we are miserable, we hate ourselves, and can easily say with St. Paul: "I do not understand my own actions. For I do not do what I want, but I do the very thing I hate. . . . I can will what is right, but I cannot do it" (Rom. 7:15, 18).

This conflict between the slavery of man's heart to its deepest love, and other values and demands, finds its most famous literary expression as the central theme of Shakespeare's *Hamlet*. Hamlet, like Charlie Brown, cannot understand why he "just can't" bring himself to do what he surely can and ought to do: "I do not know/ Why yet I live to say 'This thing's to do,'/ [Since] I have cause, and will, and strength, and means/ to do't."[16] Hamlet, St. Paul, and Charlie Brown all know what it means to die this death:

> The good which I want to do, I fail to do. . . . In my inmost self I delight in the law of God, but I perceive that there is in my bodily members a different law, fighting against the law that my reason approves and making me a prisoner under the law that is in my members, the law of sin. Miserable creature that I am, who is there to rescue me out of the body doomed to this death? (Rom. 7:19, 22–24, NEB)

"Oh, what a rogue and peasant slave am I!" (Hamlet) "Wretched man that I am! Who will deliver me. . . ?" (St. Paul) "What's wrong with me?" (Charlie Brown). "But when you don't like your own life," suggests Camus, "when you know you must change lives, you don't have any choice, do you? What can one do to become another? Impossible. One would have to cease being anyone, forget oneself for someone else, at least once. But how?"[17] The Bible would agree that it is *impossible* for "one to become another." The situation of unredeemed mankind is the situation Snoopy describes when he says, "Yesterday I was a dog. Today I'm a dog. Tomorrow I'll probably *still* be a dog. * Sigh * There's so little hope for advancement!" This is not the relatively superficial problem of *what we do*, but the deeper problem of *who we are*. In another strip he tells us: "So here I am starting a new year. But am I any different? Nope! I'm the same ol' dog! Day after day and year after year, never a change! Sometimes I marvel at my consistency!" But there is a collection of "old sayings" called the Bible that is never surprised by this consistency.

"CAN the Ethiopian change his skin or the leopard his spots?" (Jer. 13:23). "'But how is it possible,' said Nicodemus, 'for a man to be born when he is old? CAN he enter his mother's

womb a second time and be born?' " (Jn. 3:4, NEB) "CAN Satan cast out Satan?" (Mk. 3:23). "Children, how hard it is to enter the kingdom of God! It is easier for a camel to pass through the eye of a needle than for a rich man to enter the kingdom of God!" The astonished disciples did not then ask, "Then what rich man can be saved?" They knew that all men were rich in— or proud of—one thing or another. Therefore they asked, "Then WHO CAN be saved?" The answer to all of these questions is firmly negative: the Ethiopian, the leopard, a man, Satan, a camel, a rich man CANNOT—for all of these "it is impossible, but not for God; to God everything is possible" (Mk. 10:24-27, NEB). "It is impossible to surrender our lives to Jesus . . . of our own free will" (Bonhoeffer).[18] "Did we in our own strength confide, our striving would be losing" (Luther). "A drowning man cannot pull himself out of the water by his own hair. Neither can you do it. Someone else must rescue you" (Barth).[19] "Doubtless you will quote to me this proverb, 'Physician, heal yourself,' " said Christ. And the Bible certainly quotes the essence of this proverb again and again to us. For it knows that finally all our own attempts to heal our "spirits" (Greek "psyche"), rather than being healed by Christ the Physician, are as hopeless as the following little scene:

Because of [man's] radical fallenness, every movement of man's
will, even his move to get out of this predicament, is still a
movement of fallen man. He is therefore incapable of extricat-
ing himself from his plight. Only an act from outside of man,
from outside of the world and its possibilities, can effect this
transition . . . only an act of God. But this is just what the
New Testament proclaims has happened in the Christ. . . . (R.
Fuller)[20]

The Lord who created us without our help also re-creates us
without our help, quite apart from anything we can do or even
wish to do. "Man himself and of himself has neither any willing-
ness nor ability to believe" (Barth).[21] "Apart from me you can
do nothing," Christ told his disciples (Jn. 15:5). The answer of

the Gospel, the "good news," is that *God* saves man. Thus "it is not ourselves that we proclaim. . . . We are no better than pots of earthenware to contain this treasure, and this proves that such transcendent power does not come from us, but is God's alone" (2 Cor. 4:5, 7, NEB). The answer that it in any way is up to us to find the love we seek, is bad news indeed!—as in the cartoon above.

"My good Child, know this; that thou art not able to do these things of thyself, nor to walk in the Commandments of God, and to serve him, without his special grace," says the catechism of *The Book of Common Prayer.*[22] "Grace," says Pascal, "is indeed needed to turn a man into a saint; and he who doubts it does not know what a saint or a man is."[23] The saint is a man with feet planted as firmly on the world as the worldly man's. But there is a difference. The saint is no longer finally controlled nor crushed by the world. The saint has been grasped by a power that is very much in the world but much greater than the world; he is one "grasped by a power that is greater than we are, a power that shakes us and turns us, and transforms us and heals us" (Tillich).[24] It is like the difference between a man who falls to the ground in an unopened parachute and one who arrives safely at an airport in a huge jet. Both—in their own ways—are "down-to-earth" men. The difference is grace. Finally, then, it is a matter of "in whose power" we happen to be that determines whether we have a satisfactory relationship to the world. "Formerly, when you did not know God, you were in bondage to beings that by nature are no gods; but now that you have come to know God, or rather to be known by God, how can you turn back again to the weak and beggarly elemental spirits, whose slaves you want to be once more?" (Gal. 4:8, 9):

Man is man because he can recognize supernatural realities, not because he can invent them. Either everything in man can be traced as a development from below, or something must come from above. There is no avoiding that dilemma: you must be either a naturalist or a supernaturalist. If you remove from the word "human" all that the belief in the supernatural has given to man, you can view him finally as no more than an extremely clever, adaptable, and mischievous little animal. (T. S. Eliot)[25]

This is also why, we might add, that until the "supernatural" does come into man "from above," from outside man, man will continue to act like a "mischievous little animal."

6 *The Broken Heart*

Jesus turned and said to them, "If any one comes to me and does not hate his own father and mother and wife and children and brothers and sisters, yes, and even his own life, he cannot be my disciple. Whoever does not bear his own cross and come after me, cannot be my disciple." —LUKE 14:25–27

When Christ calls a man, he bids him come and die.
—BONHOEFFER[1]

Between man and truth lies mortification—you can see why we are all more or less afraid. —KIERKEGAARD[2]

God is none other than the Saviour of our wretchedness. So we can only know God well by knowing our iniquities. Therefore those who have known God, without knowing their wretchedness, have not glorified Him, but have glorified themselves.
—PASCAL[3]

                    Their great guilt,
Like poison given to work a great time after,
Now 'gins to bite the spirits.—SHAKESPEARE, The Tempest, III, iii

Batter my heart, three-personed God; for You
As yet but knock, breathe, shine, and seek to mend;
That I may rise, and stand, o'erthrow me, and bend
Your force, to break, blow, burn, and make me new.
I, like an usurped town to another due,
Labor to admit You, but oh! to no end;
Reason, Your viceroy in me, me should defend,
But is captived and proves weak or untrue.
Yet dearly I love You, and would be lovéd fain,
But am betrothed unto Your enemy.

Divorce me, untie, or break that knot again,
Take me to You, imprison me, for I
Except You enthrall me, never shall be free;
Nor ever chaste, except You ravish me.

—JOHN DONNE[4]

There's no heavier burden than a great potential!   —LINUS

ONCE UPON A TIME there was a little girl whose hands were always cold. But she thought little of this, because, as she said, "My hands always feel that way." One day, however, her hands became so cold as to make the discomfort in them unbearable. "This is terrible!" she thought. "Tomorrow I'm going to the doctor." When she saw the doctor the next day, he asked, "How do your hands feel now?" "Right now," she said, "they feel like they always have—a bit cold, but normal. But yesterday the pain was horrible, and I never want to go through that again!" The doctor then measured the "normal" temperature of her hands and said, "Good grief! You mean to tell me your hands are always like this!?" "Sure," she replied, "Aren't everyone's—more

or less?" "No," said the doctor, "everyone's aren't. Neither do yours have to be." The doctor then corrected the poor circulation in the little girl's hands; and from that day on she looked upon what she had previously thought "normal" to be the sheerest misery. And although she now knew the great pain that had once been in her hands to be none other than hell itself, she also looked upon that hell as the best thing that had ever happened to her: it had forced her to the doctor. For only the doctor could truly recognize the problem and heal it. The little girl, even with the help of her friends, could never have done this herself. (See cartoon above.)

If we have *always* had an illness, how can we ever know what life might be until we are cured of this illness? And how can we be cured of such a deep illness unless it comes to the surface in such a way that we *know* something is desperately wrong? In the meantime, what God's frozen people don't know, *does* hurt them. It hurts "just as something will sometimes obtrude itself upon the eye, and though one may be so busy . . . that for a long time one does not notice it, yet it irritates and almost torments one till at last one realizes, and removes the offending object . . ." (Dostoyevsky).[5]

We have said that all men have a "god"—that which gives meaning, direction, hope, a foundation to their lives; and that all men originate or come into life with a god that is not the true God. Three things *necessarily* follow from this: First, the god we originally serve can no longer be our god if God is to become God for us; we cannot serve two masters—God and that which is *not* God. Second, the relinquishing of a false god is not something we can do ourselves: because it is our *god*— that which we love with all our hearts and therefore will stubbornly cling to till the very end—it must be *taken from us* by a "Pow-er" outside ourselves; we must be "caused" to give it up. Nor can we surrender a false god in easy "installments—and yet one perpetually tries to do it" (Kafka).[6] The "old donkey" in us dies hard, as Luther could say. For at any one time in our lives we either love God with all our hearts or we love an *idol*— there is no other alternative. Third, when this false god is taken from us, for the first time in our lives we will know an alto-

gether different kind of hurt, a true heartbreak, a grief so deep that it was unimaginable to us before. It is true that people constantly "go through hell" for their false gods. But these "hells" are nothing when compared to the actual surrender of these gods. Thus "in the rigid obstinacy of your heart you are laying up for yourself a store of retribution for the day of retribution" (Rom. 2:5, NEB). "I suppose you're not going to change your mind?" asks Lucy. "Nope!" says Linus. "I do not change my mind easily." Then follows this little scene:

"Christianity," says Kierkegaard, as with "all radical cures, one . . . puts off as long as possible."[7] This is why no less than God himself must finally perform on us the dreadful operation of the spiritual heart transplant:

A new heart I will give you, and a new spirit I will put within you; and I will take out of your flesh the heart of stone and give you a heart of flesh. And I will put my spirit within you, and cause you to walk in my statutes. . . . Then you will remember your evil ways, and your deeds that were not good; and you will loathe yourselves for your iniquities and your abominable deeds. (Ezek. 36:26–27, 31)

Christ's message was always directed to "he who has ears to hear"; for his assumption about people in general, was the same as Isaiah's before him: "this people's heart has grown dull, and their ears are heavy of hearing" (Mt. 13:15). Spiritually speaking, then, it is only the man with the "circumcised" or broken heart who "has ears to hear." Thus Christ's beatitude was specifically extended only to the poor in spirit, the meek, the hungry, the persecuted, those who mourn, etc. Over and over in the gospels, Christ tells us that he did not come to help the proud, the righteous, the high and mighty, the healthy, wealthy, and wise; but he came only to the lost, the least, the humble, the mere nothings, the sinful, weak, poor, sick, and foolish. When the Pharisees asked Christ, "Why do you eat and drink with tax collectors and sinners?" he replied, "Those who are well have no need of a physician, but those who are sick; I have not come to call the righteous, but sinners to repentance" (Lk. 5:30–32). For this reason, the Pharisees, who considered themselves quite well and righteous, thank you! had little use for Christ. Christ's call and invitation is addressed to the brokenhearted and to them alone, for only by them can this call be heard and meaningfully understood: "Come to me, all who labor and are heavy laden, and I will give you rest" (Mt. 11:28). Why is this invitation addressed only to those who labor and are heavy laden? It is because, as Oscar Wilde could put it, "How else but through a broken heart/ May Lord Christ enter in?"[8] When our false gods finally fail us, then the heart is broken. Then, and only then, can Christ enter into our hearts and truly become our God. Not unless a man has died altogether to the old, original god of his heart, can he experience an altogether "new birth." "Truly, truly, I say to you, unless a grain of wheat falls into the earth and dies, it remains alone; but if it dies, it bears much fruit" (Jn. 12:24). There is no way a man can become

truly humble unless he is first absolutely *humbled*; there is no
way of knowing absolute joy unless one first knows what it absolutely *isn't*; there is no recognition of the true light except in
the midst of the true darkness. Only the children of darkness
who come to recognize themselves as such, can become children of light (Eph. 5:8).

> Does it occur to any child that he needs to be educated? Or
> if you took several children and let them live together, grow
> up together, would it occur to them that they needed to be
> educated? Would anything else occur to them but that they were
> just fine as they were? But a higher view, that of their parents,
> sees that they need to be educated, and so sets a standard for
> the child.

> So with man. Of course it occurs to no man or community of
> men that they are profoundly corrupted. This is quite simply im-
> possible, for one cannot be profoundly corrupted if at the same
> time, on one's own, without external help, one can see that one
> is profoundly corrupted. But something higher (Christianity) un-
> dertakes to proclaim to man that he is profoundly corrupted, and
> so sets up a standard for him.[9]

The standard set by Christianity "is spiritual but [we are] carnal,
sold under sin" (Rom. 7:14). Therefore, before the corrupted
or carnally bound heart can love God with all its heart, there
must first be a shattering breakthrough to the empty center of
the heart, the heart must first be broken or "rent" of those false
values next to it. This grievous inward experience is often symbolized in the Bible by the rending of outer garments.

"The New Testament is based exclusively upon the possibility
of a new order absolutely beyond human thought; and therefore,
as a prerequisite to that order, there must come a crisis that
denies all human thought. To understand the New Testament
Yes as anything but the Yes contained in the No, is not to

understand it at all. Life comes from *death!* Death is the source of all" (Barth).[10]

"Life has a way of slapping you down," says Schulz.[11] And as Luther could point out, "life" is only a veil for "the Lord," who also slaps us down. "Every man is a born hypocrite," said Kierkegaard; the Christian is simply that rare individual who "has all the hypocrisy knocked out of him by Providence."[12] He is rare because "what really is lacking is the power to obey, to submit to the necessary . . . to what may be called one's limit."[13] In Lucy's fist, it is often possible to see something of the dreadful judgment or wrath of God, "the might of thy hand," which says, as the Lord said to Job, "Thus far shall you come, and no farther" (Job 30:21; 38:11). Her fist often acts as a mask or instrument for "what may be called one's limit," for that "Pow-er" of Providence that knocks all the hypocrisy out of a man and brings him low enough to learn just how sorry one can *really* get. For just as a man is given a healthy slap on his "foundation" when he is born a naked child in this world, so also must he be stripped of all false gods and thus slapped on his *spiritual* foundation when he is "re-born" and fully becomes a man in the world.

"How sorry can you get?" is related to several other questions:

> You yearn to rise again? This also is legitimate and appropriate. But I have to ask you one other question: Did you ever reach the depths? Not only the depth of any inward or outward misery, but the depth where man must acknowledge that he can no longer help himself, that no man can help him, that there is absolutely no help save God's mercy? In this depth, God's mercy has already reached out for you, has already found you, and you will experience that it will lift you to the highest heights. (Barth) [14]

The experience of the broken heart is therefore no ordinary woe. Whereas before we had always had at least a foundation from which to deal with our *problems*, now we have a totally new *kind* of problem: our very foundation knocked out from

under us, there is no certain basis from which to deal with anything. This is not the question of deciding what to think on the basis of what we have always thought and taken for granted. But it is the deeper question that comes with the discovery that there are no "granteds" or certainties, that we must even decide what to be "sure" of. (See cartoon above.)

Nor are we discussing here simply the loss of *intellectual* certainty; for the broken heart is the total collapse or failure of anything and everything in which we have previously found assurance and security. When the Judgment of God appears to a man, *all* false gods are toppled. In this situation "there is nothing to hold on to," to use the words of existentialist philosopher Martin Heidegger.[15] When the foundation is removed from our lives, life ceases being a game people play and becomes a matter of grasping for straws "above 70,000 fathoms of water" (Kierkegaard). With no certain goal before us or sure foundation beneath us, we now become concerned with mere survival— "getting through the day." As Lewis Mumford has put it:

> We have lost any other basis for conduct than the will to survive, a will that becomes even feebler and more subject to suicidal turnings upon itself, as a people loses its religious sense of a goal and a purpose beyond mere existence.[16]

Modern man feels no guilt. "He feels innocent. To tell the truth, that is all he feels—his irreparable innocence" (Camus).[17] But this feeling of innocence does not save him. Being free of the feeling of having done wrong, he is nevertheless now burdened with the vague but awful feeling that something is wrong. Indeed, despair is often more intolerable for the modern despairer, as he frequently lacks any means of understanding it. He has no idea what is happening to him or what makes it happen. He is only "confused," "all mixed-up," and does not know why. He is afflicted with a "nameless woe." It is nameless because the god inside him, which he is not conscious of, has remained nameless. And now this god is dying. "Most people in my experience," says J. B. Phillips, "are not so much sinful as bewildered."[18] The bewildered man can attempt to lose himself in creativity. But finding no meaning in creativity, he then becomes destructive in his desperate desire to find something stable enough "to hold on to."

Charlie Brown is in no better shape. For he also is afflicted with the despair of "Nothingness . . . a presence within our own Being, always there, in the inner quaking that goes on beneath the calm surface of our preoccupation with things" (W. Barrett).[19] (See next cartoon.)

The inexpressible sickness of the broken heart can also seek and find expression in sickness of the body. Thus in the New Testament we frequently see Jesus healing what would seem to be purely physical and mental illnesses, on the basis of a spiritual

diagnosis. Shakespeare was pointing to this heart-body relationship when he wrote, "I would not have such a heart in my bosom for the dignity of the whole body."[20] And Charlie Brown, for one, certainly knows that indignities suffered by the heart can easily result in an undignified body:

In another cartoon, one of the girls ends a discussion with Charlie Brown by saying, "So there, Smarty! Nyah! Nyah! Nyah!" Then she turns and walks away. Says Charlie Brown, sadly clasping his stomach: "Those 'nyahs' get down into your stomach, and they just lie there and burn."

The New Testament has three major ways of talking about this "burning," or the experience of the broken heart: crucifixion, baptism, and "death" or "hell." And since the first two more properly belong to the other side of the Christian experience, we'll now take a closer look into "hell." Most of the New Testament references to "hell" point *not* to an experience that occurs to man beyond his physical death; but they refer to an "existential" reality—that is, a "living hell," the very hell that we have been discussing in this chapter, the burning that occurs *within* man *now*, while he is very much alive. For instance, when St. Paul tells us that "the wages of sin is death" (Rom. 6:23), he is apparently assuming that we are not so much punished for sin later, as we are punished by sin now. Even when the New Testament refers to "hell" as being in the future, most of these references can best be understood as anticipating that day in a man's life when his old blankets are finally destroyed or when he "will say, 'I have no pleasure in them'" (Eccles. 12:1). Certainly the Christian does not need to be told of the horrors of hell. As one who already has died the dreadful death of the old man, and continues to "die daily," the Christian has been there: he already "has passed from death to life" (Jn. 5:24). And for this reason, the Christian can tell you that the New Testament descriptions of "hell" are completely accurate: that "hell" is not a geographical locale, but is indeed an inescapable *inward* state "where their worm does not die, and the fire is not quenched" (Mk. 9:48). Furthermore, as a former "child of wrath," the Christian is in a better position for understanding the very real misery now being experienced by those whose hearts "have always been cold" and hence do not "know" it. This, then, is "all we need of hell." For the Christian not only knows that the "hell" within man *will* come to the surface and manifest itself, not only that "the Son of Man *will* send his angels, and they *will* gather . . . all causes of sin and all evildoers,

and throw them into the furnace of fire; there men will weep and gnash their teeth" (Mt. 13:41–42); but he also knows that all these things do happen—now. "The Day of Judgment," says Kafka, "in reality . . . is a summary court in perpetual session."[21]

It is not necessary, then, to think of "divine retribution" as something deferred until after death. St. Paul is speaking of a present reality when he says, "We see divine retribution revealed from heaven and falling upon all the godless wickedness of men . . . . all their thinking has ended in futility, and their misguided minds are plunged in darkness" (Rom. 1:18, 21, NEB). The "hell of fire" is precisely the same fire Christ came to baptize us with (Mt. 3:11). That is, it is the very same fire we have inside us now, consuming in us all that is not of God, thus making room for him. Hell is that deep unrest that God gives to man now, to show man that God alone is God. "For what is it like where Christ is not?" asks Luther. "What is the world if not a downright hell . . . ?"[22] Or, as T. S. Eliot could put it: "Hell is oneself, Hell is alone, the other figures in it merely projections. There is nothing to escape from and nothing to escape to. One is always alone."[23]

Charles Schulz knows something about a broken heart. For instance, an interviewer once asked him, "When did this turn-

ing about, or whatever you want to call it, happen to you in your own life?" Schulz's answer:

> I think one of the first feelings I got was when I was about eighteen. I was riding a streetcar home from a job I had in downtown St. Paul and I noticed one of the car cards which read, *Come unto me all ye who labor and are heavy laden and I will give you rest.* I was quite impressed by this scripture verse.[24]

"I know something about loneliness," says Schulz. "I won't talk about it, but I was very lonely after the war. I know what it feels like to spend a whole weekend all by yourself and no one wants you at all."[25] But whatever the source of Schulz's sensitive insight into "the tragic sense of life," this dimension of depth is constantly found in *Peanuts* and sets the strip quite apart from all that is mere child's play. Just as our time has witnessed the rebirth of the tragicomedy in the theater, in *Peanuts* we saw the first of what could truly be called a "tragicomic." Schulz's steadfast refusal to omit this crucial dimension of life, made *Peanuts* almost unique among comic strips and no doubt accounts for much of the strip's popularity. Indeed this popularity would seem to bear out the statement of Julian Hartt, who wrote: "Who then speaks most powerfully and to the men of this generation? Those poets, artists, and philosophers who preach despair and sing of bleak encounter with silence and futility and nonbeing."[26] "Nothing is funnier than unhappiness," wrote playwright Samuel Beckett;[27] and Schulz would almost always seem to subscribe to this formula. Wittingly or unwittingly, Schulz often manages to describe, with a few funny lines and drawings, the very experiences described by the existentialist theologians and philosophers under such heavy titles as "angst," "the concept of dread," "the anxiety of emptiness and meaninglessness," "the absurd," "existential despair," etc. "*Peanuts* . . . stands out among the newer strips as probably the funniest and certainly the most 'existential,' " as one recent critique of the strip could put it.[28] In order to illustrate just how "existential" *Peanuts* actually is, we will here couple some of the more characteristic strips with some of the more characteristic utterances of one of the more characteristic existentialists. Actually, we could choose any of the so-called existentialists for this

purpose, but we choose Pascal. Pascal is certainly a prototype of all modern existentialists and his *Pensées*, or "thoughts," often take the form of brief, almost cartoon-like sequences. Here we go, leading off with Pascal:

This is our true state. . . . We sail within a vast sphere, ever drifting in uncertainty, driven from end to end. When we think to attach ourselves to any point and to fasten to it, it wavers and leaves us; and if we follow it, it eludes our grasp, slips past us, and vanishes forever. Nothing stays for us. This is our natural condition, and yet most contrary to our inclination; we burn with desire to find solid ground and an ultimate sure foundation whereon to build a tower reaching to the infinite. But our whole groundwork cracks, and the earth opens to abysses. (Pensée #72)[29]

When I consider the short duration of my life, swallowed up in the eternity before and after, the little space which I fill, and even can see, engulfed in the infinite immensity of spaces of which I am ignorant, and which know me not, I am frightened, and am astonished at being here rather than there; for there is no reason why here rather than there, why now rather than then. Who has put me here? By whose order and direction have this place and time been allotted to me? . . . The eternal silence of these infinite spaces frightens me. (Pensées #205-6)

Weariness—Nothing is so insufferable to man as to be completely at rest, without passions, without business, without diversion, without study. He then feels his nothingness, his forlornness, his insufficiency, his dependence, his weakness, his emptiness. There will immediately arise from the depth of his heart weariness, gloom, sadness, fretfulness, vexation, despair. (Pensée #131)

Condition of man: inconstancy, weariness, unrest. The weariness which is felt by us in leaving pursuits to which we are attached. A man dwells at home with pleasure; but he sees a woman who charms him, or if he enjoys himself in play for five or six days, he is miserable if he returns to his former way of living. Nothing is more common than that. (Pensées #127–8)

He who does not see the vanity of the world is himself very vain. Indeed who do not see it but youths who are absorbed in fame, diversion, and the thought of the future? But take away diversion, and you will see them dried up with weariness. They feel then their nothingness without knowing it; for it is indeed to be unhappy to be in insufferable sadness as soon as we are reduced to thinking of self, and have no diversion. (Pensée #164)

Diversion—As men are not able to fight against death, misery, ignorance, they have taken it into their heads, in order to be happy, not to think of them at all. Despite these miseries, man wishes to be happy, and only wishes to be happy, and cannot wish not to be so. But how will he set about it? To be happy

he would have to make himself immortal; but, not being able to do so, it has occurred to him to prevent himself from thinking of death. (Pensées #168–9)

We run carelessly to the precipice, after we have put something before us to prevent us seeing it. (Pensée #51)

Now that we have attempted to show how "existential" *Peanuts* is by using Pascal, we will try to show how "existential" the Bible is by using *Peanuts:*

> I have become the laughingstock of all peoples, the burden of their songs all day long. . . . My soul is bereft of peace, I have forgotten what happiness is. . . . (Lam. 3:14, 17)

For the word of God is alive and active. . . . There is nothing in creation that can hide from him; everything lies naked and exposed to the eyes of the One with whom we have to reckon. (Heb. 4:12–13, NEB)

Insults have broken my heart, so that I am in despair. I looked for pity, but there was none; and for comforters, but I found none. (Ps. 69:20)

Have pity on me, have pity on me, O you my friends, for the hand of God has touched me! Why do you, like God, pursue me? (Job 19:21–22)

Alas, alas, you are like unmarked graves over which men may walk without knowing it. (Lk. 11:44, NEB)

They say, "A deadly thing has fastened upon him; he will not rise again from where he lies." Even my bosom friend in whom I trusted, who ate of my bread, has lifted his heel against me. (Ps. 41:8–9)

The Christian is always a man who has known the dreadful "existential" experience that we have attempted to describe with the aid of the Bible, *Peanuts*, Pascal, and others. For there is no "real living" without first having died this death. "We for our part have crossed over from death to life" (1 Jn. 3:13, NEB); "We know that the man we once were has been crucified with Christ, for the destruction of the sinful self, so that we may no longer be the slaves of sin" (Rom. 6:6, NEB). But this raises an important question: What can we do when we don't fit in to this scheme of things? What if we have never had this experience? What if we have never really died the death required to *really* live? What can we do when such a life seems to be passing us by? The Bible is quite clear in answering this question. It tells us that nothing is worse for us than "lukewarmness," that it is even better to be "cold" than to be "lukewarm" (Rev. 3:15–16). This means, then, in the words of Joshua, "if you be unwilling to serve the Lord, choose this day whom you will serve, whether the gods your fathers served . . . or the gods . . . in whose land you dwell" (24:15). The point is: make a decision in fear and trembling about what you will love and serve, and then *love it!* with all your heart. This kind of decision will necessarily be made in "fear and trembling," for you will have *no* certainty whether it is the right decision for reaching the happiness you desire. You will have only your own inmost heart to go by and to be true to. If you have *any other* standard for choosing, you have obviously already decided that this standard is god. And how do you know that *this* is true? But *choose now*, and give yourself completely to your choice. If you love even a *false* god with all your "mind and heart and strength," you will learn that much

sooner that it is indeed a false god. Therefore, "whatever your hand finds to do, do it with your might" (Eccles. 9:10). This is why Zorba could say to his boss:

> "It's all because of doing things by halves . . . saying things by halves, being good by halves, that the world is in the mess it's in today. Do things properly by God! One good knock for each nail and you'll win through! God hates a half-devil ten times more than an archdevil!"
>
> That evening, when he came in from work, he lay down on the sand, exhausted. . . .
>
> "Why all the hurry, Zorba?"
>
> He hesitated a moment.
>
> "Why? Well, I want to see whether I've found the right slope or not. If I haven't, we're done for. Don't you see, boss? The sooner I see if we're dished, the better it'll be for us."[30]

An interviewer once asked Schulz: "If you were talking to a classroom full of children, what would you want to say to them?" His answer: "I would tell them how important it is to get involved now in the things they like to do. Drifting around on the fringes won't help them grow."[31] To the children of this world who, for one reason or another, find themselves unwilling to serve the Lord, the Bible offers no advice for a way to live or what to live for in the world. But it does advise them how to live in the world: it says, *live in it—now—passionately:*

By the power of Love, the Christian has been rescued from what Christ called the "sickness unto death" (Jn. 11:4), the dreadful experience in which there is "no way out" (Kafka), "no exit" (Sartre), "no excuse" (St. Paul). But the Christian still fears this infinite abyss literally more than anything in the world. With Mitya in *The Brothers Karamazov*, the Christian can say, "What does it matter that I will work . . . in Siberian mines for twenty years. That does not frighten me anymore. I am afraid of something entirely different, and that is my only great anxiety. I am afraid that the man who has been resurrected in me may leave me again."[32] And so it is that the Christian's fear of the Lord, the infinite, gives him a kind of courage in facing worldly dangers that the ordinary man does not have. For he knows now that the world itself is only a lesser danger and can be conquered by Love through the power of Love.

What the natural man considers horrible . . . this for the Christian is like a jest. Such is the relation between the natural man and the Christian; it is like the relation between a child and a man: what the child shudders at, the man regards as nothing. The child does not know what the dreadful is; this the man knows and he shudders at it. The child's imperfection consists, first of all, in not knowing what the dreadful is; and then again . . . in shuddering at that which is not dreadful. And so it also is with the natural man, he is ignorant of what the dreadful truly is, yet he is not thereby exempted from shuddering; no, he shudders at that which is not the dreadful; he does not know the true God, but this is not the whole of it, he worships an idol as God. Only the Christian knows what is meant by the sickness unto death. He acquires as a Christian a courage which the natural man does not know—this courage he acquires by learning fear for the still more dreadful. Such is the way a man always acquires

courage; when one fears a greater danger, it is as though the
other did not exist. But the dreadful thing the Christian learned
to know is "the sickness unto death." (Kierkegaard)[33]

"From a real antagonist boundless courage flows into you"
(Kafka).[34] As we can see, however, Lucy is not Snoopy's *real*
antagonist, the one from whom "boundless courage flows." She
is only a *little* devil. Snoopy's *real* antagonist, we will discuss in
more detail in the next chapter.

7 Good News of a Great Joy Which Will Come to All the People

Someday I'll get you, Red Baron!   —SNOOPY

The seventy-two came back jubilant. "In your name, Lord," they
said, "even the devils submit to us." [Jesus] replied, "I watched
how Satan fell, like lightning, out of the sky."
                                              —LUKE 10:17, 18, NEB

Every man is a virtual brother of Christ, because the whole world
is healed in and through Christ. Every man has his destination
in Christ. . . . Even before he becomes a Christian he is in
continuity with God in Christ, but he has not yet discovered
it. He realises it only when he begins to believe.   —BARTH[1]

It is implicit in the New Testament statement concerning the
incarnation of God in Christ that all men are taken up, enclosed
and borne within the body of Christ and that this is just what
the congregation of the faithful are to make known to the world
by their words and by their lives. What is intended here is . . .
the summoning of the world into the fellowship of this body of
Christ, to which in truth it already belongs.   —BONHOEFFER[2]

"Karamazov," cried Kolya, "can it be true what's taught us in
religion, that we shall all rise again from the dead and shall live
and see each other again, all. . . ?"
"Certainly we shall all rise again, certainly we shall see each
other and shall tell each other with joy and gladness all that has
happened!" Alyosha answered half laughing, half enthusiastic.
"Ah, how splendid it will be!" broke from Kolya.
                                              —DOSTOYEVSKY[3]

UP TO THIS POINT we have only discussed how the children of *Peanuts* start their days as "children of wrath, like the rest of mankind" (Eph. 2:3). Being well aware of this wrath ourselves, most of us are like Charlie Brown: it's how these days end up that now bothers us. And from the Christian point of view, how our days end up is decisively and uniquely and irrevocably bound to what happened on "this day":

"Gospel" means "good news." And this cartoon contains the whole of the Gospel *in nuce*—the Gospel "in a nutshell." For Christianity is in the world to proclaim the "good news of a great joy which will come to all the people"! (Lk. 2:10). All the people? That's right! *All* the people! Christianity is not, nor has it ever been, the "bad news" of a cosmic penal system bent on selling fire insurance for eternity. It is instead the "good news" that any and all penalties against us have been dropped, that there will certainly be no fire for anyone but only great joy for all, and that men may begin even now to live in this joy by living toward this future. The only fire that will ever exist for any of us is the fire we talked about in the last chapter: the "hell"—recognized or unrecognized—that most certainly exists within us now inasmuch as we attempt to live our lives on any other basis than the assurance of Christianity's "good news." Just as the "angel of the Lord" appeared to the shepherds by night, the message of the Gospel comes to us only in our awareness of our nights; and our earthly lives will remain "in the night" unless we actually believe this message enough to stake our entire lives and deaths on it. Thus Christianity not only assures us of the future but also points to the way of being sure of this future through actual participation in it now. The Christian is one "to whom the Spirit is given as firstfruits of the harvest to come" (Rom. 8:23, NEB). The Christian message assures all of us that no less than God himself loves us, will always love us without qualification, and that finally nothing "will be able to separate us from the love of God in Christ Jesus our Lord" (Rom. 8:39). Therefore, "Be not afraid!" Indeed, such news seems to be too good to be true. Our inclination is either to laugh at it or else to interpret it as being something not quite so good after all. Not only does the *all-inclusiveness* of this message

seem incomprehensible to us, but even "the conception of a future life has become a jest, a claim so precarious that no one honors it, nay, no one even any longer issues it; it tickles our sense of humor to consider that there was once a time when this conception transformed the whole of life" (Kierkegaard).[4]

Christianity proclaims, however, that the scornful, derisive laughter of "Lucy-fer" is not the last word; that life is not finally a cruel joke in which we are the punch lines.

> Christianity is a proclamation of joy. It is not a mixed message of joy and terror, salvation and damnation. . . . It does not proclaim in the same breath both good and evil, both help and destruction, both life and death. It does, of course, throw a shadow. We must not overlook or ignore this aspect of the matter. In itself, however, it is light and not darkness . . . . The Yes cannot be heard unless the No is also heard. But the No is said for the sake of the Yes and not for its own sake. In substance, therefore, the first and last word is Yes and not No. (Barth)[5]

Christ's coming into the world was the great "Yes" of God to all men of all times. "As God is true, the language in which we address you is not an ambiguous blend of Yes and No. The Son of God, Christ Jesus . . . was never a blend of Yes and No. With him it was, and is, Yes. He is the Yes pronounced upon God's

promises, every one of them" (2 Cor. 1:18, 19, NEB). So who needs Santa Claus? Or even a "Great Pumpkin"? Or finally even human love, with all their "ambiguous blends of Yes and No"— the kind of love that loves us "if." "Contrary to human mercy," says Barth, "even in its kindest expression, God's mercy is almighty. . . . It brings light, peace, joy. We need not be afraid that it might be limited or have strings attached. His 'yes' is unequivocal, never to be reversed into 'no.' "[6]

That our eternal destinies should be left up to us—"if you're good"—what overwhelmingly "bad news" this would be, especially in view of what frail little children all of us are. Or, as Melville could put it, "Oh God! that man should be a thing for immortal souls to sieve through!"[7] But the good news is that our Father knows what we finally need and want; and he fully intends that, as evil as we all are, we shall all finally have this "outrageous happiness" which we continue to seek for in the wrong places.

> What man of you, if his son asks him for bread, will give him a stone? Or if he asks for a fish, will give him a serpent? If you then, who are evil, know how to give good gifts to your children, how much more will your Father who is in heaven give good things to those who ask him! (Mt. 7:9–11)

So finally there is a string attached then! We must "ask." Not at all! The very same Evangelist can tell us, "Your Father knows what you need before you ask him" (Mt. 6:8). For oftentimes, like poor, starving dogs, we do not know who or how to ask, or even what to ask for:

"Man cannot commit a sin so great as to exhaust the infinite love of God," Dostoyevsky's saintly Zossima tells a woman who has committed an unspeakable crime and is afraid to die. "Can there be a sin which could exceed the love of God? . . . Believe that God loves you as you cannot conceive; that He loves you with your sin, in your sin . . . . All things are atoned for, all things are saved by love. If I, a sinner, even as you are, am tender with you and have pity on you, how much more will God."[8] "Peter . . . asked him, 'Lord, how often am I to forgive my brother if he goes on wronging me? As many as seven times?' Jesus replied, 'I do not say seven times; I say seventy times seven'" (Mt. 18:21, 22, NEB). This is not arithmetic, but a biblical way of saying, "I say infinitely." Could it be that Peter's Lord requires more of his children than he asks of himself? Could such a Lord even think of banishing his children from his forgiveness—especially "forever"? Would this not make God the great celestial hypocrite? Apparently even "children of wrath" find it difficult to sustain this kind of cruelty:

In the following cartoon, Linus asks two very important questions, both of which the Bible does a better job of answering than Lucy:

The answer to Linus' first question, "Why don't you try to understand me?" has already been discussed in previous chapters: "A man gifted with the Spirit can judge the worth of everything," says the New Testament (1 Cor. 2:15, NEB); but "the natural

man does not receive the gifts of the Spirit of God . . . and he is not able to understand them because they are spiritually discerned" (1 Cor. 2:14). Linus' second question, "Aren't I worth more than a *bug?!!*" comes up for answer in the New Testament when Christ says, "Are not sparrows two a penny? Yet without your Father's leave not one of them can fall to the ground. As for you, even the hairs of your head have all been counted. So have no fear; you are worth more than any number of sparrows"—or bugs, we assume! (Mt. 10:29, 30, NEB).

John Updike's short story "Pigeon Feathers" deals with a little boy, about the age of Linus, who is troubled about "Heaven"— he wants to be assured that there is one and that he will go there. In his Sunday catechetical class, David commits the "indiscretion" of asking his pastor about it.

> "David, you might think of Heaven this way: as the way the goodness Abraham Lincoln did lives after him."
> "But is Lincoln conscious of it living on?" He blushed no longer with embarrassment but in anger . . . . at being betrayed, at seeing Christianity betrayed. . . .

When David's mother later discovers him trying to read his grandfather's Bible, she is alarmed as "she had assumed that Heaven had faded from his head years ago."

> "David," she asked gently, "don't you ever want to rest?"
> "No. Not forever."
> "David, you're so young. When you get older, you'll feel differently."
> "Grandpa didn't. Look how tattered this book is."
> "I never understood your grandfather."
> "Well, I don't understand ministers who say it's like Lincoln's goodness going on and on. Suppose you're not Lincoln?"
> "I think Reverend Dobson made a mistake. You must try to forgive him."
> "It's not a *question* of his making a mistake. It's a question of dying and never moving or seeing or hearing anything ever again."
> "But"—in exasperation—"darling, it's so greedy of you to want more. When God has given us this wonderful April day, and given us this farm, and you have your whole life ahead of you—"
> "You think, then, that there is a God?"
> "Of course I do" . . . .

"He made everything? You feel that?"

"Yes."

"Then who made Him?"

"Why, Man. Man." The happiness of this answer lit up her face radiantly, until she saw his gesture of disgust. She was so simple, so illogical; such a femme.

"Well that amounts to saying there is none. . . . Mother, good grief. Don't you see"—he rasped away the roughness in his throat —"if when we die there's nothing, all your sun and fields and what not are all, ah, *horror?* It's just an ocean of horror."

Nothing or no one is able to help David "build his fortress against death . . . . He was alone. In that deep hole." The story is finally resolved when David is given the job of shooting the pesky pigeons that live in the barn on his family's farm, a job he does not care for. But as David is burying the dead birds, Updike describes the following experience, which echoes the saying of Christ: "You are worth more than any number of sparrows":

He had never seen a bird this close before. The feathers were more wonderful than dog hair, for . . . the feathers . . . were trimmed to fit a pattern that flowed without error across the bird's body. . . . Yet these birds bred in the millions and were exterminated as pests. Into the fragrant open earth he dropped one broadly banded in slate shades of blue, and on top of it another, mottled all over in rhythms of lilac and gray. . . . As he fitted the last two, still pliant, on the top, and stood up, crusty coverings were lifted from him, and with a feminine, slipping sensation along his nerves that seemed to give the air hands, he was robed in this certainty: that the God who had lavished such craft upon these worthless birds would not destroy His whole Creation by refusing to let David live forever.[9]

Nobody cares much for sparrows, yet not one of them even falls to the ground apart from the will of God. "Look at the birds of the air," said Christ; "they do not sow and reap and store in barns, yet your heavenly Father feeds them. You are worth more than the birds!" (Mt. 6:26, NEB). How much more then will God, whose sovereign power governs the rise and fall and feeding of all things, "always stick up" for even the lowest of men, who nevertheless is also the man Christ died for.

The joyful "Good News!" of Christianity, then, is that God's salvation falls freely upon *all* men—there is nothing that can finally separate any of us from this joy. God is not only the Source from whom everyone comes, but he is also the ultimate Goal of everyone. "I'm going back to where I came from," says Peppermint Patty, the little girl from another neighborhood. "That must be a nice thing to be able to do," comments Charlie Brown. We are assured that it is "nice." But this is nicer: The New Testament also promises us that *all* will *return* to where all came from: "For in making *all* mankind prisoners to disobedience, God's purpose was to show mercy to *all* mankind . . . . Source, Guide, and Goal of *all* that is—to him be glory for ever! Amen" (Rom. 11:32, 36, NEB). That's good news! *Everybody dance!*

The announcement of God's totally free and unmerited gift of unqualified salvation for "everybody," is indeed a cause for the happiest dancing. But immediately this question arises: what's to keep us from "overdoing it"? What's to keep us from abusing this good news? As Shermy says to Charlie Brown, "If there *is* a Santa Claus, he's going to be too nice not to bring me anything for Christmas no matter *how* I act . . . Right? *Right!*" Replies Charlie Brown: "*Wrong!* But I don't know where!" If Christianity proclaims the final redemption of all men, then why can't I go and do as I please, "live it up," since everybody is headed for the same ultimate unity with God anyway? Since we are assured that God is going to be too nice to exclude anyone from his kingdom, why can't we forget about God for now and in the meantime live our lives to the fullest? This objection to the proclamation of God's universal forgiveness is totally unthinking. For, in the first place, how does anyone know this promise is true? There is only *one* way of knowing: the experience of the fullest life that comes to us *now* only through obedience to God *now*. The moment we find ourselves disobedient, we inevitably lose the experience of *abundant* life that assures us of *eternal* life. Apart from responsible obedience here and now, we have no assurance

of what the future holds or who holds it; our lives are once again
thrown into the chaos of uncertainty. And as Luther could say,
"uncertainty is the most miserable thing in the world."[10] Only
through obedience now do we know "the fullest life" now; and
only through the fullest life are we made sure of eternal life for
us and for all men. He that does not actively love God, has no
actual assurance of God's love for him. Both the Christian and
non-Christian, all, are destined for eternal life with God. But there
is a basic difference: the Christian knows it. By staking his life
on an event that occurred in the past, God's decisive revelation
of himself in Christ, the Christian is given a joy in the present
that also assures him of another "great joy which will come to all
the people"—in the future. So then, when we say there is a "hell"
of a difference between the Christian and the non-Christian, this
is the hell we mean:

"For us there is one God, the Father, from whom all being comes,
towards whom we move . . . . But not everyone knows this" (1
Cor. 8:6, 7, NEB). The job of the Christian, then, the "wise guy"
who "knows this," is simply to acquaint the "others" with the
same knowledge: that God has already secured their salvation;
and that men can begin to know and enjoy this salvation even

now by abandoning their shaky little foundations that are "driving them crazy," and instead basing their lives on the firm footing that is Christ alone. From the point of view of the Christian, non-Christians are people who think they are their own captains "perishing on a stormy sea. But in reality they are not in a sea where one can drown, but in shallow water, where it is impossible to drown. Only they do not know it" (Brunner) :[11]

The Christian, along with all his fellow men, is on his way home to the Father. But the Christian *knows* this and knows moreover that much of the fun can be in getting there, that it is not necessary to go through a hell on earth to get to the eternal destiny of us all—heaven. This he knows in the very act of attempting to lighten the load for others along the way by sharing with them the same happy knowledge. This knowledge is the good news of

a victory already won not just for part of the world, for those who believe or who are good; but it is the knowledge that "God was in Christ reconciling the world to himself" (2 Cor. 5:19). "Behold, the Lamb of God, who takes away the sin . . ."—Whose sin? The sin of the Christian or the righteous or those who believe in him? These only? The Lamb who will take away sin *if?* —"who takes away the sin of the world!" (Jn. 1:29).

So what will heaven be like? Who knows? Who can understand or even conceive of such a thing? All we are given to know is that it will be *heaven*, "that the sufferings of this present time are not worth comparing with the glory that is to be revealed to us" (Rom. 8:18). As long as we are assured that heaven will be heaven, why worry about the details? However, we can easily say what heaven will *not* be. In the words of Emil Brunner:

> Eternal life is not an unending continuance of this life—that would perhaps be Hell—but eternal life is a quite different life, divine, not mundane, perfect, not earthly, true life, not corrupt half-life.[12]

But to say that "hell" is the internal combustion that exists in the heart of a man who lives without the Spirit of God in his heart, is not yet to exhaust the ways in which the New Testament

speaks of the terrible wrath of God. It is not enough simply to
"spiritualize" damnation by saying that it is only to be understood as an inner reality of our lives—whether in our consciousness or the dis-ease still lurking below consciousness. The New
Testament quite obviously and seriously also raises the terrifying
specter of an eternal damnation existing beyond man's physical
death. And yet, at the same time, it cannot be denied that the
New Testament repeatedly and openly and joyously affirms that
God "has made known to us in all wisdom and insight the
mystery of his will . . . as a plan for the fulness of time, to unite
all things in him, things in heaven and things on earth" (Eph.
1:9, 10). How can this seeming contradiction be held together?
As we have said, the assurance of God's universal salvation for
all men must be based on active faith in Christ alone, or else it
is no assurance at all. Therefore, any false basis for this confidence
must be radically called into question. Thus in the gospels, Christ
never unequivocally condemns anyone to an eternal damnation
that exists on the other side of death. This kind of hell is mentioned only as a possibility, albeit a very strong possibility, if our
destinies should be determined according to what we may de-
serve. The attitude typical of Christ in this matter is: "fear him
who can destroy both soul and body in hell" (Mt. 10:28); or,
"how are you to escape being sentenced to hell?" (Mt. 23:33).
And although neither of these statements clearly condemns anyone to a hell beyond death, they do raise the question: What
assurance do you have that you will escape this kind of judgment?
How do you know you will not be so destroyed? Thus it was
important to suggest the existence of a hell after death; for even
in the time of Christ it was possible to see death as "mere oblivion," as the one, great, final certainty of life. Among the Jews,
there were the Sadducees, "who say that there is no resurrection."
Among the Romans, there was the philosophy of Stoicism, which
considered suicide virtuous and death the end. Among the many
Charlie Browns of the time, there was simply the age-old yearning
of Job:

> Why is light given to him that is in misery, and life to the bitter
> in soul, who long for death, but it comes not . . . who rejoice

exceedingly, and are glad, when they find the grave? Why is light given to a man . . . whom God has hedged in? (Job 3:20–23)

For those whose lives are already a living hell, the prospect of the grave as "mere oblivion" must seem sweet indeed. But for those who know what life *is* when lived in obedience to God, mere oblivion could only be the *worst* news: "It is only when one loves life and the world so much that without them everything would be gone, that one can believe in the resurrection and a new world" (Bonhoeffer).[18] But in strongly calling into question the finality of death, Christ continued "to cast fire upon the earth" (Lk. 12:49). The purpose of this fire was to consume and deny certainty to all false gods, all false securities, all easy ways out. Christ himself was to be the only security and certainty, and hence all other so-called certainties must first be repudiated, questioned, and destroyed. The suggestion of eternal damnation in the New Testament is there only to help form a background of darkness against which the *light* must stand in order to be recognized as such. Christ never says that apart from faith in him one is sure to end up in hell; but he does make quite clear that apart from faith in him there is *nothing* sure—whether in life or death or after death. Hamlet is the representative figure in

literature who wished desperately to blow out the candle of his life, "to die—to sleep." And yet he could not. "For in that sleep of death what dreams may come"?[14] he asked. Indeed, who knows what dreams may come beyond the boundary of death? "Who knows whether the spirit of man goes upward and the spirit of the beast goes down to the earth?" (Eccles. 3:21). Who knows what the darkness holds? Hence neither Charlie Brown nor Hamlet is eager to play the suicidal "night game" of Macbeth:

> Out, out, brief candle!
> Life's but a walking shadow, a poor player,
> That struts and frets his hour upon the stage
> And then is heard no more.[15]

But what of those doom-saying Vulture-Evangelists who are ready to send the world to hell in a handbasket unless it "Gets right with God!" The best that can be said of them is that their god is too small. Nicolas Berdyaev tells us that the existence of an actual hell is

incomprehensible, inadmissible and revolting. It is impossible to be reconciled to the thought that God could have created the world and man if He foresaw hell, that He could have predetermined it for the sake of justice, or that He tolerates it as a

special diabolical realm of being side by side with His Own Kingdom. From the divine point of view it means that creation is a failure. The idea . . . is altogether unthinkable and, indeed, incompatible with faith in God. A God who deliberately allows the existence of eternal torments is not God at all but is more like the devil. Hell . . . is a fairy tale; there is not a shadow of reality about it; it is borrowed from our everyday existence with its rewards and punishments. The idea of an eternal hell . . . is one of the most hideous and contemptible products of the triumphant herdmind. . . . From the point of view of God, there cannot be any hell. To admit hell would be to deny God.[16]

In ascribing any lack of mercy on the part of our Father, we are only creating a god in our own image, a god who is, as we are, quick to anger and slow to show mercy. For we know that our Father is precisely the opposite:

For the mountains may depart and the hills be removed, but my steadfast love shall not depart from you, and my covenant of peace shall not be removed, says the Lord, who has compassion on you. (Is. 54:10)

It has certainly been true in the history of the Church that "wherever the body is, there the vultures will be gathered to-

gether" (Mt. 24:28). In times when the greatest spiritual darkness has prevailed in men's lives, there has always been a host of vulture-like evangelists, or "friends," all too eager to swoop down into this vacuum and proclaim the gloomy "good news" of doom, as if this vacuum itself were not doom enough. Men do not need the "good news" of hell if they already live their deaths there. It is just at this point that men will indeed be willing to listen to the Gospel, to the good news of God's salvation and forgiveness for all men in "the new Adam," the new "all men"— Christ. For "as in Adam all men die, so in Christ all will be brought to life" (1 Cor. 15:22, NEB). But the Vulture-Evangelist, like Lucy, "enjoys being the bearer of bad news!" No one knows how to mock the Vulture-Evangelist better than Snoopy:

If there is one thing a Vulture-Evangelist really hates, it is not to be taken in utter seriousness. And this is because he takes himself so seriously. Theologically speaking, it is because he does not really believe that God is God, but he believes that man is God, for, in his view, man is capable of deciding his own eternal destiny. Man is himself the master of his fate and captain of his soul. The Vulture-Evangelist preaches salvation by God's grace and damnation by man's works, forgetting that he cannot have

it both ways. Thus the Vulture-Evangelist wears the morosely gloomy face of his own "bad news," the bad news of a scornful, judging, deadly No. For as Luther could say, "No one judges and thinks so harshly of others as do those who are devoted to human exertions and works."[17] Hence the Vulture-Evangelist has actually placed his faith or taken his stand on man and what man is able to do. He forgets that God is the Lord and ruler of all of man's existence—even of man's puny little "decisions." For it is God himself who "has mercy upon whomever he wills, and he hardens the heart of whomever he wills" (Rom. 9:18). This is why, says Luther, "one should exercise mercy, for we are all made of the dough of which prostitutes and fornicators are made. If we stand, we stand by grace alone; otherwise our piety stands on a wisp of straw and soon collapses."[18]

"Peculiar Christendom," says Karl Barth, "whose most pressing problem seems to consist in this, that God's grace in this direction should be too free, that hell, instead of being amply populated, might one day perhaps be found to be empty."[19] Mark Twain saw the humorous incongruity of the Vulture-Evangelists when he said they preach the "good news" of "what a beautiful place heaven is and how nearly impossible it is to get there, and . . . what a dreary place hell is, and how easy it is to go there."[20] And thus the Vulture-Evangelists can do much harm to the church's proper proclamation of the *good* news by misrepresenting this message and placing unnecessary stumbling blocks before such men as Camus, who, out of sheer human honesty and decency, would like to drive "out of this world a god who [has] come into it with dissatisfaction and a preference for futile sufferings."[21] The Vulture-Evangelists, who try to scare "hell" out of men by scaring it into them, are worthy of the statement Christ made to the scribes and Pharisees:

> But woe to you . . . hypocrites! because you shut the kingdom of heaven against men; for you neither enter yourselves, nor allow those who would enter to go in. Woe to you . . . hypocrites! for you traverse sea and land to make a single proselyte, and when he becomes a proselyte, you make him twice as much a child of hell as yourselves. (Mt. 23:13-15)

It is no accident that there is a strong correlation between emotional instability and those men and women who live their lives under the threat of an actual "hell-fire." Again, this is because the heresy of eternal damnation is based on self-righteousness, or self-worship, and hence lays such an intolerable responsibility on the individual self—the responsibility for one's own eternal destiny. This is why John Donne could say, in speaking of men's fear of hell, "Even in this inordinate dejection thou exaltest thy self above God, and makest thy worst better than his best, thy sins larger than his mercy."[22] And so it is that the Vulture-Evangelist, the "leaping variety," believes in a kind of "do-it-yourself" redemption, a redemption by one's own "decision" or efforts. This is why when he finally falls and has to be rescued by a gracious power quite outside himself, it will be a humiliating experience.

A good Vulture-Evangelist, or even one of his proselytes—a mere Vulture, hates to accept charity!

The Christian message is finally and basically and supremely positive in its affirmation, and the Church should never be afraid to say so. "We cannot," says Barth,

> at all reckon in a serious way with *real* "outsiders," with a "world come of age," but only with a world which *regards* itself of age (and proves daily that it is precisely not that). Thus the so-called "outsiders" are really only "insiders" who have not yet understood and apprehended themselves as such. On the other hand, even the most persuaded Christian . . . must and will recognize himself ever and again as an "outsider." So . . . . what we have

to say to them—and first to ourselves—is a strange piece of news in any case. Let us see to it that it really is the great piece of news —the message of the eternal love of God directed to us men as we at all times were, are, and shall be. Then we shall certainly be very well understood by them, whatever they may or may not do with it.[23]

Charles Schulz once was asked, "Can humor and faith go together?" "It's almost a necessity!" he replied. "Those who find no humor in faith are probably those who find the church a refuge for their own black way of looking at life . . . . Humor is a proof of faith, proof that everything is going to be all right with God, nevertheless."[24]

Christianity, like comedy, is a "narrow escape." This is why Christianity's proclamation is of a "divine comedy." Both Christianity and comedy are concerned with a difficulty; and hence the "narrowness" involved. But both also involve a "happy ending"; and hence the joy, the laughter, the "escape." Neither of these elements should ever be forgotten or minimized. But just as comedy ceases being comedy when the narrowness outweighs the escape, so Christianity ceases being Christianity when the problem is taken more seriously than the final outcome. The final outcome, however, as Schulz pointed out in the above statement, is "that

everything is going to be all right with God, *nevertheless*." For it is essential to understand that God has already forgiven and elected all men to salvation "not with a natural Therefore, but with a miraculous Nevertheless" (Barth).[25] When we say that God loves all men and that finally he will make "all things subject to him, and thus God will be all in all" (1 Cor. 15:28, NEB), we are not saying what man is like but what God is like. "All I want is what I have coming to me! All I want is my fair share!" Linus tells Lucy just before Christmas. "Santa Claus doesn't owe you anything!" she tells him. Likewise "God does not have to do anything at all" (Barth).[26] God neither has to forgive us because it may be "expected of him," nor does he owe us forgiveness out of any "moral obligation." We are forgiven always out of God's own gracious freedom and choice, in spite of who we are or who we can be or what we have done. It is fatal to faith to look upon God's forgiveness as something "we have coming to us." In such cases we are trusting not in the goodness of God, but in some goodness of our own. If we were finally to receive what we have coming to us, it would probably be something quite less than what we had expected. God's gracious forgiveness is "free"—that is, unmerited, undeserved, and under no necessity. Lesser deities give only because they have to:

"I'm sure I have a good life ahead of me," Lucy smilingly tells Charlie Brown. "I'm sure I'm going to be happy, and have everything go just right for me all the days of my life!" "What makes you so sure?" he asks her. "It's only fair!" she shouts. But God is the "wholly other" whose ways are not our ways. He is under no compulsion to do what he does. Nor is he ruled by human standards of fairness and decency and justice. As a matter of fact, from the human point of view, God's mercy would often seem to be "unfair" in the equality of its final bounty to all. In the parable of the Prodigal Son (Lk. 15), both the obedient and the disobedient sons are loved equally by their father. In the parable of the Laborers in the Vineyard (Mt. 20), the same wage is paid at the end of the day both to those who worked all day "in the scorching heat" and to those who worked only an hour at the end of the day. The explanation given is: "Friend, I am doing you no wrong . . . . I choose to give to this last as I give to you. Am I not allowed to do what I choose with what belongs to me? Or do you begrudge my generosity?" God does what he does out of his own free choice and pleasure, and for no other reason. If God should *have* to do something, then obviously he would not be God but only the subject of some higher power. Therefore when we "all appear before the judgment seat of Christ" (2 Cor. 5:10), none of us will be able to do more than this:

Thus the prospect of going before the judge, says Barth,

> . . . can only be consoling for us if and when we hold fast to
> this one fact that Christ has accepted these very ones who have
> not deserved it of him, that he forgave those who nailed him to
> the cross and mocked him as he was being crucified, that he
> has loved us too as his enemies, and loves us and will love us
> still. The great, effective consolation when we face the coming
> judgment is that the judge is the one who has taken our side
> like this, that we may believe in the one who is like this, place
> our hopes in the one who is like this, and love the one who is
> like this. This expensive consolation cannot be had more cheaply
> than this. But it is to be had like that, at once, completely and
> with utter certainty.[27]

Having then in Christ this certainty of the future, what is
the Christian to do in the meantime? He is under orders, quite
simply, to "hate what is evil, hold fast to what is good" (Rom.
12:9):

To say that it is possible to see the devil in the figure of the dreaded "Red Baron" should be "no wonder, for even Satan disguises himself as an angel of light" (2 Cor. 11:14), and "the Prince of Darkness is a gentleman," as Shakespeare can tell us— a gentleman traditionally symbolized in red. Also, it is quite obvious that for Snoopy at least, the Red Baron *does* represent the forces of evil in the world. For instance, in one cartoon, after getting shot down for the umpteenth time, Snoopy grimly makes his way back to his outfit, muttering to himself, "Curse the Red Baron and his kind! Curse the wickedness in this world! Curse the evil that causes all this unhappiness!" But not only is Snoopy's *real antagonist* very much like the Christian's, but Snoopy is engaged in exactly the same *kind* of struggle "the church militant" is engaged in: "the First World War"—a war of the *past*. And the first war for the world that was fought on the *cosmic* scale, was also the *last* "world war." For the Church is here to proclaim that this struggle has *already* been decisively fought and won for all times in Jesus Christ. "In the world you will have trouble. But courage! The victory is mine; I have conquered the world" (Jn. 16:33, NEB). In the meantime, then, the Christian soldier has one task and one task only: to proclaim in all he says and does the good news of the great victory *already* won. The war is over! The forces of light have defeated the forces of darkness! You can come out of your dark, muddy trenches now and live as free men in the clear light of day! In recounting an incident after World War II, Karl Barth writes:

Did you read in the paper recently that two Japanese soldiers were found in the Philippines, who had not yet heard, or did not believe, that the war had ended fourteen years ago? They continue to hide in some jungle and shoot at everybody who dares approach them. Strange people, aren't they? Well, we are such people when we refuse to perceive and to hold true what the Easter message declares to be the meaning of the Easter story. Sin and death are conquered; God's free gift prevails, his gift of eternal life is for us all. Shall we not very humbly pay heed to this message? . . . He, Jesus Christ . . . made his wondrous history our own! He in whom the kingdom of the devil is already destroyed! In whom the kingdom of God and of his peace has

already come, to us, to you and me, to us all, on the earth and in the whole world![28]

This, then, is who the Church is: "a chosen race, a royal priesthood, a dedicated nation, and a people claimed by God for his own, to proclaim the triumphs of him who has called you out of darkness into his marvellous light" (1 Pet. 2:9, NEB):

Snoopy's encounters with the Red Baron are comical for the same reason that the Christian is involved in a divine comedy: regardless of how narrowly perilous and difficult the situation becomes for both of them, we know they will always *finally* escape; the war in which they are fighting has *already* been fought and won; the final outcome is assured long before the individual skirmishes ever begin. Both Snoopy and the Christian may get shot down time after time; but we know, as they do, that "Someday I'll get you, Red Baron!" We know this because we know that "the Red Baron" has, in actual fact, already been got. "For our fight," just as Snoopy's, this little peanut-sized "hound of heaven" who persistently dogs the Red Baron, "is not against human foes, but against cosmic powers, against the authorities

and potentates of this dark world, against the superhuman forces of evil in the heavens" (Eph. 6:12, NEB).

> The New Testament is concerned solely with the manner in which the reality of Christ assumes reality in the present world, which it has already encompassed, seized and possessed. There are not two spheres, standing side by side, competing with each other and attacking each other's frontiers. If that were so, this frontier dispute would always be the decisive problem of history. But the whole reality of the world is already drawn into Christ and bound together in him. . . . (Bonhoeffer)[29]

Thus the job of the Christian, in everything he does, is to make known the good news of the victory already won. He is concerned only with improving "the meantime," with the increase of joy on the earth: "Thy kingdom come, Thy will be done, on earth as it is in heaven."

"For to you is born this day in the city of David a Savior, who is Christ the Lord," reads Linus to Charlie Brown in the Christmas cartoon we have already seen. It is important that all of us —Linus, Charlie Brown, everyone—understand to whom this statement is directed, the "you" for whom a Savior has been born. For it is true that this

> promise says to those who hear or read it: Thou mayest not hear or read at this point something said about another. Thou art not in the audience, but in the centre of the stage. This is meant for thee. Thou art "this" individual. . . . It was for thee that Jesus Christ Himself bore the divine rejection in its real and terrible consequences. Thou art the one who has been spared from enduring it. And it is for thee that Jesus Christ is the elect man of God and arrayed in divine glory. Eternal life and fellowship with God await thee. Jesus Christ died and rose for thee. It is thou who art elect with Him and through Him. (Barth)[30]

But it was just on your account, Linus! Whether or not you understand what has happened, or whether or not you are a good and obedient child, all of this happened just for you.

8 *Jesus—The Dog God*

> I have only one word to say, but if the power were given me to say that single word, that single phrase in such a fashion that it would remain fixed and unforgettable—my choice is made; I know what I would say: "Our Lord Jesus Christ was nothing, oh, remember this, Christendom." —KIERKEGAARD[1]

Interviewer: "As a person of faith, what do you feel there is in the Christian faith that speaks most clearly to the world today?"

Charles Schulz: "Always Jesus," he answers firmly. "I think the minute we begin to get away from Jesus himself, we begin to cloud our theology. I am a firm believer in the theology of 'Lord, let us see Jesus and Jesus only.' This is why I refuse to go out and speak to groups as a so-called celebrity, because I think anyone who becomes religious because somebody else is religious, is already on the wrong track. A person should be converted because he has seen the figure of Jesus and has been inspired by him. And this is the only thing that makes a person Christian."[2]

Kafka suddenly stood still and stretched out his hand.
  "Look! There, there! Can you see it?"
  Out of the house . . . ran a small dog looking like a ball of wool, which crossed our path and disappeared around the corner . . . .
  "A pretty little dog," I said.
  "A dog?" asked Kafka suspiciously, and slowly we began to move again.
  "A small, young dog. Didn't you see it?"
  "I saw. But was it a dog?"
  "It was a little poodle."

"A poodle? It could be a dog, but it could also be a sign. We Jews often make tragic mistakes."

"It was only a dog," I said.

"It would be a good thing if it was," Kafka nodded. "But the *only* is true only for him who·uses it. What one person takes to be a bundle of rags, or a dog, is for another, a sign. . . . There is always something unaccounted for."

We walked in silence. . . . I said:

"Bloy writes that the tragic guilt of the Jews is that they did not recognize the Messiah."

"Perhaps that really is so," said Kafka. "Perhaps they really did not recognize him." —CONVERSATIONS WITH KAFKA[3]

If the Dog can be a Christ-symbol for Eliot, why not for Schulz?
—ROBERT MCAFEE BROWN[4]

Two things alone have still the power to avert the final plunge into the void. One is the miracle of a new awakening of faith, and the other is that force which the Bible calls the "restrainer" . . . that is to say, the force of order, equipped with great physical strength, which effectively blocks the way of those who are about to plunge into the abyss. . . . What the west is doing is to refuse to accept its historical inheritance for what it is. The west is becoming hostile towards Christ. This is the peculiar situation of our time, and it is genuine decay. . . . The task of the Church is without parallel. . . . The world has known Christ and has turned its back on Him, and it is to this world that the Church must now prove that Christ is the living Lord. . . . The Church, as the bearer of a historical inheritance, is bound by an obligation to the historical future. . . . In devoting herself to her proper task . . . the Church strikes a blow at the spirit of destruction. The "restrainer," the force of order, sees in the Church an ally, and, whatever other elements of order may remain, will seek a place at her side. Justice, truth, science, art, culture, humanity, liberty, patriotism, all at last, after long straying from the path, are once more finding their way back to their fountain-head. The more central the message of the Church, the greater now will be her effectiveness. —BONHOEFFER, *Ethics*[5]

He who does not find or receive God in Christ will never find him. He will not find God outside of Christ, even should he mount up above the heavens or descend below hell itself, or go

beyond the limits of the world. God declares that here, in Christ's human nature, which he assumed through his birth . . . shall be his dwelling place. If thou believest this, it is well for thee.

—LUTHER[6]

WE HAVE SAID THAT the Christian is finally distinguished from the non-Christian by something the Christian knows about the finale of history: eternal salvation has already been made sure once and for all time and for all men through Jesus Christ. As Harvey Cox has put it:

> Christian theology, unlike the Old Testament vision, claims that the seizure of power has already taken place. The revolutionary deliverer has come and has won the decisive battle. For this reason, all of history . . . . is a permanent crisis in which the defeated old regime still claims power while the victorious new regime has still not appeared publicly on the balcony. The New Testament looks forward not to the victory of Jesus, since that has already been won, but to the day when "every knee shall bow and every tongue confess" that Jesus is Victor.[7]

This view of history is, as Cox says, the expressed understanding of the New Testament. So it would probably be safe to assume, then, that the New Testament is a nice document to have.

Unfortunately, however, not all documents carry the same authority, even if they should seem to give us the same guarantees. Therefore we must now begin to close in on *how* the Christian knows what he knows. For *what* he knows includes the knowledge that there is only *one* way of knowing it. Otherwise, the Christian believes, nothing is *truly* known nor is there really any true knowledge. What is *the* way of knowing our absolution from all blame? Bonhoeffer puts it this way: "God Himself . . . absolves the world . . . . Now there is no more godlessness, no more hatred, no more sin which God has not . . . Himself . . . expiated. Now there is no more reality, no more world, but it is reconciled with God and at peace. God did this in His dear Son Jesus Christ."[8] Jesus Christ, then, is not only *the truth* of God that gives men life now and knowledge of life forever, but he is himself also *the way* to this truth. "For all the promises of God," says St. Paul of Christ, "find their Yes in him. That is why we utter the Amen through him, to the glory of God" (2 Cor. 1:20). Christ himself "is the mediator of a new covenant, or testament" through whom all of us now "may receive the promise of the eternal inheritance" (Heb. 9:15, NEB). It is through Christ and Christ alone that men may now have the assurance of God's final redemption of all men:

> [God's] purpose is that all men should be saved and come to realize the truth. And that is, that there is only one God, and only one intermediary between God and men, the Man Jesus Christ. He gave himself as a ransom for us all—an act of redemption which happened once, but which stands for all time as a witness to what he is. (1 Tim. 2:3–6, Phillips)

Thus, as in the last chapter we talked about Christ as One with

the Father *to whom* all men will finally return and find redemption, we now want to discuss Christ as the One *through whom* all must finally learn of the Father (Rom. 11:36).

"Come unto me *now*," Jesus says in effect to those who hear him, "and I will *now* give you joy—a joy that will also be your assurance of the great joy which will ultimately come to all the people." With these two promises offered, why do people not flock to him? He is literally offering, through his own mediation, *everything* we have ever hoped for: outrageous happiness now and forever. And yet the reaction of all the world to the "one mediator between God and man," is exactly the opposite. As he could say to his disciples, "If the world hates you, bear in mind that it hated me first . . . . he who hates me, hates my Father" (Jn. 15:18, 23, NEB).

Why is it that likewise "the world," "everybody," hates Jesus, "the middleman"? It is because conversation between Jesus and the children of this world always follows the pattern of the conversation between Jesus and "the rich young man." For if the doctrine of original sin teaches us anything, it is that *all* of us come into the world as "rich young men." The "riches" of the rich young man just happened to be money and possessions. If his blanket had not been his possessions, he would have been clutching some

other blanket—as *all* of us do originally. All of us come to Jesus dragging along our "riches," our blankets, our false gods of one kind or another that we have carefully held on to from the beginning, and the conversation goes about like this: " 'Good Master, what must I do to win eternal life?' Jesus said to him. . . . 'One thing you lack: go, sell everything you have, and give to the poor . . . and come, follow me.' At these words his face fell and he went away with a heavy heart" (Mk. 10:17, 21, 22, NEB). Jesus, being the "middleman" between God and man, could refer to himself as "the door." As such, he is very much like the door in the following cartoon:

Who's going to open the door? God is going to open the door, God *has* opened the door, and the door that is now open is Jesus himself: "Truly, truly, I say to you, he who does not enter the sheepfold by the door but climbs in by another way, that man is a thief and a robber . . . . I am the door; if any one enters by me, he will be saved" (Jn. 10:1, 9). But what makes us angry as we stand before this door, is the very same thing that made Charlie Brown angry: there is no getting through this door while still wrapped up in our false securities. All of us must first be completely stripped of all false gods or false securities before

ve can go through that narrow door called "Jesus." "We must hrow off every encumbrance, every sin to which we cling" (Heb. 2:1, NEB). For only then can we "go in and out and find pasture," ife, joy. Therefore we hate Jesus, "the door," "the middleman." Ie offers us everything any of us could desire—joy, peace, eternal ife. And yet he insists that we first stop worshiping whatever it s that now means most to us. There is no exception to this rule. Ne all come to Jesus desperately clinging to our false gods, asking im the question of how we can get more out of life. But his nswer to us is always the same: let go of the god you now have which is precisely to "take up one's cross") and come, follow ne. "If we obey God, we must disobey ourselves," says Melville; and it is in this disobeying ourselves, wherein the hardness of beying God consists." Accordingly, all initial confrontations be-ween Jesus and the world will invariably look like this:

The Family Man: Sir, I will certainly follow you if I can have your promise that this will not threaten any of my family rela-tionships, which I value most highly.

Jesus: "He who loves father or mother . . . son or daughter more than me is not worthy of me." (Mt. 10:37)

The Moralist: Sir, more than anything else, I am concerned with a high standard of morality and ethical conduct for myself, for my country, and for all men. I will follow you if you will give us a lofty code of ethical teachings, a sanctified system of moral laws to live by, good works to do and charitable rules to follow. "What must we do, to be doing the works of God?"

Jesus: "This is the work of God, that you believe in him whom he has sent." (Jn. 6:28, 29)

The Superstitious: Sir, if you really are of the supernatural, then give us some supernatural sign or miracle, and then I will follow you. After all, seeing is believing and miracles don't happen every day.

Jesus: "An evil and adulterous generation seeks for a sign . . . . Blessed are those who have not seen and yet believe." (Mt. 16:4; Jn. 20:29)

The Rationalist or "The Greek": I think, sir, that if you are the truth, then it will necessarily be a rational truth that you represent.

Could you please demonstrate the rational wisdom behind your arguments. For more than anything, I trust in reason.

St. Paul: "We proclaim Christ . . . folly to Greeks." (1 Cor. 1:23, NEB)

The Pelagian or "Self-Righteous": Sir, I will be very happy to follow you if you will only keep in mind that this is a decision I am making myself out of my own "free-will" and choice. Hence when I do choose to come to you, at least part of the righteousness will be my own. You have no right to claim all the credit. You cannot deny me this.

Jesus: "You did not choose me, but I chose you . . . . Apart from me you can do nothing." (Jn. 15:16; 5)

Linus: "I believe in the 'Great Pumpkin.' The way I see it, it doesn't matter what you believe just so you're sincere!"

Peter (speaking of Jesus): "There is salvation in no one else, for there is no other name under heaven given among men by which we must be saved." (Acts 4:12)

The Religious Man: If you will show us what rites we are to perform and what observances we are to keep, I, of course, will follow you.

Jesus: "Go and learn what this means, 'I desire mercy, and not sacrifice.'" (Mt. 9:13)

The Lover: Well spoken! What really is important is love! Oh, 'tis love that makes the world go round! We should all simply love each other as we love ourselves. Right?

Jesus: "A new commandment I give to you, that you love one another . . . as I have loved you." (Jn. 13:34)

The Humanist: Sir, pardon me, but I don't understand why you are so important in all of this. If there is a truth, then it must be freely available to us all—even something born in us . . . or else, perhaps, freely distributed by the government. Otherwise it simply wouldn't be fair—much less democratic. And how can you say this is "new"? Hasn't truth always been the same?

Jesus: "I am the way, and the truth, and the life; no one comes to the Father, but by me. If you had known me, you would have

known my Father also; henceforth you know him and have seen him." (Jn. 14:6, 7)

Caesar: If you will outline for me your social program for "the New Tomorrow," I most certainly will follow you.

Jesus: "You always have the poor with you, and whenever you will, you can do good to them; but you will not always have me." (Mk. 14:7)

The Objectivist: Surely there must be some objective, unifying principle of authority to prove that you are you. There must be either a Bible or a Pope or a church or a set of doctrinal beliefs to trust in. You can't expect us simply to trust in you—without some external guarantee.

Jesus: "Do you say this of your own accord, or did others say it to you about me? . . . Who do you say that I am?" (Jn. 18:34; Mt. 16:15)

The Ancestor Worshiper: "Lord, let me first go and bury my father."

Jesus: "Follow me, and leave the dead to bury their own dead." (Mt. 8:21, 22)

The Hedonist: For me, life is a real kick just the way it is. What can you do to improve what I already have?

Jesus: "If any one comes to me and does not hate . . . his own life, he cannot be my disciple. Whoever does not bear his own cross and come after me, cannot be my disciple. If any man would come after me, let him deny himself and take up his cross and follow me. For whoever would save his life will lose it; and whoever loses his life for my sake and the gospel's will save it." (Lk. 14:26, 27; Mk. 8:34, 35)

Regardless of whatever direction we come to Jesus from, he immediately tells all of us that we are going in exactly the *opposite* direction that *life* is in, and in order to find this *real* life we must turn around and follow *him*—the way and the life. Otherwise, he tells us, the life we lead will *not* be life indeed—as in the cartoon above.

Is there any wonder, then, that "everyone hates the 'middleman' "? Is there any wonder that the "middleman" met his death at the hands of an angry mob? As Bonhoeffer could say, "In the end, there are only two possibilities of encountering Jesus: either man must die or he kills Jesus."[9] This is why a good Christian sermon will always have something in it to offend everyone—namely, Jesus, the "stone of offense" (Is. 8:14). For when men come to Jesus, the teacher, and ask him how they can make "the honor roll," and the teacher has the audacity to tell them that they all must first "die," and that only then "if anyone serves me, he . . . will be honoured by my father" (Jn. 12:24-26, NEB)— none of this is calculated to make the teacher the most popular person in the world.

It is the height of folly to assume that Jesus "accepts people for what they are." Again, the invitation to "come to me" is not extended to one and all, but only to those "who labor and are heavy-laden." "Unless you become like children," "unless you repent," "unless one is born anew," "unless you eat the flesh of the Son of man and drink his blood," "unless you believe that I am he," "unless you abide in me," "unless your righteousness exceeds that of the scribes and Pharisees, you will never enter the kingdom of heaven." Do any of these stipulations sound as if Christ "accepts people for what they are"? It is true that God was in Christ reconciling the entire world to himself. Finally, therefore, all men will enter and be accepted into God's kingdom of heaven. But we are now abandoned from the knowledge of this acceptance "unless . . . ."

And so we hate the "middleman" because we are required to give up our false gods before we can come to him. But, as Kafka could say, "We are sinful not merely because we have eaten of the Tree of Knowledge, but also because we have not yet eaten of the Tree of Life."[10] Thus there is one other reason for our hatred:

"Come hither unto me, all ye that labor and are heavy laden, and I will give you rest." Halt now! But what is there to impose a halt? . . . The halt is imposed . . . by something infinitely more decisive: by the INVITER.[11]

These are the words with which Kierkegaard stops talking about the offensiveness of giving up our original false gods for Jesus, and begins talking about Christianity's offense proper—Jesus himself. For look at the Inviter! Who is it that bids us relinquish our false gods and come to him?

"Come hither, hither, all ye that labor and are heavy laden; oh, come hither; behold how He bids you come, how He openeth his arms!"

Oh, when these words are uttered by a fashionable man in a silk gown, with a pleasant and sonorous voice which sounds agreeably from the lovely, vaulted ceiling, a silken man who bestows honor

and repute upon all who hear him; oh, when a king says this who is clothed in purple and velvet . . . —then indeed thou wilt agree that there is some sense in what he says. But make what sense out of it thou wilt, one thing is sure, it is not Christianity, it is exactly the opposite, as contrary to Christianity as could be—for remember who the Inviter is.[12] (See cartoon above.)

Was Jesus, the man, ever a "great" man? Did he ever get to be "King"? Only at the time of his execution as a common criminal and with the utmost mockery and scorn, was this title given to him. Then who is the Inviter? Who is the one who bids us to "repent," to make an about-face from the direction in which we are going, and to follow him? To follow him to what? To follow him to crucifixion—crucifixion of that very thing we hold most dear. Who is it then? Oh, no! Not him! Not the dog!

The central teaching of Jesus was the doctrine of the Incarnation, the doctrine of the God-man: "I and the Father are one . . . . No one comes to the Father, but by me . . . . He who has seen me has seen the Father" (Jn. 10:30; 14:6, 9). These words are extremely difficult for *anyone* to swallow. Indeed, it was just for statements such as these that Jesus met his death: the people "sought all the more to kill him, because he . . . called God his Father, making himself equal with God" (Jn. 5:18). For Jesus calls us not only to repentance, to the "letting go" of the false gods we come to him with; but he goes one more *difficult step farther*: he also calls us to believe in *him alone* as the decisive, absolutely unique, once and for all, full revelation of God to man. This is extremely difficult for us, because Jesus was careful to give men *no external guarantee* that he was, in fact, God in the flesh. Otherwise, he realized, we would not be worshiping *him*, but would only be worshiping or trusting in the guarantee, whatever it might be.

But sinful man is extremely clever. Because when confronted with the hard, difficult, irrational, "nothing to go on" decision of whether or not this particular flesh-and-blood man, Jesus, was actually God, man can very cleverly sidestep this decision by imputing to Jesus that attribute which sinful man *already* worships or else greatly admires. Whenever we come to Jesus as "rich men," whatever these riches may be, we will attempt to invest him with the same riches in order that we can continue to cling to them rather than to him. Thus "Christ is always betrayed by the kiss" (Bonhoeffer).[13] The nominal Christian, then, will see Jesus as a name, a representative, a symbol, a personification, a prototype, a figure, a model, an exemplar for some-

thing else. The nominal Christian pays homage to something *about* Jesus, rather than worshiping the man himself. For this reason, nominal Christians will extol the moral teachings of Jesus, the faith *of* Jesus, the personality *of* Jesus, the compassion of Jesus, the world view *of* Jesus, the self-understanding *of* Jesus, etc. None of these worships *Jesus* as the Christ, but only something *about* him, something peripheral to the actual flesh-and-blood man. This is why when the almighty God came into the world in Jesus, he came as *the lowest of the low,* as weakness itself, as a complete and utter *nothing,* in order that men would be forced into the crucial decision about *him alone* and would not be able to worship anything *about* him. Kierkegaard's famous analogy tells of a king who falls in love with a humble maiden, a subject of his realm who is literally a nothing, a nobody. He could give the order and have her brought to his palace at once. But he does not do it. For he wants her to return his love. He does not want her to love something *about* him, that he is the great and mighty king, etc.; but he wants her to love *him,* simply for who he is in himself. Therefore the king goes to her. And he goes not as the king, but he goes as the humblest of men, a man as humble and lowly as his beloved herself. Likewise, in order to reach down to us nothings, God himself became a nothing in Jesus: "For the divine nature was his from the first; yet he did not prize his equality with God, but made himself nothing, assuming the nature of a slave. Bearing the human likeness, revealed in human shape, he humbled himself, and in obedience accepted even death—death on a cross" (Phil. 2:6–8, NEB). Man is man, a mere nothing; but God nevertheless loves man and chose equality with man, to become a nothing also, in order to talk to man, so that man could then become something.

But, as we said, men no longer see Jesus as a mere nothing to be worshiped in and of himself; they now want to find some aspect about him that they already worship. Thus it is no longer adequate simply to talk of the doctrine of the "God-man," since we are so inclined to see the man Jesus only as a symbol for ourselves or for our own systems of value. Therefore we must once more recapture and hold the powerfully prophetic vision of Isaiah, who could see the Christ as "the Dog God," as the almost less than human Messiah, as an utter nothing:

> His appearance was so marred, beyond human semblance, and his form beyond that of the sons of men . . . . He had no form or comeliness that we should look at him, and no beauty that we should desire him. He was despised and rejected by men; a man of sorrows, and acquainted with grief; and as one from whom men hide their faces he was despised, and we esteemed him not. (Is. 52:14; 53:2, 3)

How does this description compare with most of the pictures of Jesus seen in churches and church literature?—"preferably sentimental: the gentle look, the kindly eye, or whatever else may occur to such a silly parson" (Kierkegaard).[14] When Love came into the world in bodily form, it did not come in the form of the easily recognized and overwhelming lover, who would only reflect our own desires and hence leave us no choice to make. But the Messiah came in a form that demands the deepest kind of decision from each of us—"Who do you say that I am?" (Mt. 16:15). Such a decision might not have been difficult to make, and hence would have required no faith, were it not for the fact that the Messiah came unexpectedly as a dog among men.

When we look at the word GOD from one perspective, it would seem almost to be the opposite of God—DOG. Similarly, Christianity proclaims that in Jesus and Jesus alone can we see God —and yet when we look honestly at the New Testament's picture of Jesus, without seeing him as the Christ of faith or remaking him in our own images, we see just the opposite of what we might easily expect—a "nothing," a "slave," a lowly dog of a man. And in this way *faith* is demanded from us. "For we walk by faith, not by sight" (2 Cor. 5:7). As for the Old Testament, it is especially in Isaiah's vision of the Messiah as the Dog God that we are enabled to see more clearly the actual object of the Christian faith's devotion: the man Jesus and him alone. And in this way the object of faith is better protected from those who would have faith in some attribute of Jesus, rather than faith in the man himself. This is why Bonhoeffer could say of Jesus:

God allows himself to be edged out of the world and on to the

cross. God is weak and powerless in the world, and that is the way, the only way, in which he can be with us and help us.[15]

Only for faith does Jesus, "the very stone which the builders rejected," become the Christ, "the head of the corner." Therefore whenever the Church is absent-minded enough to proclaim only the glorified and triumphant "cornerstone," the Christ of faith, faith will be made impossible for others. For faith is always faith in the humiliated, crucified Jesus, the *rejected* stone, "a stone that will make men stumble, a rock that will make them fall" (1ᵉ Pet. 2:7-8). And many *will* fall. But it is far better to offer men the hard, clear-cut choice that makes real decision necessary and faith possible, than to offer them a 'watered-down "choice" that is much easier but exists only among alternatives that make little difference anyway. The choice offered by Christianity cannot be clearer: this lowly man; this ugly, uneducated, insignificant Rabbi from out of the sticks of Nazareth; this self-asserting, gloomy carpenter's son, "whose father and mother and brothers and sisters they knew" (Donne);[16] this "authoritarian" itinerant preacher and vagabond, with no credentials and no place to lay his head—was God! was the man in whom "the complete being of God, by God's own choice, came to dwell. Through him God chose to reconcile the whole universe to himself . . . —to reconcile all things . . . through him alone" (Col. 1:19, 20, NEB)! Why, says Kierkegaard with mock horror, "if this insane thing were possible, that an individual was God, then logically one must worship this individual. A greater philosophical bestiality cannot be conceived."[17] Nevertheless, this is the "bestial" decision laid before men: the dogma of the Dog God—that this wretched, humiliated outcast, this "stumbling stone," was either God, or he was not. Thus the

choice is made brutally clear; and thus Christ could say of himself: "He that is not against us is for us" (Mk. 9:40); and "He
who is not with me is against me, and he who does not gather
with me scatters" (Mt. 12:30). (See cartoon above.)

"The connection of Christ with Snoopy becomes annoying only
if one forgets how annoying faith in Christ is as such," says
Swiss theologian and *Peanuts* fan W. Neidhart.[18] And why is
faith in Christ annoying? Again, it is because a real face-to-face
encounter with the object of faith, Jesus, will invariably disap-
point us in our preconceived ideas of what God should be like.
God will *always* be an annoyance when he reveals himself to us
sinful men. For all of our preconceived ideas of what he should
be, only represent those false gods that we are still hanging on
to and that still come between ourselves and him. Therefore in
revealing himself as a complete *nothing*, when all false gods are
—by definition—"really something," we are all forced to give up
our false gods, our "hangups," and likewise to become nothing,
before we can go to him. Thus we are annoyed or "offended."
And this is precisely why Jesus, the Dog God, could say, "Blessed
is he who takes no offense at me" (Lk. 7:23). In *Training in
Christianity*, Kierkegaard describes some of the different hangups
men can have as they confront the lowly Jesus with their own
ideas of the kind of person a Messiah should be. One such man
is a real Lucy:

Literally He is nothing . . . . What has He done to provide for His
future? Nothing. Has He any definite job? No. What prospects
has He? None. To speak only of a minor consideration—what will
He do to pass the time when He grows older? . . . Why, He cannot even play cards. He enjoys some popular favour . . . . which in

the twinkling of an eye can be transformed into disfavour—To join myself to Him—no, I thank you. Praise God, I have not yet entirely lost my wits.[19]

Another one of Kierkegaard's men who is hung up by the nothingness of Jesus, the Dog God, has this to say:

No, let us be men. Everything is good in moderation; too little and too much spoils all . . . . —and as for this man, His downfall is obviously a sure thing. So I have seriously taken my son to task, warning and admonishing him that he should not drift into evil ways and join himself to that person. And why should he? Because all are running after Him. Yes, but who are these "all"? Idle and unstable people, street loungers and vagabonds who find it easy to run. But not very many who have their own houses and are well to do, and none of the wise and respected people after whom I always set my clock . . . . And if we look at the clergy, who surely must understand such matters best— . . . Pastor Green said yesterday evening at the club: "That life will have a terrible ending." And he is a chap that doesn't only know how to preach. One should not hear him on Sundays in church, but on Mondays at the club—I only wish I had half of his knowledge of the world. He said quite rightly and as from his very heart, "it is only idle and unstable people that run after Him." And why do they run

after Him? Because He is able to perform some miracles. But who knows whether they really are miracles, or whether He can confer the same power on His disciples? In any case a miracle is a very uncertain thing, whereas certainty is certainty. Every serious father who has grown up children must be truly concerned lest his sons be seduced and carried away to throw in their lot with Him and with the desperate men who follow Him, desperate men who have nothing to lose.[20]

When man and Christ are joined in the faith relationship, they will always come together as a couple of "nothings." Man must be "a nothing" in that, having all false gods stripped from him, he has *nothing* else to cling to; Christ appears as "a nothing" in order to furnish man with *nothing* other than Himself to worship.

And why does the Dog God dance? Because he is, as one of the newer hymns of the church can tell us, "The Lord of the Dance":

> I danced for the scribe and the pharisee,
> But they would not dance and they wouldn't follow me,
> I danced for the fisherman, for James and John,
> They came with me and the dance went on.
>
> I danced on the Sabbath and I cured the lame,
> The holy people said it was a shame
> They whipped and they stripped and they hung me high
> And they left me there on a cross to die.
>
> (Chorus) Dance then wherever you may be
> I am the Lord of the Dance said he
> And I'll lead you all wherever you may be,
> And I'll lead you all in the dance said he. (Etc.)[21]

But it is important to remember that the joyful dance of the Dog God comes to us only in following and worshiping him, the very one who is nothing—whipped, stripped, and left on a cross to die. Then and only then will the saying of Jesus become true for us: "How blest you are when men hate you, when they outlaw you and insult you, and ban your very name as infamous, because of the Son of Man. On that day be glad and dance for joy; for assuredly you have a rich reward in heaven" (Lk: 6:22, 23, NEB).

The only thing that is radically "new" in the New Testament is the man Jesus himself and who he is said to be—God in flesh and blood. "To this man thou shalt point and say, 'Here is God'" (Luther).[22] The story of the virgin birth of Jesus is only one means the New Testament uses in pointing to the radical newness of the Savior that has been brought into the world. The Christ was no new, improved model of anything that had been done before. For in Christ, God brought the altogether new and final eon of history into being.

For instance, all of the so-called "teachings" of Jesus are also taught—many of them word for word—in the Old Testament. And only a casual knowledge of the other religions of the world will reveal that many of his "teachings" are also found there.

And so, as Kierkegaard could say, "It is 1,800 years since Christ lived, so He is forgotten—only His teaching remains—that is to say, Christianity has been done away with."[23] For what is absolutely unique in the New Testament is not the ethical or moral teachings of Jesus, nor anything else about or surrounding the man. But what *is* unique is the witness the New Testament bears to *this man himself:* "In the beginning was the Word, and the Word was with God, and the Word was God. . . . And the Word became flesh and dwelt among us, full of grace and truth; we have beheld his glory, glory as of the only Son from the Father" (Jn. 1:1, 14). Thus Christ did not come into the world to be "a nice guy," or to "make trivial remarks" or even to chase the sticks of moral casuistry. He came into the world as the decisive, final, once and for all, self-revelation of God to history. This is why Kierkegaard could say:

> Mediocrity goes on interpreting and interpreting Christ's words until it gets out of them its own spiritless, trivial meaning—and then, after having removed all the difficulties, it is tranquillized, and appeals confidently to Christ's words! It quite escapes the attention of mediocrity that hereby it generates a new difficulty, surely the most comical difficulty it is possible to imagine, that God should let Himself be *born,* that Truth should have come into the world . . . in order to make trivial remarks.[24]

Christianity holds that the actual historical man, Jesus of Nazareth, is the one and only channel of access, "the one mediator,"
that man now has, or will ever have, to God. "No one comes to
the Father, but by me" (Jn. 14:6). Hence it is literally true for
Christianity that "the medium *is* the message," that the way
is also the *truth* and the *life*, that the means is also the end, that
"The Helper is the help" (Kierkegaard).[25] No more than anyone else does the Christian pretend to understand the scandal-
ous and "ridiculous" narrowness of "the door," the man Jesus,
through whom all must reach the Father. All he knows is that
it is a true and essential part of his faith. If Christ is not
absolutely essential to faith as "the way," then he is not essential to faith in *any* way at all. And if Christ is not *essential* to
faith, what right do we have to call this faith Christ-ian? But
Christianity believes that in the historical Jesus of Nazareth, and
in him only, we are at this point and in this person "in touch"
with God. To say that the Spirit of God must flow to all the
world through this one tiny, historical point, is like saying that
a huge, tri-state, metropolitan area could suddenly be plunged
into complete darkness because of the failure of one very small
"breadbox-size fuse."[26] And yet this is exactly the power failure
that occurred in 1965, throughout 80,000 square miles of north-
eastern United States and Canada. And so it is that through
Jesus alone "the true light that enlightens every man was coming into the world. . . . to all who received him, who believed
in his name, he gave power to become children of God" (Jn.
1:9, 12). "The argument becomes still clearer . . ." says the
New Testament in speaking of "Jesus, on whom faith depends
from start to finish," "and a better hope is introduced, through
which we draw near to God" (Heb. 7:15, 19; 12:2, NEB). Again,
the Christian can give no *objective* reason for why this is so.
Otherwise, he would cease worshiping his Lord and begin trusting in the "reason" or the proof or the objective authority. The
Christian can only give a *subjective* reason for why he knows the
man Jesus to be the only channel of God's Holy Spirit between
God and men. The Christian knows what he knows entirely
from the subjective *experience* of his encounter with Jesus. He
can only say with the man who, like himself, was born blind

and was also cured by Jesus: "All I know is this: once I was blind, now I can see" (Jn. 9:25, NEB).

It may be humiliating for us to have to follow a lowly dog. But Jesus is the only Seeing Eye dog of the spirit that blind humanity has. "What Jesus means to me is this," says Schulz: "In him we are able to see God, and to understand his feelings toward us."[27]

> Not only do we know God by Jesus Christ alone, but we know ourselves only by Jesus Christ. We know life and death only through Jesus Christ. Apart from Jesus Christ, we do not know what is our life, nor our death, nor God, nor ourselves. Thus without the Scripture, which has Jesus Christ alone for its object, we know nothing and see only darkness and confusion in the nature of God, and in our own nature. (Pascal)[28]

Again, it is important to be clear that the Christian worships nothing "about" or "of" Jesus. He worships the historical "body and blood" Jesus; he worships the historical man, Jesus himself. This is why Christ could say, "unless you eat the flesh of the Son of man and drink his blood, you have no life in you" (Jn. 6:53). This is why the central sacrament of the Church is the

Eucharist, or Holy Communion, the sacrament in which precisely *this body* and *this blood* are remembered and pointed to as *the* source of communion with God. "Flesh and blood" is a means used in Jewish writing to say "humanity" as contrasted with divinity.[29] For it is only through the concrete, historical, flesh-and-blood *humanity* of Jesus that man has contact with God. "There is . . . one concrete formula which says everything that is essential in all brevity and accuracy: *Revelation* (in its definitive form) *is Christ himself*," says Jesuit theologian Werner Bulst.[30] "To say revelation is to say, 'The Word became flesh' " (Barth).[31] The situation of mankind before Jesus came into the world is the same situation described by Bonhoeffer in a letter from a Nazi prison, written just before Christmas, 1943: "Life in a prison cell reminds me a great deal of Advent—one waits and hopes and putters about, but in the end what we do is of little consequence, for the door is shut, and it can only be opened from the outside."[32] The situation of mankind before Jesus came into the world is also described in the following cartoon:

For it is true "that Jesus, whom they knew to be that Carpenter's Son, and knew his work, must be believed to have set up a frame that reached to heaven, out of which no man could, and in which any man might be saved" (Donne).[33] "There is no way

from us to God," says Karl Barth.[34] Then how do we get to God? You can't get there from here! But fortunately for us, there is a way from God to man; and this way is the way given to man in the historical person of Jesus of Nazareth. Jesus is that kiss planted by God on the nose of the world in order to break up the vicious circle of the world's self-contained "crab-in." The door of the prison cell Bonhoeffer spoke of above is opened only, as Bonhoeffer could say, in "the word of the revelation of God in Jesus Christ. This word does not proceed from any man's own heart or understanding or character; it comes down to man from heaven, from the will and mercy of God." "Behold," says Christ, "I stand at the door and knock" (Rev. 3:20):

X marks the spot where revelation has taken place, the point of contact between God and man, "the still point of the turning world" (Eliot).[35] Indeed, "X" is the whole point of Xianity. The historical Jesus himself is precisely the place of God's unique self-disclosure to man; there is no other. To have missed this is to have "missed the whole point" of Christianity. Beside him, all else is "beside the point." Without him, Christianity is utterly pointless.

The relation between us and God, between this world and His

world, presses for recognition, but the line of intersection is not self-evident. The point on the line of intersection at which the relation becomes observable and observed is Jesus, Jesus of Nazareth, the historical Jesus,—"born of the seed of David according to the flesh." The name Jesus defines an historical occurrence and marks the point where the unknown world cuts the known world . . . . At this point, time and things and men are . . . exalted inasmuch as they serve to define the neighborhood of the point at which the hidden line, intersecting time and eternity, concrete occurrence and primal origin, men and God, becomes visible. The years A.D. 1–30 are the era of revelation and disclosure; the era which ; . . sets forth the new and strange and divine definition of all things (Barth).[36]

Since the time man became man, he has been searching for *the* place of salvation, *the* place of comfort. The question of "Where can I find God?" is not just Job's question; it is the question behind all human activity. But Job put the question this way: "Oh, that I knew where I might find him, that I might come even to his seat!" (Job 23:3). Charlie Brown, on the other hand, a sort of modern-day Job-Everyman, makes one more of his futile attempts to find God and "come to his seat," in this cartoon:

But Christianity proclaims that the basic question of man, "Where can God be found?" has been *answered*—it has been

answered decisively and for all history in the historical man Jesus. The Christian no longer asks this question, as the disciples once did. At this "point," Jesus seems almost to have lost patience with them: "How can you say, 'Show us the Father'? Do you not believe that I am in the Father and the Father in me?" (Jn. 14:9, 10).

> No man can look with undivided vision at God and at the world of reality so long as God and the world are torn asunder. Try as he may, he can only let his eyes wander distractedly from one to the other. But there is a place at which God and the cosmic reality are reconciled, a place at which God and man have become one. That and that alone is what enables man to set his eyes upon God and upon the world at the same time. This place does not lie somewhere out beyond reality in the realm of ideas. It lies in the midst of history as a divine miracle. It lies in Jesus Christ, the reconciler of the world. (Bonhoeffer).[37]

Since the Church began, one of the most dangerous and persistent heresies it has had to fight is the *docetic heresy*—the heresy that attempts to make Christ's incarnation easily acceptable by seeing Jesus as a "transparent envelope," as the "embodiment" of an abstract idea of one kind or another. This heresy is rampant in the Church today, especially in Protestantism. Docetism is the heresy in which, as Bonhoeffer could say,

> a particular religious idea is first held and then applied to the historical Jesus. . . . It understands Jesus as the support for or the embodiment of particular ideas, values and doctrines. As a result, the manhood of Jesus Christ is in the last resort not taken seriously, although it is this very theology which speaks so often of the man. It . . . brings Jesus more than ever into the field of speculation. . . . The understanding of the man as the support for a particular idea bypasses his real existence. It confuses the real man with an ideal man and makes him a symbol.[38]

Thus the heresy of docetism attempts to avoid what Kierkegaard called the "scandal of particularity" of the Christian faith, the scandal which says that "In the Christ of Israel this Word has become *particular*, that is, Jewish flesh" (Barth).[39] Since the docetist, like all of us, would much rather avoid worshiping Jesus, the *hard fact* at the center of the Christian faith, he then

draws a picture of Jesus on the canvas of "airy nothing." He does not base his faith on this event in history, but he worships an abstraction, an idea, a concept. And he feels that in this way he has finally escaped the judgment of God.

Docetism, like all heresies of the Church, is concerned with "winning," or "catching" more and more followers. Likewise the Church is chiefly concerned that it "might win the more" (1 Cor. 9:19). But, as Kierkegaard has pointed out, "The method which has been increasingly followed in the course of the centuries is as follows: the standard for being a Christian has been lowered, so that all the more. have been caught"[40]—or "won." And what is the basic standard for being a Christ-ian? "What must I do to be saved?" is another way the New Testament asks the same question. The answer, the standard, is Christ himself: "Believe in the Lord Jesus, and you will be saved" (Acts 16:30, 31). But this answer, this standard, is the most difficult thing about Christianity to swallow. Just here, at *the point of Jesus*, is *the* "stumbling-stone," *the* "rock of offense" of our faith. Obviously, then, to "win more," we must lower this standard, we must get rid of the *dog*. And so it is that we see everywhere in the churches today what one journalist called "the ugly spectre

of sell-out theology." But the question then becomes: if we really are willing to sell Snoopy out "just to win a few ball games," will the ball games we then win be the same games, and will they be worth winning?

It is true that the Church might win a few insignificant ball games if it were to get rid of its Lord, the lowly "stumbling-block" of its faith. But on the other hand, "What will a man gain by winning the whole world, at the cost of his true self?" (Mt. 16:26, NEB). Jesus referred to himself as "the truth"; and "in the Church we are concerned with truth, and today with an urgency such as probably has not been the case for centuries. And truth is not to be trifled with. If it divides the spirits, then they are divided. To oppose this commandment for the sake of a general idea of 'peace' and 'unity' would be a greater disaster for all concerned than such division" (Barth).[41] Fortunately, however, Snoopy was not traded. ("Betrayed" would probably be a better word.) As a matter of fact, by a peculiar set of circumstances he actually became the new manager of Charlie Brown's team. And as the new manager, Snoopy again began to bear many striking resemblances to the Dog God, the "new manager" of the New Testament. For in "Jesus, the mediator of a new covenant," God has promised to shake every man to his very

foundation, "in order that what cannot be shaken may remain" (Heb. 12:24, 27).

The nominal Christian would usually rather not think of the "gentle Jesus" as being rough to play for. Again, however, this is only one of our many attempts to make a nice controllable household pet of God, to take the divine into our possession and bring it under our management. But "Snoopy"—like Jesus —"is kind of frightening because he is so uncontrollable" (Schulz).[42]

What does the Church think of Christ? The Church's answer is categorical and uncompromising, and it is this: That Jesus Bar-Joseph, the carpenter of Nazareth, was in fact and in truth, and in the most exact and literal sense of the words, the God "by whom all things were made". . . . He was not merely a man so good as to be "like God"—He *was* God. Now this is not just a pious commonplace . . . . For what it means is this, among other things; that for whatever reason God chose to make man as he is—limited and suffering and subject to sorrows and death—He had the honesty and the courage to take His own medicine. Whatever game He is playing with His creation, He kept his own rules and played fair. He can exact nothing from man that He has not exacted from Himself. He has Himself gone through the whole of human ex-

perience, from the trivial irritations of family life and the cramping restrictions of hard work and lack of money to the worst horrors of pain and humiliation, defeat, despair, and death. When he was a man, he played the man. He was born in poverty and died in disgrace and thought it well worth the while. (Sayers)[43]

But if there was one thing that Jesus, the Dog God, hated more than anything about the game he played, it was *losing*. For this purpose he came into the world: "to seek and to save the lost" (Lk. 19:10). For it was his Father's "will that I should not lose even one of all that he has given me" (Jn. 6:39, NEB).

Occasionally the question will arise as to the "historicity of Jesus," the question as to whether such a man actually ever lived. This question can never be a serious threat to the Christian. The Christian lives his life totally by faith, rather than "sight" (which includes historical research). And the Christian's faith tells him not only that *this man was God*, but also that *this man was*. "Faith needs no confirmation from history . . . . historical investigation is irrelevant before the self-attestation of Christ in the present," says Bonhoeffer. "By the miracle of [Christ's] presence in the church he bears witness to himself here and now as the one who was historical then."[44] In any case, historical investigation can never be *absolutely* sure of any of its con-

clusions, whatever they may turn out to be. These "conclusions" may change tomorrow, and usually do. Fortunately, however, faith does not need to wait for the conclusions of historical research. Faith is certainty *now*, for it is the certainty present in the heart. To use Pascal's famous dictum:

> The heart has its reasons, which reason does not know . . . . It is the heart which experiences God, and not the reason. This, then, is faith: God felt by the heart, not by the reason.[45]

Faith, then, does not stand back and ask academically the essential questions concerning Jesus; it does not trust in reason's power to prove or disprove that this man *lived* or *was God*. This would only be to trust in reason as God. Faith knows Jesus to be the Christ only by the direct relationship of trust in *him*. The Christian is a member of the *body* of Christ, which clings only to him and thus knows him by *direct experience*. The Christian is *part of* Christ, "the tree of life." Thus Jesus could say:

> I am the vine, and you the branches. He who dwells in me, as I dwell in him, bears much fruit; for apart from me you can do nothing. He who does not dwell in me is thrown away like a withered branch. The withered branches are heaped together, thrown on the fire, and burnt. (Jn. 15:5, 6, NEB)

To follow him meant cleaving to him bodily. That was the natural consequence of the Incarnation. Had he been merely a prophet or a teacher, he would not have needed followers, but only pupils and hearers. But since he is the incarnate Son of God who came in human flesh, he needs a company of followers, who will participate not merely in his teaching, but also in his Body . . . . It is certain that there can be no fellowship or communion with him except through his Body. For only through that Body can we find acceptance and salvation. (Bonhoeffer)[46]

Or, as Snoopy could put it, "If somebody likes you, he pats you on the head."

In addition to being largely indifferent to the academic question of whether Jesus actually lived, the Christian faith is not particularly concerned with the *details* of Jesus' life. The fact that Jesus lived, that *this man was God incarnate*, is infinitely more important to faith than any of the individual events surrounding his birth or life or death. Whatever the actual events in Jesus' life may or may not have been, faith knows it has been given enough information to put the believer "in touch," or "in communion," with this particular historical man. And this, for the Christian, is what is essential. Jesus was the Savior at his *birth*, quite apart from anything that was to happen later in his life. Again, Jesus was not God "because" of something he said or did. This would only be worshiping something a man said or did and not the *man* himself. There is only one "because": Jesus was God because it pleased God to be this flesh-and-blood man. The fact that the Christian worships *Jesus* as the Christ and not anything *about* him, is the basis for Kierkegaard's famous statement that "If the contemporary generation had left nothing behind them but these words: 'We have believed that in such and such a year God appeared among us in the humble figure of a servant, that he lived and taught in our community, and finally died,' it would be more than enough."[47] Luther was making the same point when he said:

It is not enough nor is it Christian, to preach the works, life and words of Christ as historical facts, as if the knowledge of these would suffice for the conduct of life . . . . For the humanity would be no use, if the divinity were not in it; yet on the other hand,

God will not and cannot be found except through and in this humanity.[48]

Therefore, says Luther, "Know that there is no other God besides this man, Christ Jesus."[49] This is why Vincent van Gogh, who knew his Bible as well as the colors on his palette, could say:

> The consolation of that saddening Bible which arouses our despair and our indignation—which distresses us once and for all because we are outraged by its pettiness and contagious folly—the consolation which is contained in it, like a kernel in a hard shell, a bitter pulp, is Christ.[50]

The "kernel" of the New Testament, the New Testament's one, firm, hard, irreducible standard for judging *all* things, was not "sincerity," as Linus might hope; but it was to

> test the spirits to see whether they are of God; for many false prophets have gone out into the world. By this you know the Spirit of God: every spirit which confesses that Jesus Christ has come in the flesh is of God, and every spirit which does not confess Jesus is not of God. (1 Jn. 4:1-3)

All of the teachings of Jesus, all of his mighty works and miracles, indeed all of his life, was finally directed to one purpose:

to draw attention to himself so that men might make the most decisive of all decisions: "Who do you say I am?" Both in parable and in direct teaching, both in word and deed, his entire life was calculated to "rivet thine attention upon Him, that thou mayest be offended at the contradiction and the thoughts of thy heart may be revealed in the act of choosing whether thou wilt believe or not" (Kierkegaard).[51] The "contradiction," the absolutely incomprehensible paradox presented to us, was this: this lowly nothing, this nobody, this absolute dog of a man said he was God. "Have I been with you all this time, and yet you do not understand me . . . ? He who has seen me has seen the father" (Jn. 14:9, Moffatt). This is the decision about Jesus that he himself long ago placed before us. The rest is now up to us.

What is the hard, basic, bedrock proclamation of Christianity? Is it the glorious resurrected Christ, or Christ the great teacher, or Christ the fearless prophet and wonder-worker? It is none of these. But it is the proclamation of the humiliated, despised, rejected, crucified Jesus, who nevertheless—was God. This lowliness will always offend, annoy, "bug" us as long as we are quite sure of ourselves and self-possessed. But for those who have found it necessary to let go of themselves, for those who have been crucified with Christ and are therefore willing to stoop

so low as even to this lowly one himself, this lowly Jesus is the power of God for transforming even the hardest of us: "For Jews demand signs and Greeks seek wisdom, but we preach Christ crucified, a stumbling block to Jews and folly to Gentiles, but to those who are called, both Jews and Greeks, Christ the power of God and the wisdom of God" (1 Cor. 1:22–24).

I sought a way of acquiring strength . . . but I found it not until I embraced that Mediator between God and man, the man Christ Jesus, who is . . . God blessed forever, calling unto me, and saying, I am the way, the truth, and the life . . . . For I did not grasp my Lord Jesus—I, though humbled, grasped not the humble One; nor did I know what lesson that infirmity of His would teach us. . . . He intended . . . that they might go no further in self-confidence, but rather should become weak, seeing before their feet the Divinity weak . . . and wearied, they might cast themselves down upon It . . . . (Augustine) [52]

Over the past few years, I have spoken to many people about "Jesus—the Dog God." But I shall never forget the person who seemed to be most delighted with this concept, a little black woman from a small, struggling church on Chicago's West Side. She said to me, "I thank my God that my Savior was a dog like me. He was nothing and I'm nothing, and that's how we got together."

9 You Shall GOD Your Neighbor As Yourself

Rakitin says that one can love humanity without God. Well, only a snivelling idiot can maintain that.
—DOSTOYEVSKY, *The Brothers Karamazov*[1]

From Christ alone must we know what we should do. But not from him as the preaching prophet of the Sermon on the Mount, but from him as the one who gives us life and forgiveness, as the one who has fulfilled the commandment of God in our place, as one who brings and promises the new world. . . . Thus we are completely directed towards Christ. —BONHOEFFER[2]

To say that love is a feeling or anything of the kind is really an un-Christian conception of love. That is . . . the erotic and everything of that nature. But to the Christian love is the works of love. Christ's love was not an inner feeling, a full heart and what not, it was the work of love which was his life.
—KIERKEGAARD[3]

We can do worse than remember a principle which both gives us a firm Rock and leaves us the maximum elasticity for our minds: the principle: Hold to Christ, and for the rest be totally uncommitted. —H. BUTTERFIELD[4]

The love I speak of is not our love for God, but the love he showed to us in sending his Son. . . . If God thus loved us, dear friends, we in turn are bound to love one another.
—I JOHN 4:10, 11, NEB

"GOD WAS IN CHRIST reconciling the world to himself, no longer holding men's misdeeds against them" (2 Cor. 5:19, NEB). That's good news, Charlie Brown! For you're part of the world; you're a "men." It was a narrow escape, but the final verdict handed down is: "Not Guilty." For just "as one man's trespass led to condemnation for all men, so one man's act of righteousness leads to acquittal and life for all men" (Rom. 5:18). The trouble is, though, as St. Paul could point out, "not all have responded to the good news" (Rom. 10:16, NEB):

"For Isaiah says, 'Lord, who has believed our message?' We conclude that faith is awakened by the message, and the message that awakens it comes through the word of Christ" (Rom. 10:17, NEB). In the last chapter we talked about how faith comes to men only as faith *in* and *through* Jesus Christ, the historical Jesus of Nazareth. This is why the New Testament places so much significance upon "the name" of Jesus. For "this name" designates this *particular* historical man, this precise *point* in time and space, apart from which nothing can be truly known about God, about the world, or about oneself.

In Jesus Christ the reality of God entered into the reality of this world. The place where the answer is given, both to the question

concerning the reality of God and to the question concerning the reality of the world, is designated solely and alone by the name Jesus Christ. God and the world are comprised in this name. In Him all things consist (Col. 1:17). Henceforward one can speak neither of God nor of the world without speaking of Jesus Christ. All concepts of reality which do not take account of Him are abstractions. (Bonhoeffer)[5]

In this chapter we want to continue to bear down on the question of *how* the Christian knows what he knows. We have said that he lives with the happy assurance of the ultimate salvation of himself and of all men; and we have said that he knows this good news only in and through "the name," the person, of Jesus Christ. Therefore, the next question should go about like this:

It is in Shakespeare's *Romeo and Juliet*, that Juliet asked her famous question, "What's in a name?" And for the New Testament, what's in the name of Jesus is the fact that "there is no other name under heaven given among men by which we must be saved" (Acts 4:12). But now that we know this, what do we do? For an answer without the knowledge of how to implement it, is really no answer at all. For example: "You worry too much, Charlie Brown," Lucy tells him at her psychiatric booth. "No wonder your stomach hurts. You've got to stop all

this silly worrying!" "How do I stop?" he asks. Says Lucy: "That's your worry! Five cents, please!!" A similar but far more hopeful scene occurs in *The Brothers Karamazov*. (Incidentally, this is one book no one should postpone reading any longer. Linus, of course, has read it. And when asked by Lucy if he was not bothered by "all those Russian names," he has some good advice: "No, when I come to one I can't pronounce, I just bleep right over it!") In this scene, "a lady of little faith" is speaking to Zossima, Dostoyevsky's saintly old monk:

> "They say that [faith] comes from terror at the menacing phe-
> nomena of nature, and that none of it's real. And I say to myself,
> 'What if I've been believing all my life, and when I come to die
> there's nothing but the burdocks growing on my grave? . . . It's
> awful! How—how can I get back my faith? But I only believed
> when I was a little child, mechanically, without thinking of any-
> thing. How, how is one to prove it? I have come now to lay my soul
> before you and to ask you about it. If I let this chance slip, no one
> all my life will answer me. How can I prove it? How can I convince
> myself? Oh, how unhappy I am! I stand and look about me and see
> that scarcely anyone else cares; no one troubles his head about it, and
> I'm the only one who can't stand it. It's deadly—deadly!"
>
> "No doubt. But there's no proving it, though you can be con-
> vinced of it."
>
> "How?"
>
> "By the experience of active love. Strive to love your neighbour
> actively and indefatigably. In as far as you advance in love you
> will grow surer of the reality of God and of the immortality of
> your soul. If you attain to perfect self-forgetfulness in the love
> of your neighbour, then you will believe without doubt, and no
> doubt can possibly enter your soul. This has been tried. This is
> certain."[6]

Zossima's answer, as far as it goes, would certainly be the answer of the New Testament. But we must go further with this answer, because when the New Testament uses the word "love," it means something quite specific. In this day and age, "love" is probably the most wishy-washy word we use. It can mean "wishy" to one person, "washy" to another, with one thousand distinct variations in between. It is still true that "love covers a multitude of sins" (1 Pet. 4:8), but nowadays it most often does this by

simply being a name for them. So, then, what does the New Testament mean when it uses this word? Nobody knew better than Bonhoeffer:

A love which embraces only the sphere of personal human relations . . . can never be the love of the New Testament. If, then, there is no conceivable human attitude or conduct which, as such, can unequivocally be designated by the name "love," . . . then it is an . . . open question what else the Bible can mean by "love." The Bible does not fail to give us the answer. We know this well enough, but we continually misinterpret it. It is this: "God is love" (1 Jn. 4:16). First of all . . . this sentence is to be read with the emphasis on the word God, whereas we have fallen into the habit of emphasizing the word love. God is love; that is to say not a human attitude, a conviction or a deed, but God Himself is love. Only he who knows God knows what love is; it is not the other way round; it is not that we first of all by nature know what love is and therefore know also what God is. No one knows God unless God reveals Himself to him. And so no one knows what love is except in the self-revelation of God. And the revelation of God is Jesus Christ. "In this was manifested the love of God toward us, because that God sent his only begotten Son into the world, that we might live through him" (1 Jn. 4:9) . . . . Love has its origin not in us but in God. Love is not an attitude of men but an attitude of God. "Herein is love, not that we loved God, but that he loved us, and sent his Son to be the propitiation for our sins" (1 Jn. 4:10). Only in Jesus Christ do we know what love is, namely, in His deed for us . . . . Love is inseparably bound up with the name of Jesus Christ as the revelation of God. The New Testament answers the question "What is love?" quite unambiguously by pointing solely and entirely to Jesus Christ. He is the only definition of love. But again it would be a complete misunderstanding if we were to derive a general definition of love from our view of Jesus Christ and of His deed and His suffering. Love is not what He does and what He suffers, but it is what He does and what He suffers. Love is always He Himself. Love is always God Himself. Love is always the revelation of God in Jesus Christ.

When all our ideas and principles relating to love are concentrated in the strictest possible manner upon the name of Jesus Christ this must, above all, not be allowed to reduce this name to a mere abstract concept. This name must always be understood in the full concrete significance of the historical reality of a living

man . . . . Love is the reconciliation of man with God in Jesus Christ. The disunion of men with God, with other men, with the world and with themselves, is at an end. Man's origin is given back to him. Love, therefore, is the name for what God does to man in overcoming the disunion in which man lives. This deed of God is Jesus Christ, is reconciliation.[7]

Jesus said to his disciples, "I give you a new commandment: love one another; as I have loved you, so you are to love one another" (Jn. 13:34, NEB). At first glance, there would seem to be nothing "new" about this commandment at all. For instance, one of the commandments we find in the Old Testament is: "You shall love your neighbor as yourself" (Lev. 19:18). But Christ's new commandment was not merely to "love others as you enjoy loving yourself." ("Others" may not have the same tastes, as someone has observed.) The new commandment was to "love one another as I have loved you." And how, exactly, had Christ loved these very disciples to whom he was speaking? He had loved them by bringing them into an altogether new and special relationship with his Father through himself. Therefore, when the Christ-ian loves another man, he does precisely the same thing, no more or no less: he attempts, in all that he does, to bring also this man into this new relationship with God through Christ. And in this way, Christ himself defines Christ-ian love, defines who our neighbor is, and defines who we are. No one can "love his neighbors" as they should be loved, unless he first has some idea of what his neighbor essentially needs. And the Christ-ian is a person convinced that the "one thing needful" by all men is—Christ, is Love, is God. Therefore, when a Christian loves a man, he "Gods" him, he "Christs" him; he does everything he does to the one end that this other person may also come to enjoy, and keep enjoying, this new and special relationship to God through Christ. " 'What must we do, to be doing the works of God?' Jesus answered them, 'This is the work of God, that you believe in him whom he has sent' " (Jn. 6:28, 29). And the way to believe is to obey; and to obey is to dedicate our lives to the increase of this belief among as many others as possible. In this way and in this only, do we love others as he, Christ, has loved us, the members of his Church.

"The underlying motive both of the call of Jesus and of the exhortation of the apostle . . . is the same," says Bonhoeffer, "—to bring their hearers into the fellowship of the Body of Christ."[8] This, then, is the answer to the question of "Now that I know God's name was Jesus, what do I do?" The Christian has been given only this one thing to do. But this is plenty. For Jesus' commandment was not to love just a select few whenever we happen to feel like it; it was a commandment to love *all* men *always*: "Go forth therefore and make all nations my disciples; baptize men everywhere in the name of the Father and the Son and the Holy Spirit, and teach them to observe all that I have commanded you. And be assured, I am with you always, to the end of time" (Mt. 28:19, 20, NEB).

"The world belongs to Christ, and it . . . has need, therefore, of nothing less than Christ himself" (Bonhoeffer).[9] Therefore, to "keep the faith" is to be constantly giving it to others. To be a true lover is to be dedicated to making true lovers of others. Snoopy is not seen so often on top of his doghouse with his nose pointing heavenward for nothing:

Religion may be a private affair, but the work and word of God are the reconciliation of the *world* with God, as it was performed

in Jesus Christ . . . . Revelation is undoubtedly the affair of the general public in the most comprehensive sense. What is spoken into human ears demands proclamation from the housetops. (Barth)[10]

The Christian, then, is one who does all things at all times for one purpose only: that faith in God through Jesus Christ might increase in the world. Everything—without exception—that the Christian does "must aim at one thing: to build up the church," to "help to build up the [Christian] community" (1 Cor. 14:5, 6, 12, 27, NEB). "Whether you eat or drink," says St. Paul, "or whatever you are doing, do all for the honour of God . . . . regarding not [one's] own good but the good of the many, so that they may be saved" (1 Cor. 10:31, 33, NEB). All things for God's greater honor? All things! But what if you are not a "religious" person? What if you are something as "worldly" as an actress, for instance. What if, as Salinger's Zooey Glass tells his sister Franny, "Somewhere along the line . . . you not only had a hankering to be an actor or an actress but to be a good one. You're stuck with it now. You can't just walk out on the results of your own hankerings . . . . The only thing you can do now, the only religious thing you can do is act. Act for God, if you want to—be God's actress, if you want to. What could be prettier? You can at least try to, if you want to—there's nothing wrong in trying."[11] But what if you are doing something that you do not want to do, and perhaps must even do it for people whose primary concern stands quite apart from God and the "building up" of his Church?

There are many of you in this congregation who think to your-selves: "If only I had been there! How quick I would have been to help the Baby [Jesus]! I would have washed his linen. How happy I would have been to go with the shepherds to see the Lord lying in the manger!" Yes, you would! You say that because you know how great Christ is, but if you had been there at the time you would have done no better than the people of Bethlehem. Childish and silly thoughts these are! Why don't you do it now? You have Christ in your neighbor. You ought to serve him, for what you do to your neighbor in need you do to the Lord Christ himself. (Luther)[12]

"Even the merest gesture is holy if it is filled with faith," said Kafka.[13] Whether the Christian's activity is obviously very close to the work of "building up the Christian community," or whether it outwardly seems quite far from this intention, the Christian's attitude toward his Lord remains the same. For the commandment of his Lord has been well expressed in the words of the popular song:

> When we're far apart or when you're near me,
> Love me with all your heart as I love you.
> Don't give me your love just for a moment, or an hour,
> Love me always as you loved me from the start—
> With every beat of your heart![14]

"Men need a fixed pole they can look to for direction," says Bonhoeffer.[15] And the Christian has one—he has the fixed pole that gives not only orientation and direction to his life, but it also gives life itself. This is the fixed pole of the turning world that is the historical Jesus of Nazareth. The Christian's entire life is one that points, in his greatest and smallest deeds, to this place in history and says, "There was God!" The Christian never stops moving toward this point, but orients all his life in this direction—with "every beat of his heart." Whenever the

Christian stops living *from* and *in* and *to* this direction, then the bottom falls out of his life again. He is like Peter, who discovered that he was able to walk across the rough sea as long as he kept moving toward Jesus. For as soon as Peter ran out of faith and *stopped*, he sank like the Rock he was.

It is also impossible to "love without thinking." The Christian's relationship to his Lord is always a relationship first of all of the *heart*. This is because it is only the heart that loves and is most basic to man, and that directs and controls all else in a man's life. Therefore, when one loves with all one's heart, all the "soul and mind and strength" will necessarily follow, will also be brought into the service of this love. And this is why, though our relationship to Christ is never one based primarily on our "heads," or on critical intelligence, we are nevertheless commanded to use our heads entirely for His sake; this is what they are for. Thus Jesus commanded his disciples to "be wise as serpents and innocent as doves" (Mt. 10:16). Whenever our heads begin questioning God, then we have stopped loving God and started loving our heads, which are not God. But the head *does* ceaselessly ask how best to serve God. Therefore, no one who "loves without reservation," can also "love without thinking."

"Do you love Gila monsters?" Lucy asks him, not quite believing he could "love every living creature." "I've never heard of a Gila monster," he replies, "but if I knew what it was, I'd love it!!!" This is a good example of why one should never love without thinking. One should always think at least twice before loving a Gila monster.

Both faith and love, then, are nothing more or less than present and active *obedience* to God through Christ. "Faith is the obedience of the *pilgrim* who has his vision and his trust set upon God's free act of reconciliation. . . . Love is the obedience of the *witness* who is summoned to announce this transition. The witness announces God's victorious deed, offered to all his brothers and sisters far and nigh so that they might greet it as their light" (Barth).[16] The Christian's only ruling passion is that more men might know more of God's victorious deed through Christ, that the Church "might win the more" (1 Cor. 9:19), that "faith increases" in the world (2 Cor. 10:15). For this reason, the Christian can never simply be content with the faith he has. Again, he only "has" it in the very act of increasing it among others. "He must increase, but I must decrease," is the Christian's attitude as he looks upon Christ. The Christian who is not absolutely preoccupied with the increase of his master's Church is like the lazy servant in one of Christ's para-

bles, who had been entrusted with the management of his
master's property. When the master returned and found that
the servant had only kept the entrusted money intact, the master
said:

> "You're a wicked, lazy servant! . . . you ought to have put my
> money in the bank, and when I came I should at any rate have
> received what belongs to me with interest. Take his thousand
> dollars away from him and give it to the man who now has the
> ten thousand!" (For the man who has something will have more
> given to him and will have plenty. But as for the man who has
> nothing, even his "nothing" will be taken away.) "And throw this
> useless servant into the darkness outside, where he can weep and
> wail over his stupidity." (Mt. 25:26–30, Phillips)

For those who might have difficulty visualizing someone being
thrown outside where he "weeps and wails over his stupidity,"
we here offer the following modern parable:

"Let all things be done for edification," says St. Paul. But if the command to edify others is the only command the Christian lives by as ultimate and final, what of all the other command-ments, rules, regulations, moral laws, maxims, and "thou shalt nots" that are so frequently associated with the Christian faith? Are these just out the window, or what? St. Paul answered this question very succinctly when he wrote to the saints in Corinth: " 'We are free to do anything,' you say. Yes, but is everything good for us? 'We are free to do anything,' but does everything help the building of the community?" (1 Cor. 10:23, 24, NEB). St. Paul was quite clear as to the Christian's relationship to "the law," to "the old written code," or to any set of moral laws or commands that claims to be the ultimate guide for conduct to be followed at all times. The Christian was clearly and simply "free of the law" (Rom. 7:3, NEB), "no longer under law" (Rom. 6:14, NEB), free from all slavish obedience to any code of ethics or set of moral standards, regardless of how sanctified these rules or "commandments" might be in the light of the past or in the light of culture or in the light of society. "But now," he said, "having died to that which held us bound, we are discharged from the law, to serve God in a new way, the way of the spirit, in contrast to the old way, the way of a written code" (Rom. 7:6, NEB).

When asked if Christians "are free to do anything?" St. Paul could answer in all frankness, "Yes." When he could say that the purpose of his entire ministry was "that I might by all means save some," he meant what he said: "by all means." For the New Testament it was simply not true that "the end does not justify the means." When accused of being "a glutton and a drinker," Jesus, rather than denying this charge, confessed that "the Son of Man came eating and drinking. . . . And yet," he said, "God's wisdom is proved right by its results" (Mt. 11:19, NEB). Some-thing has got to be the "end," the "ultimate," the "result"; some one thing has got to be "God" for us. And to say that "the end does not justify the means" is to apotheosize or to make the means themselves god; it is to raise some moral code or ethical standard to the level of God himself. And God is no one's moral code, however lofty this code might be. God is the Tran-

scendent One, the "wholly other," who stands as judge over all rules of conduct, and who meets us only in and through Jesus Christ. And in Jesus Christ the Christian is no longer a slave to anyone's law. "For the law was given through Moses; grace and truth through Jesus Christ" (Jn. 1:17). What then is the Christian's attitude toward "the law"? As St. Paul can tell us, "the law is holy, and the commandment is holy and just and good" (Rom. 7:12). Here we have it, then: the law is holy and just and good and filled with wisdom; the law is a good guide; but it is not the final guide—it is not God. Therefore Christians, who worship God only, are finally—"when the chips are down" —free from the law. Legal and moral codes—which cannot heal or forgive or finally give life, but can only bind and constrain and finally kill—the Christian is no slave to. But the Christian is a slave to Jesus Christ. " 'We are free to do anything'. . . . Yes, but is everything good for us? 'We are free to do anything,' but does everything help the building of the community?" Woe will come to those "Christians" who in their "freedom" flout the law only to become slaves of something much crueler. Woe will come to those "Christians" who are free from the law but forget they are slaves of Jesus Christ and are thereby commanded to do everything for the building of his community. But in this new commandment, Christians are perfectly free to use any and "all means"—as long as these means are for this one goal, this one supreme purpose. The Christian, then, can say with Snoopy: "I'm the kind who'll do anything to prove a point!"— so long as this point is the point. "You, my friends, were called to be free men; only do not turn your freedom into licence for your lower nature, but be servants to one another in love. For the whole law can be summed up in a single commandment: 'Love your neighbour as yourself'" (Gal. 5:13, 14, NEB). And as we have seen, "love," for the New Testament, means God, means Jesus Christ.

The Christian has been told that he "must be perfect, as your heavenly Father is perfect" (Mt. 5:48). But he finds that he cannot obtain the required perfection through the law, "for the law made nothing perfect" (Heb. 7:19). And so the Christian's situation then becomes like Charlie Brown's when Patty says to him: "I can't really like you because you're not perfect.

I'm sorry, Charlie Brown, but that's just the way I feel." "But I'm *pretty* perfect," he protests. And this is as close to perfection that the Christian discovers he can come—*through the law.* He may be a very, very, very good man. Perhaps he has even managed to keep *all* of the commandments of the law, as St. Paul said he had (Phil. 3:6). And yet he knows something vitally essential is still lacking; for his goodness, as great as it may be, still does not satisfy him or give him the happiness he desires. As a matter of fact, the harder he tries to find fulfillment and perfection under the rules of the law, the unhappier he becomes. And so, as Paul could finally say, "the very commandment which promised life proved to be death to me" (Rom. 7:10).

This is why in the gospels we see Jesus making the law so incredibly hard for men. As we have said, Jesus' intention in strongly suggesting the existence of eternal damnation, was only one method he used to produce the dark background necessary for the true light (Jesus) to be clearly seen and recognized. Similarly, his intention in pressing "the righteousness of the law" to its logical and ultimate and miserably unsatisfying extremes, was to drive people to *him*—"the righteousness of God" (Rom. 3:21). For instance:

You have heard that it was said to the men of old, "You shall not kill; and whoever kills shall be liable to judgment." But I say to you that every one who is angry with his brother shall be liable to judgment; whoever insults his brother shall be liable to the council, and whoever says "You fool!" shall be liable to the hell of fire. (Mt. 5:21–22)

What one man in ten thousand is not here already done for? It would be easy to imagine the frantic attempts there have been to water down passages such as this one. Nevertheless, *the law* stands as read: everyone who becomes so much as *angry* with his brother is "liable to judgment." Or, what is probably an even more impossible demand goes like this: "You have heard that it was said, 'You shall not commit adultery.' But I say to you that every one who looks at a woman lustfully has already committed adultery with her in his heart" (Mt. 5:27, 28). According to the law, even the best among us are doomed—even Linus:

Likewise, Jesus pushed the law to its inevitable extremes. This he did in order to make its demands next to impossible for us. But even if we could or did fulfill these demands, fulfillment of the law would be of little use. For the law remains good and holy, but it is still not God; it is still not capable of fulfilling us— that is, it is not capable of giving us the happiness, the "life," the "perfection" we seek from it. Only Christ can give us this. This is why the New Testament can speak of Jesus as having fulfilled the law for us: "Think not that I have come to abolish the law and the prophets," said Jesus; "I have come not to abolish them but to fulfil them" (Mt. 5:17). And what does this mean for us? It means that "now, quite independently of law, God's justice has been brought to light. The Law and the prophets both bear witness to it: it is God's way of righting wrong, effective through faith in Christ for all who have such faith. . . . For all alike have sinned, and are deprived of the divine splendour, and all are justified by God's free grace alone, through his act of liberation in the person of Christ Jesus. . . . For our argument is that a man is justified by faith quite apart from success in keeping the law" (Rom. 3:21–24, 28, NEB). "What does it mean to fear and love God?" asks Karl Barth. "What does it mean to believe?"

> Being certain Jesus Christ is God but we are men, we will do well not to try to imitate Jesus . . . and thus to believe as Jesus believed. However, the meaning of the first commandment . . . must be that we believe in Jesus Christ, that we—since the Word became flesh . . . acknowledge his representative faith, which we will never realize, and allow it to count as our life . . . . And we will keep and fulfill the Law and all its commandments if we have faith in Jesus Christ; that means the faith which clings to him and remains true to him, simply because he is the eternal incarnate Word, which has accomplished all things. This faith includes all obedience. Our works, great and small, internal and external, are accepted if they take place as works of this faith—and they are rejected if they do not.[17]

Then how does the Christian, who is free from the rules of the law, respond to all of the things he possesses and all that happens to him—the body that is his, the stomach that gets hungry,

the blood that boils with anger, the lusts that are as much a part of his body as hunger? What does he do with all that he has and all that comes his way? He sees *all*—the bitter and the sweet, the hard and the easy, everything—as a gift God has given him to be used for *one purpose*: thy kingdom come, thy will be done on earth as it is in heaven. No longer does he allow passions and circumstances to rule him. No longer is he a slave to any of these, but he *uses* them all *obediently*: to increase among men the joy that comes, and will only come, through their own obedience to God. Finally, this is the only *ultimate rule* the Christian lives by. In achieving this end, he is perfectly free to use "all means" and all his creativity. And because it is only in the very act of increasing others' joy that the Christian receives joy, he sees all that comes his way, everything, as a wonderful gift from God; for all is seen as an *op-portunity*, an *occasion*, for obedience to God. The Christian is not ashamed of or afraid to express his passions, which are also God's good gifts—his desire for pleasure and love, his hunger, his anger; but he is careful to use all of these passions obediently. For "this is man's happiness: to live for God's glorification" (Barth). Thus the Christian does not seek pleasure merely for pleasure's sake, but neither does he reject pleasure because it

is pleasure. For the Christian, any occasion is an occasion for obedience; and therefore any occasion is an occasion for joy. "For everything that God created is good, and nothing is to be rejected when it is taken with thanksgiving" (1 Tim. 4:4, NEB)—as in the above cartoon.

The Christian, then, no longer attempts to get in touch with God through "legal righteousness," which says: "The man who does this shall gain life by it" (Rom. 10:5, NEB). He has learned that giving "life" is simply something "the law could never do" (Rom. 8:3, NEB). Instead the Christian is in touch with God through faith in Jesus. Faith is simply that which says with its lips and its heart: "Jesus is Lord" (Rom. 10:9, NEB). That is, Jesus "is our righteousness" (1 Cor. 1:30, NEB). This is why Jesus, the Dog God, was such an offensive threat to all the holy, patriotic, good people of his time who believed in and lived by legal righteousness, or "righteousness which is based on the law." They were afraid of what they saw coming: "Christ is the end of the law" (Rom. 10:4). And so it was that the poor souls of Jesus' time, those who had absolutely nothing to lose, were not afraid of being put in touch with God by actually touching Jesus, the Dog God. On the other hand, the scribes and Pharisees, who lived according to legal righteousness, and hence knew their hands were clean, actually considered Jesus and his disciples to be unclean, as well as a threat to their own tradition. Consequently, in Jesus' time, just as today, the sheep were separated from the goats by whether or not they were willing to "touch the Dog":

> Wherever he went . . . they laid out the sick . . . and begged him to let them simply touch the edge of his cloak; and all who

touched him were cured. A group of Pharisees, with some doctors of the law . . . met him and noticed that some of his disciples were eating their food with "defiled" hands—in other words, without washing them. (For the Pharisees and the Jews in general never eat without washing the hands, in obedience to an old-established tradition . . . .) Accordingly, these Pharisees and the lawyers asked him, "Why do your disciples not conform to the ancient tradition, but eat their food with defiled hands?" He answered, "Isaiah was right when he prophesied about you hypocrites in these words: 'This people pays me lip-service, but their heart is far from me: their worship of me is in vain, for they teach as doctrines the commandments of men.' You neglect the commandment of God, in order to maintain the tradition of men." (Mk. 6:56; 7:1-3, 5-8, NEB)

Any morality, new or old, that is not squarely based on Christ himself, upon his new commandment to "love others as *I* have loved you," is from the Christian perspective not new, not truly moral, and—by definition—not Christ-ian. Any humanism, new or old, that is not firmly based on God's supreme gift to humanity through "the new man," the very humanity of God himself in Christ, is neither new nor human. The truly new man lives only for the new purpose of increasing belief in God's new covenant established with all humanity through Christ. "The new man lives in the world like any other man. Often there is little to distinguish him from the rest. Nor does he attach much importance to distinguishing himself, but only to distinguishing Christ for the sake of his brethren" (Bonhoeffer).[18] The fundamental error of modern times is its attempt to bridge the endless yawning abyss that exists between man and God, man and man, and man and himself, with anything other than the man Jesus of Nazareth himself. Between man and man, it is only Jesus that "has made the two one, and in his own body of flesh and blood has broken down the enmity which stood like a dividing wall between them" (Eph. 2:14, NEB). Without the flesh-and-blood man Jesus between man and man, this wall still stands.

The path . . . to the "God-given reality" of my fellow-man or woman with whom I have to live leads through Christ, or it is a blind alley. We are separated from one another by an unbridgeable gulf of otherness and strangeness which resists all our attempts to overcome it by means of natural association or emotional or spiritual union. There is no way from one person to another. However loving and sympathetic we try to be, however sound our psychology, however frank and open our behaviour, we cannot penetrate the

→

incognito of the other man, for there are no direct relationships, not even between soul and soul. Christ stands between us, and we can only get into touch with our neighbors through him. (Bonhoeffer)[19]

Only the Christian is capable of truly giving or capable of giving the true gift. By virtue of his faith in the hard, matter of fact of Christmas, that in the infant Jesus God was born in the world, the Christian has found the full-fillment for which he had been seeking. He is no longer the dry sponge with the unquenchable thirst that he once was. He knows that "whoever drinks the water that I shall give him will never suffer thirst any more. The water that I shall give him will be an inner spring always welling up for eternal life" (Jn. 4:14, NEB). Having thus been given, the Christian is enabled to give. Indeed, he *must* give if this inner spring is not to be frustrated and again made stagnant and dead. And what the Christian gives will be the one thing that he has in abundance and yet is most precious to him: this same life-giving spirit. Unfortunately, however, the spring, the source, the fountain of this nourishment, the child who was born at Christmas, is no longer understood as the one who really has something to give.

"Those thinkers," says Chesterton, "who cannot believe in any gods often assert that the love of humanity would be sufficient for them; and so, perhaps, it would, if they had it."[20] For just as we are incapable of loving God without at the same time loving our neighbors, we are likewise incapable of loving our neighbors without also loving God—and loving God first. The love of God must claim priority, for it is only God's love through faith in Christ that gives man the power to love. The family of man, isolated from obedience to God, can neither love itself nor give itself the power to love.

In Jesus Christ, true God and true man . . . rests our hope for a real humanity. Not by ourselves, but insofar as we are members of the Body of Christ—and thus only—are we men according to God. In order to avoid the misfortune of mankind's being lost because it does not fulfill the meaning of its creation, in order to be man, in order to fulfill the true humanism, then we must believe in Jesus Christ. There is no humanism without the Gospel. (Barth)[21]

And, as we have said, love not only comes to us through Jesus Christ alone, but also "my children, love must not be a matter of words or talk; it must be genuine, and show itself in action" (1 Jn. 3:18, NEB):

When is it easiest to believe, and when is the comfort of faith the greatest? When the lover says, "I will do it," or when he has done it? No, not until he has done it, not till then is doubt made impossible, as impossible as it possibly can be . . . not till then, is the comfort at hand which makes the doubt of the forgiveness of sins as impossible—yes, as impossible as it possibly can be; for then it is only for faith that this comfort exists. (Kierkegaard)[22]

When Christians turn their attention to the "politics of God," that is, to the question of which strategy to use in order best to bring more men to faith, they will sometimes abuse their freedom in the gospel, in their allegiance to Christ alone, by tending to reflect that aspect of God's love that utters a harsh "No!" This is especially true of those Christians who have lived their former lives under the law that says, "Always be nice." Finding a new freedom in the gospel which says that one does not necessarily *have* to be "nice" to obey God, they use this as an excuse to be the heels they have always wanted to be in the first place. However, as a general—but never ultimate—rule, being a heel for Christ's sake is poor strategy. It is true that God's love for us has shown itself at times to be the harsh and unrelenting "No!" of an angry Father—a "No!" that says, "Thus far shall you come, and no farther," and "You shall have no other gods besides me!" But the Christian has learned to see this No as only a lesser part of a far more predominant Yes. Therefore, to be an accurate reflector of God's attitude toward us, the Christian's attitude should also be dominantly positive and gracious. Whether he says Yes or No, the Christian is *always* commanded to love. But because God's love for us has appeared overwhelmingly in the form of Yes, so also should the Christian's attitude be toward his fellow man. This more "positive approach" of common human charity and kindness is "the more excellent way" that St. Paul is championing when he says that "Love is patient and kind; love is not jealous or boastful; it is not arrogant or rude. Love does not insist on its own way . . . ," etc. (1 Cor. 13). Generally speaking, the attitude of the New Testament is that "you must forgive as the Lord forgave you" (Col. 3:13, NEB). That is, the day-to-day life of common human love and

graciousness is usually the most effective way the Christian has of pointing to the infinitely greater love and graciousness of his Lord. What does all this mean in more specific terms? It means, for one thing, that "Vengeance is mine, I will repay, says the Lord" (Rom. 12:19). Or, as St. Paul could say:

> If a man is weak in his faith you must accept him without attempting to settle doubtful points. For instance, one man will have faith enough to eat all kinds of food, while a weaker man eats only vegetables. The man who eats must not hold in contempt the man who does not, and he who does not eat must not pass judgement on the one who does; for God has accepted him. Who are you to pass judgement on someone else's servant? Whether he stands or falls is his own Master's business; and stand he will, because his Master has power to enable him to stand. (Rom. 14:1–4, NEB)

With "an alarming frequency" (Linus) it is possible to see in Lucy those "defenders of the faith" and their "secularized offshoots . . . the existentialist philosophers and the psychotherapists, who demonstrate to secure, contented, happy mankind that it is really unhappy and desperate, and merely unwilling to realize that it is in severe straits it knows nothing at all about, from which only they can rescue it. . . . They make it their object first of all to drive men to inward despair and then all

is theirs."[23] But, as Bonhoeffer could also point out, most of the attempts by faith defenders to bring idolators to grief, are actually attempts on their part to play God by supposing they possess a power that finally belongs to God alone. As Barth could put it, "The presence of *Yahweh* is necessary to make a man say 'Woe is me! for I am undone.' "[24] Actually, the world will always be filled with enough "judgment" and "wrath" and unhappiness without the Christian feeling that he must add his share. In any case, the power to rid either himself or others of idols is in no sense the Christian's own, but belongs solely to God.

Thus the Christian will usually be able to be a more effective "communicator" of the Christian message when he acts as a forthright minister of the good news of God's love, rather than attempting to play the presumptuous role of the thundering prophet of God's angry judgment upon all false gods. Not only is the more "positive approach" a better mirror of what God is actually like, but this approach also has the paradoxical ability to bring true judgment to bear. This is what St. Paul was getting at when he could say, "If your enemy is hungry, feed him; if he is thirsty, give him a drink; by doing this you will heap live coals on his head" (Rom. 12:20, NEB). And thus the role of the Church, both in its dealings with individuals and with society

as a whole, will usually be just the opposite of Lucy's. That is, in order to bring to light and help cure what is really the deeper problem, the Church will first be concerned to do all it can to relieve more superficial sufferings.

"It is for the love of Christ, which belongs as much to the hungry man as to myself, that I share my bread with him and that I share my dwelling with the homeless. . . . To provide the hungry man with bread is to prepare the way for the coming of grace" (Bonhoeffer).[25] And so, what does our Father require us? Not much more, really, than the kind of thing we see in Charlie Brown's relationship with *his* dad:

"To do justly . . .   to love mercy . . .

and to walk humbly with thy God" (Mic. 6:8 KJV)

Suppose a brother or a sister is in rags with not enough food for the day, and one of you says, "Good luck to you, keep yourselves warm, and have plenty to eat," but does nothing to supply their bodily needs, what is the good of that? So with faith; if it does not lead to action, it is in itself a lifeless thing. (Jas. 2:16, 17, NEB)

A soft answer turns away wrath. (Prov. 15:1)

You have learned that they were told, "An eye for an eye, and a tooth for a tooth." But what I tell you is this: Do not set yourself against the man who wrongs you. If someone slaps you on the right cheek, turn and offer him your left. If a man wants to sue you for your shirt, let him have your coat as well. If a man in authority makes you go one mile, go with him two. Give when you are asked to give; and do not turn your back on a man who wants to borrow. You have heard that they were told, "Love your neighbour, hate your enemy." But what I tell you is this: Love your enemies and pray for your persecutors; only so can you be children of your heavenly Father. (Mt. 5:38–45, NEB)

This "new system of human relations" is not new simply because it is found in the New Testament. It is also found in many of the other religions of the world, as well as in the Old Testament. But it is new and it is Christ-ian insofar as it is used to serve *him*, Christ, the *new* man, who alone makes the New Testament truly new. Only when all of our strategies and ethical codes and systems of human relations are brought exclusively into the service of Christ, for the sole purpose of pointing to him as God, are they truly "new" or truly Christ-ian. As Bonhoeffer could say:

> Evil becomes a spent force when we put up no resistance. By refusing to pay back the enemy with his own coin, and by preferring to suffer without resistance, the Christian exhibits the sinfulness of contumely and insult. Violence stands condemned by its failure to evoke counter-violence. When a man unjustly . . . requires me to go the other mile, I go willingly, and show up his exploitation of my service for what it is. To leave everything behind at the call of Christ is to be content with him alone, and to follow only him. By his willingly renouncing self-defense, the Christian affirms his absolute adherence to Jesus, and his freedom from the tyranny of his own ego. The exclusiveness of this adherence is the only power which can overcome evil.[26]

Thus we must also remember that any code of morals, along with everything else in creation, has been created for the service of Christ alone; not Christ for the moral code. "The Son of man is lord even of the sabbath," Jesus could say of himself (Mk. 2:28). Only Christ is ultimate; only he is Lord. There-

fore, our deification of any code of ethics will only mean our own deaths.

If our love for one another does not have Christ in it, it is not true love, nor is it Christian, nor is it finally capable of healing either him that gives or him that takes. Another way of saying this is that the Christian looks upon himself as "simply [one of] God's agents in bringing [others] to the faith" (1 Cor. 3:5, NEB); and he looks upon all "others" as men for whom Christ came into the world. This is why Kierkegaard could say:

> The majority of men are subjective towards themselves and objective towards all others, terribly objective sometimes—but the real task is in fact to be objective towards oneself and subjective towards all others.[27]

Schulz has frequently been asked why *Peanuts* does not "seem to deal with controversial issues . . . . like war, or sex, or something similar," as one student so aptly put it. The answer to this question, of course, as Schulz indicated in his reply, is that *Peanuts* is more concerned with gospel than with law. The strip refuses to give us little homilies or moral lessons or rules to live

by, but goes straight to the heart of the matter where the question and the answer lie. For example, Schulz cites "Charlie Brown's adulation of the little red-haired girl [which] touches upon the fact that there are some people—maybe all of us— who never really get to meet the little red-haired girl."[28] *Peanuts*, then, like all real art, is a *metaphor* for the universal; it is more interested in the larger implications than the specifics. As Thoreau could say, "There are a thousand hacking at the branches of evil to one who is striking at the root."[29] And, we believe, such a one is Schulz. For it is rare when we see the moralizing game played in *Peanuts*, whether in the social or religious or political fields. This is one comic strip that is really playing a deeper, far more crucial game than "right and wrong": it is concerned with the "game" of good and evil. For this reason, it is very easy to apply to Schulz the statement T. S. Eliot made of Baudelaire: "In . . . an age of bustle, programmes, platforms, scientific progress, humanitarianism and revolutions which improved nothing, an age of progressive degradation, [he] perceived that what really matters is Sin and Redemption."[30]

"It has almost come to the point," said Kierkegaard, "that one must make use of art in the most various ways to get Christendom to display any sympathy for Christianity. But by the help of art, whether it be the art of the sculptor, or of the orator, or of the poet, we get at the very most only 'admirers,' who, while incidentally they are admiring the artist, are led by his presentation to admire Christianity. But yet the admirer is in the strictest sense no true Christian, only the follower is such."[31] Having come with us this far might indeed indicate that the reader has some admiration for what has been said and done. But Kierkegaard's point is well taken; for Jesus does call us to be his followers, rather than his admirers. The command to "Follow me" was the first and last word Jesus spoke to his disciples (Mk. 1:17; Jn. 21:22). Therefore we should point out that if the reader has followed *us* up to this point and has understood what we have attempted to say, then he should have a rather clear idea of just *who* it is that bids us follow him as well as what it means to follow this person. If this is the case, then the reader cannot turn away from this page without first having made a decision, a decision that will require all his life, one way or another. For the most crucial of all questions is here put to you—a question that Jesus put to his disciples and that he now puts to you through this book: "Who do *you* say that I am?"

10 *Blessed Are the Poor in Spirit*

My dear friends, do not be bewildered by the fiery ordeal that is upon you, as though it were something extraordinary. It gives you a share in Christ's sufferings, and that is cause for joy.

—1 PETER 4:12, 13, NEB

The life of the spirit is not that which shuns death and keeps clear of destruction: rather it endureth death and in death is sustained. It only achieves its truth in the midst of utter destruction.

—BONHOEFFER[1]

So shalt thou feed on Death, that feeds on men,
And Death once dead, there's no more dying then.

—SHAKESPEARE, Sonnet 146

Religion happens first inside the person. . . . I think we all have a time when we become aware of something and it is at this point that some react by what Jesus called being born again. Now, being born again may be going to the altar at a Sunday evening service and it may merely be a turning around spiritually in your life, just facing toward more mature things. It doesn't matter what you call it, but there is some kind of experience which happens to those who then decide that they want to do something for God or want to be closer to him.   —SCHULZ[2]

Delight,—top-gallant delight is to him, who acknowledges no law or lord, but the Lord his God, and is only a patriot to heaven.

—MELVILLE[3]

The Christian: we must be agreed that we do not mean the Christians, not the multitude of the baptized, nor the chosen few who are concerned with Religion and Social Relations, nor

even the cream of the noblest and most devoted Christians we might think of: the Christian is the Christ. The Christian is that within us which is not ourself but Christ in us. "Christ in us" . . . is not a psychic condition, an affection of the mind, a mental lapse, or anything of the sort, but is a presupposition of life.
—BARTH[4]

"THE STONE WHICH THE BUILDERS REJECTED has become the chief cornerstone. This is the Lord's doing; it is marvelous in our eyes. This is the day which the Lord has made; let us rejoice and be glad in it" (Ps. 118:22–24). And so it is that the marvelous, joyful day of the Lord is bound eternally to "the stone which the builders rejected"—Jesus Christ. When Christ was born, the angel announced: Unto you is born *this* day a Savior! "And every time someone really becomes a Christian," says Kierkegaard, "the same thing is said: unto you is born this day a Savior."[5] The long-awaited most important day in a person's life, never occurs unless Christ is born within that person on "this day."

And why won't it? Part of the fault belongs to the Church: it has sold out its gospel, its Dog, to win a few ball games. But the fault belongs not strictly to the Church alone; for "in everyone we find a clever fear of really having anything to do with God, because in having to do with God they become nothing" (Kierkegaard).[6] Christianity proclaims two absolutely fundamental essentials to *really* having anything to do with God: "I decided to know nothing among you except Jesus Christ and him crucified" (1 Cor. 2:2). For no one can really know God without first knowing Jesus Christ; and no one can really know Jesus Christ unless he has also been crucified, unless he has also taken up his own cross to follow Jesus. Therefore the moment of decision for Jesus Christ, the "this day" in our lives that is our most important day, is also the day and moment of our crucifixion, of being reduced to nothing. And to endure our cross without realizing that it is precisely *here*, on the cross with us, that our Savior is to be found, for it is *only* here that we would be desperate enough to reach out to him—this is unrelieved hell and despair. To endure the endless moment of nothingness in which we are stripped and made nothing, without realizing that our Lord Jesus Christ was stripped and *became* nothing in order to meet us precisely here: *in* our nothingness —this is a difficult moment to treasure!

This moment, difficult to treasure when we are experiencing it, is the same kind of moment Isaiah spoke of when he said:

> For a brief moment I forsook you, but with great compassion I will gather you. In overflowing wrath for a moment I hid my face from you, but with everlasting love I will have compassion on you, says the Lord, your Redeemer. (Is. 54:7, 8)

A man is like a bottle of medicine: he was created for the purpose of healing people. And God himself has placed a label on this bottle that He never forgets to heed: "Shake Well Before Using." We have talked about how all of us must first be shaken loose from our old, original false gods before we can be brought to grasp the true God—God in Jesus Christ. Hence a Christian can "never forget that our old selves died with him on the cross that the tyranny of sin over us might be broken" (Rom. 6:6, Phillips) and that we might reach out to the man on the cross with us and thus find newness of life in holding fast to him. Thus "you must regard yourselves as dead to sin and alive to God, in union with Christ Jesus" (Rom. 6:11, NEB). The crucifix is the most powerful image of the Christian church. For the Christian, literally everything can be seen there. "I, when I am lifted up from the earth," said Jesus, "will draw all men to myself" (Jn. 12:32). And with outstretched arms, Jesus does bid all men to come to him, and thence to go and carry him with them into all the nations. The Christian sees God's love for all men, for herein God suffered even death for all men— even for those who crucified him. In the man Jesus, the Christian sees *the single fixed point* of intersection between the horizontal dimension of time with the vertical dimension of eternity; the vertical dimension of God intersecting the horizontal di-

mension of man. The Christian sees in the crucifix the new
tree of life, the flesh-and-blood fruit of which must be eaten
if one is to overcome his old sickness—the sickness symbolized
by fruit once eaten from a tree *forbidden* to be eaten of.
The Christian clearly sees here the image of his own sinfulness
and his own crucifixion; for he remembers that the primacy of
whatever false god he had worshiped till then, had to be re-
linquished before the man on the cross could truly become his
God. In short, the Christian sees in the crucifix: sinful man,
God's perfect love for man, and *Jesus in death*—the only way
between God and man. Whenever Charlie Brown-Everyman finds
himself completely stripped of all false gods, whenever he really
hits bottom and begins to feel the oldness of his "old self," then
we invariably find him leaning against a tree. This, then, is
precisely where his Savior must meet him—and does meet him:

When any man suddenly finds himself "up a tree," or "out on
a limb," and screaming with pain and horror because of having
been betrayed, there is someone to meet and help him precisely
in this place and in these circumstances. The last sound that
Jesus uttered on the "tree of calvary" was not a beatific word of
forgiveness and comfort to those below him, but it was the terrible

scream of outrage and doubt and pain: "And Jesus cried again with a loud voice and yielded up his spirit" (Mt. 27:50).

The disciples had pinned on Jesus all their hopes for the new "neighborhood championship" of Israel. They had left all they had to follow him. And Jesus had carefully instructed them about his kingdom, which he was just beginning to bring into the world. And yet, up until the very end of Jesus' life, the disciples apparently did not understand. The kingdom they wanted from him belonged to this world; his kingdom was not of this world. This meant that one thing was still needed before they could truly worship and fully understand him: the crucifixion of the false hopes they had placed on him, their hopes for a worldly, triumphant New Israel. And this meant the crucifixion of Jesus himself. Only in his own total defeat would they find the defeat they needed to forget "the New Israel" and to fully turn to him alone. And thus when Jesus died, the disciples died with him—inwardly. Everything was lost; he had let them down. And yet it was not until their own crucifixion occurred that "the boys" finally began to understand. A cruel means of instruction, perhaps, to kill the false hopes of one's followers in order that true hope might live. But "that's the way it goes"; they would

never have learned otherwise. And certainly no less cruel was it
for the one *actually* defeated, the teacher, the Dog God himself.

When a man finally has to bear his own cross, this cross can
only become meaningful and redemptive if it is seen as the
sword God uses to cut us loose from the tyranny of false gods.
Then, in following the One who continues to set us free by the
cross, this sword becomes meaningful indeed and will be a redemptive force the New Man will always wish to live under and
to conquer by. The cross "must be understood not as an event
external to us, but as one which takes place in our existence.
The cross means our being crucified with Christ" (Fuller).[7]

But because of all men's natural and quite understandable re-
luctance to die, to be crucified, the church itself (a body of men)
has an equally stubborn tendency to forget its message of the
cross: that the cross is *the* way to the Christ who is *the* way to
God. Consequently, the church turns to a message of cheaper
and easier grace, representing Jesus as no more than a helpful,
friendly guide in obtaining our *real* goals. The result of this
distortion—a distortion calculated to win more by "lowering
the standard"—is just the opposite of what sell-out Christianity
intends: its superficial message appeals superficially to only a
few and deeply to no one. A young woman in her twenties once

said to me: "When I was sixteen I went through hell. I was so confused I didn't know which way was up. Nobody could understand—my parents, my friends, I didn't, nobody. Finally I went to our minister. I could have gotten down on my knees and begged that man to help me. But all he could say to me was something like, 'Buck up! This is just a stage you're going through.' . . . I haven't been back to church since." There are countless young people such as this girl, as well as countless adult men and women Willy Lomans, who everyday are being "overwhelmed by excessive sorrow" (2 Cor. 2:7). They are not getting the message that God himself became nothing and died in order to meet *them* precisely here—in their deaths, in their nothingness, and thus to raise them to newness of life. It is true of the New Testament that "in order to hear what the document is saying we must approach it with the right questions. The right question . . . is the question of human existence, a question motivated by what St. Augustine called man's . . . restless heart. The New Testament message is seen as the answer to this quest, and is to be expounded as such" (Fuller).[8] If the New Testament message is *not* proclaimed as such, then scenes like the one that follows are bound to take place with greater and greater frequency. For when Linus loses his blanket, then *he* is surely lost.

It is precisely to the depths of downfall, of guilt and misery, that God stoops down in Jesus Christ . . . precisely the dispossessed the humiliated and exploited, are especially near to the justice and mercy of God . . . it is to the undisciplined that Jesus Christ offers His help and His strength . . . the truth is ready to set upon firm ground those who stray and despair. (Bonhoeffer)[9]

The church is doomed if it does not remember to whom Jesus' good news was specifically directed, for it is only by these that it can be clearly heard and appreciated: "The Spirit of the Lord is upon me, because he has anointed me to preach good news to the poor. He has sent me to proclaim release to the captives and recovering of sight to the blind, to set at liberty those who are oppressed . . ." (Lk. 4:18). The church then should be more like Snoopy: totally loyal; but when it comes to character . . .

Likewise the church should be "a poor judge of character," for there are always more possibilities for real character among the poor. The church will accomplish nothing of significance among proud, strong, "rich men"; but its ministry of reconciliation will be fulfilled (and hence the church will be fulfilled) only among

"the *least* of my brethren," among those who are already one
with Christ in his weakness and loneliness and humility.

> Then the King will say to those at his right hand, "Come, O
> blessed of my Father, inherit the kingdom prepared for you from
> the foundation of the world; for I was hungry and you gave me
> food, I was thirsty and you gave me drink, I was a stranger and
> you welcomed me, I was naked and you clothed me, I was sick
> and you visited me, I was in prison and you came to me. . . .
> Truly, I say to you, as you did it to one of the least of these
> my brethren, you did it to me." (Mt. 25:34–36, 40)

One of Charlie Brown's few real triumphs and accomplishments
came on one occasion at camp when he quit trying to be something, acknowledged that he was nothing, and simply became
the friend of another little nothing, Roy.

> God is the God of the humble, the miserable, the oppressed, and
> the desperate, and of those who are brought even to nothing;
> and his nature is to give sight to the blind, to comfort the broken-
> hearted, to justify sinners, to save the very desperate and damned.
> (Luther)[10]

Then what of the church? Does this not mean that it has already incurred the wrath and judgment of God by continually
ignoring the genuinely *poor in spirit*, "the least of these my

brethren," who are crucified before its very eyes every day? And we are not simply speaking of the economically poor. For there are many "whose humble means match not their haughty spirits." The first step in making the church's message "relevant" is not to change the proclamation, but to pay more attention to whom it is proclaimed. "Do not be haughty, but associate with the lowly" (Rom. 12:16). For "the Gospel is a terror to the great, learned, holy, and powerful because they all despise Christ. It is a comfort to the lowly to whom alone Christ is revealed" (Luther).[11] Therefore—

> Is it nothing to you, all you who pass by? Look and see if there is any sorrow like my sorrow which was brought upon me, which the Lord inflicted on the day of his fierce anger. (Lam. 1:12)

Look and see if there is any sorrow like Charlie Brown's. Here is precisely the profoundly heavy-laden spirit to whom Christ's invitation to serve and to love could be most meaningfully heard and understood—if the message were only gotten to him. But "how are they to believe in him of whom they have never heard?" asks St. Paul (Rom. 10:14). As Thornton Wilder could put it, "The very angels themselves cannot persuade the wretched and blundering children on earth as can one . . . broken on the wheel of living. In Love's service only the wounded soldiers can serve."[12] No one could possibly meet this requirement better than Charlie Brown:

Then how does grief become good for the Christian? Initially in a person's life, this happens in only one way:

> Only when a man has become so unhappy, or has grasped the misery of this existence so profoundly that he can truly say, "For me life is worthless"—only then can he make a bid for Christianity. And then life can have worth in the highest degree. (Kierkegaard)[13]

In Christianity, *all* of life has worth in the highest degree because *all* of life takes on meaning: the bitter as well as the sweet, the wins as well as the losses. Whether he wins or loses, the Chris-

tian knows from the mere fact of playing the right game with
all his might, that the final outcome will be a win to end all
losses. This is why St. Paul could say of the Church: "For no
one of us lives, and equally no one of us dies, for himself alone.
If we live, we live for the Lord; and if we die, we die for the
Lord. Whether therefore we live or die, we belong to the Lord"
(Rom. 14:7, 8, NEB). This is the testimony of a man who found
the highest degree of value and satisfaction in both living and
dying! And why? Because the game he played was "for the
Lord." Think, then, of how it must feel to be trapped in a
game that finally has no purpose, no meaning, no importance:

"Don't be discouraged, Charlie Brown," Schroeder tells him.
"These early defeats help to build character for later on in life."
"For what later on in life?" asks Charlie Brown. "For more defeats!" replies Schroeder. Charlie Brown then invests in five
cents' worth of Lucy's psychiatric help. At first her advice sounds
a bit more sophisticated: "Adversity builds character. Without
adversity a person could never mature and face up to all the
things in life!" "What things?" he asks. "More adversity!" she
says. Is this all there is to man's existence: facing adversity with
"maturity" and then—nothing? Are we really alone in a mean-

ingless universe? Is there finally no one who even knows about our defeats? Is God dead? The Christian hardly thinks so. In speaking of a series of drawings he did on the subject of "security," Schulz put it this way: "Perhaps the way I feel about God is best told in the last cartoon of that series. Linus is kneeling with his arms on his bed, and the caption reads, 'Security is knowing you are not alone.' "[14] And how does the Christian finally know he is not alone? Again, we will let Linus speak:

It is "through Christ," says St. Paul, that "we . . . have access to the Father in the one Spirit. Thus you are no longer aliens in a foreign land, but . . . members of God's household. You are built upon the foundation . . . and Christ Jesus himself is the foundation-stone. . . . In him you too are being built with all the rest into a spiritual dwelling for God" (Eph. 2:18–22, NEB). Thus the Christian is built into God by being built into Christ by the presence of God's Holy Spirit becoming built into him. And when God is thus built into a person, this person will then know he is not alone but is the built-in son of a Father who loves him. Christ has as much as said to the Christian: "So that you may know that I (the Son) am the way to the truth (the Father, who loves—and will finally save—all men),

I will now give you the life" (the Holy Spirit). Christ's "purpose in dying for all," says St. Paul, "was that men, while still
in life, should cease to live for themselves, and should live for
him who for their sake died and was raised to life" (2 Cor. 5:15,
NEB). The Christian *knows* that Christ died for the eventual
salvation of all men and was raised to life, because in the very
act of living *for* this Christ, Christ is now raised in—and raises
—the Christian; "and if a man does not possess the Spirit of
Christ, he is no Christian" (Rom. 8:9, NEB). Christ's Spirit living in a man is the Holy Spirit, the Comforter, the Counselor,
the point at which the Trinity meets man *personally*. The Holy
Spirit is called "the Comforter" in the New Testament because
this is exactly what "he" does: he brings joy, comfort, fulfillment, certainty and "life" to man's empty and broken heart:
"He who believes in the Son of God has this testimony in his
own heart. . . . The witness is this: that God has given us
eternal life, and that this life is found in his Son. He who
possesses the Son has life indeed; he who does not possess the
Son of God has not that life" (1 Jn. 5:10–12, NEB). The Holy
Spirit is also called "the Counselor" in the New Testament
because, by his actual presence or absence, he "leads" the Christian in the course of the Christian's actions and thinking. Thus
Jesus could say to his disciples: "These things I have spoken to
you, while I am still with you. But the Counselor, the Holy
Spirit, whom the Father will send in my name, he will teach
you all things, and bring to your remembrance all that I have
said to you" (Jn. 14:25–26). Without the presence of Christ's
Spirit in him, which is given to the Christian in the very act of
obedience, the Christian discovers that he "falls back into fear"
(Rom. 8:13–17). And thus the alternating presence or absence

of God's Spirit in him is the Christian's teacher, counselor, and guide. The Christian is guided in his endeavors by the fact that "God opposes the proud, but gives grace to the humble" (1 Pet. 5:5)—as in the above cartoon.

In this way, the Christian comes to look upon suffering as a positive force and actually as an *especially* gracious gift from God. "We rejoice in our sufferings," said St. Paul; and this is because the Christian learns "obedience in the school of suffering" (Rom. 5:3; Heb. 5:8, NEB). So it is again true that "in everything God works for good for those who love him," but especially in grief does he work for good. That is, the Christian does not value suffering or anxiety or grief for its own sake, but only for the extreme *good* that can come from extreme *grief*. As Paul could put it, "we felt in our hearts that we had received a death-sentence. This was meant to teach us not to place reliance on ourselves, but on God who raises the dead" (2 Cor. 1:9, NEB). St. Paul, like every Christian, was a great opportunist: every time he found himself in hot water, he simply used it for bathing purposes. But, to mix our metaphor, this is the way the Christian always learns to harness his own internal combustion and put it to a genuinely positive use. For as Christ said, the ability of the Comforter to dispel discomfort would teach his disciples *all* things—even "sound theology":

What is the Holy Spirit like? Complete joy is one way Jesus describes his Spirit, "and no one will take your joy from you" (Jn. 15:11, NEB; 16:22).

"Joy," for the New Testament, meant a far more profound fulfillment than either "pleasure" or "peace of mind" or what we ordinarily think of as "happiness." Joy meant the fulfillment of man's inmost being, a fulfillment that could be effected only by God through Christ in the person of God's Holy Spirit. As Tillich could say:

Joy is more than pleasure; and it is more than happiness. Happiness is a state of mind which lasts for a longer or shorter time and is dependent on many conditions, external and internal. In

the ancient view it is a gift of the gods which they give and take away again. In the American Constitution, "the pursuit of happiness" is a basic human right. In economic theory the greatest happiness of the greatest number of people is the purpose of human action. In the fairy tale, "they lived happily ever after." Happiness can stand a large amount of pain and lack of pleasure. But happiness cannot stand the lack of joy. For joy is the expression of our essential and central fulfillment. No peripheral fulfillments and no favorable conditions can be substituted for the central fulfillment. Even in an unhappy state a great joy can transform unhappiness into happiness.[15]

Nor is the Bible interested in "peace of mind" as such. It is only interested in the peace of God, which can sometimes be deeply disturbing to the mind—but never to the heart. "For God hath not given us the spirit of fear; but of power, and of love, and of a sound mind" (2 Tim. 1:7, KJV).

"Peace" is another word Jesus uses for the Holy Spirit: "Peace is my parting gift to you, my own peace, such as the world cannot give. Set your troubled hearts at rest, and banish your fears" (Jn. 14:27, NEB). The New Testament also calls the Spirit "the light of men. The light shines on in the dark, and the darkness has

never quenched it" (Jn. 1:4, 5, NEB). Apparently, then, "fellowship and participation in the Holy Spirit" must look something very much like the peace and light Linus finds in this cartoon:

"Choose something like a star," Robert Frost says of God, "to stay our minds on and be staid."[16] For it is only God's own Spirit that can stay our restless minds. "Freedom" is another term the New Testament uses to describe God's gift of the Holy Spirit. "If . . . you are truly my disciples," said Jesus (and one should never forget this "if") ". . . you will know the truth, and the truth will make you free . . . . So if the Son makes you free, you will be free indeed" (Jn. 8:31, 32, 36). But to be "free indeed" did not mean "freedom of choice" or freedom to do as we please. As a matter of fact, discipleship to Jesus meant being a slave to him, to place one's neck under his yoke. But his yoke

was the only "easy, light yoke." Slavery to any other god was to labor under a heavy, burdensome yoke. Therefore freedom in Christ's Spirit was freedom from the heavy yoke of false gods.

The yoke surrounding the hearts of those who labor and are heavy-laden under the bondage of sin, is heavy indeed. As far as freedom from unhappiness is concerned, their hearts might as well be buried under a huge mountain. The mountain of unhappiness surrounding the heart of the unfaithful man is the same mountain Jesus said would become as light as a feather for the man with

> faith in God. Truly, I say to you, whoever says to this mountain, "Be taken up and cast into the sea," and does not doubt in his heart, but believes that what he says will come to pass, it will be done for him. (Mk. 11:22, 23)

The difference between the man of faith and the man of unfaith is finally a difference in lightness of Spirit. The man of the world has the cares of the world on his shoulders to weigh him down. But the man of faith—being a follower of the Dog God and hence having nothing and being nothing—is extremely light in relation to the world. The world's terrible hold on man, the depressing law of gravity which finally overcomes everything of the world, is no longer the law the faithful man lives by. Instead he lives on the basis of an unseen Spirit, which, from the point of view of the worldly man, must seem utterly impossible and incredible. "While," says Karl Barth in speaking of faith, "seen from the viewpoint of an outsider, it hovers in mid-air, it depends actually upon God's living word . . . ."[17]

To such surrender to the grace of God and to the neighbor, the gospel promises freedom, power, life. If man gives himself up to the grace of God he is released from all anxiety for himself and his security, and in such freedom he gains a quite new power. (Bultmann)[18]

"Being loved gives one certain wings, a certain surprising courage and energy. Then one is more of a *complete* man than otherwise. And the more one is this, the better," said van Gogh, a favorite of Snoopy's and also a man who thought of himself as only "a big rough dog."[19]

The presence of the Holy Spirit in the heart of the Christian is the final criterion for all that he does and knows and believes. "The only assurance that faith tolerates is the Word itself which

comes to me through Christ" (Bonhoeffer).[20] The witness borne by God's Spirit to the Christian's spirit goes much deeper than mere reason. It is "the peace of God, which passes all understanding" (Phil. 4:7). For this reason, the experience of the God's Spirit in man's heart is very much like the merely human experience of being in love. The true lover is overwhelmed by the experience of love. It could never occur to him to ask whether he is really in love or whether real love is in him. For the true lover it is quite simply the case that "You ain't livin' if you don't know it." The true lover knows it, because more real than anything else to him is the love that lives in his own heart. For this reason, no one else ever needs to tell him what true life and true love are. He knows. He knows in the same way that all men finally "know" anything—by their own personal experience. The man in love with God has simply been given a richer and deeper amount of data than other men.

"There is only one proof of the truth of Christianity and that, quite rightly, is from the emotions" (Kierkegaard).[21] For this reason it is impossible for the true lover to ever doubt his love. To question, to say "if"—as all our various "rich men" said to Jesus in laying down their conditions for him—is not truly to love the intended love, but is to judge on the basis of a more

deeply trusted love. And what we trust solely on the basis of our hearts, our emotions, there will our true loves be. Therefore when one is a true lover—that is, *totally* dedicated to one's love—there can be no doubts or "ifs" or conditions. It would simply be impossible for him even to think of loving another—as long as he remains a true lover and loves with *all* his heart. Schroeder is such a totally dedicated, true lover:

The inspiration (the "in-spirit-ion") of the Holy Spirit is like being lost and then being found; it is like losing our lives and then having them for-given. Loving God through Christ is not something the Christian may do if he so chooses; it is something he *must* do; he has no choice. For he discovers that only in this way is he taken off of the hook of life and set free. And, as Linus can tell us, "In all this world there is nothing more inspiring than the sight of someone who has just been taken off the hook!"—unless of course it is the inspiration of having just been taken off the hook oneself. And for this reason, "the gift of the Holy Spirit" is very much like finding our long lost—but true—securities:

This is why the entire New Testament is an intensely *personal* document. It is not the effort of a group of men who are out to prove something to us by the force of their rational arguments. But it is the *testimony*, or *testament*, of a group of *witnesses*— witnesses who are bent on simply reporting to us the experience of a love that overtook them and overwhelmed them, a peace that passed all their understanding, and a peace that they in turn would pass on to us. It is a testament marked "PERSONAL."

11   *Just Who's in Charge Here?*

There remains just a word to be said about the suspicion that this simple obedience involves a doctrine of human merit.
—BONHOEFFER[1]

I have always regarded religion as gratitude. We live on an earth which is not ours but belongs to God. We are his creatures. We worship him out of a feeling of gratitude for what he has done for us and for his guidance, his protection, his leading.—SCHULZ[2]

Grace and gratitude belong together like heaven and earth. Grace evokes gratitude like the voice of an echo. Gratitude follows grace like thunder [follows] lightning . . . . this correspondence cannot fail. Its failure, ingratitude, is sin . . . . Radically and basically all sin is simply ingratitude.   —BARTH[3]

There is a great difference between disciples and true disciples. We recognize them by telling them that the truth will make them free; for if they answer that they are free, and that it is in their power to come out of slavery to the devil, they are indeed disciples, but not true disciples.   —PASCAL[4]

This is my absolute opinion: he that will maintain that man's free-will is able to do or work anything in spiritual cases be they never so small, denies Christ. This I have always maintained . . . and thereby will I remain, for I know it to be the truth, though all the world should be against it.   —LUTHER[5]

At the present time a "remnant" has come into being, selected by the grace of God. But if it is by grace, then it does not rest on deeds done, or grace would cease to be grace.
—ROMANS 11:5–6, NEB

Know that the Lord is God!
It is he that made us, and we are his.   —PSALM 100:3

THE FOUR "FREEDOMS" WE HAVE DISCUSSED thus far are: *First*: the
freedom from false gods that no man originates with, simply because of the "natural-born" idolatry of his heart. Man is a slave
to the idol he initially worships because it is his *god*—it means
everything to him; he is bound to this god with all of the passion
of his heart. From this original basis man wills to do many different things. But everything *he does* is based on *who he is*—an
idolator, a natural-born "child of this world," who cannot stop
being who he is by the power of his own will. Satan cannot cast
out Satan. Thus what we do is *always* based on the god we serve
(or "who we are"); not the other way round. "I'll never forget
Will Durant's line on the Apostle Paul," says Schulz. " 'He had
to be what he was to do what he did.' And this is the same with
all of us."[6] Schopenhauer's view that "A man can do what he
wants, but not want what he wants" is, said Albert Einstein, a
realization that "mercifully mitigates the easily paralyzing sense
of responsibility and prevents us from taking ourselves and other
people all too seriously; it is conducive to a view of life which,
in particular, gives humor its due."[7] And so it does:

Second: we talked about what Dostoyevsky called "the dreadful freedom," the freedom that comes in having all of our false gods broken, shaken and stripped from us so that we have "nothing to hold on to." *Third:* we have discussed the freedom the Christian finds in being shaken free from the heavy burdens of idolatry and, after passing through the dreadful freedom of having nothing to cling to, in finally coming to rest under the "easy yoke" of obedience to Christ. *Fourth:* we have said that the man who worships only Jesus as the Christ is free to use any means that more expediently brings others to believe that "Jesus is Lord." "All things are lawful unto me, but all things are not expedient" (1 Cor. 6:12, KJV). And now, *fifth,* we want to discuss the so-called "freedom of the will," or freedom from necessity, a freedom no man has, not even in the smallest actions; a freedom that can only be attributed to the Creator and to none of his creation. Or, to put it another way, we now want to discuss more specifically the sovereignty of God and his grace by which men are saved.

Holden Caulfield has just been kicked out of his third prep school and has gone to the home of "old Spencer," his history teacher, to say good-by:

> "I'll drop you a line, sir. Take care of your grippe, now."
> "Good-by, boy."
> After I shut the door and started back to the living room, he yelled something at me, but I couldn't exactly hear him. I'm pretty sure he yelled "Good luck!" at me. I hope not. I hope to hell not. I'd never yell "Good luck!" at anybody. It sounds terrible, when you think about it.[8]

The idea of "luck" is terrible to think about because it is based

on the pagan notion of fate, or chance, in which the entire universe is understood to be fatalistically controlled by blind, impersonal forces. And so when we yell "Good luck!" to somebody, we are reminding him that though perhaps we care for him, the *world itself* does not. (See cartoon above.)

The Christian and what physicist Albert Einstein called "the serious scientist" (that is, the scientist who "takes the hypothesis of causality really seriously") are in complete agreement that "a man's actions are determined by necessity, external and internal, so that in God's eyes he cannot be responsible, any more than an inanimate object is responsible for the motions it undergoes" (Einstein).[9] But the Christian also has an interest in metaphysics, or that which goes "beyond physics," and believes that finally all of the universe's necessity is created, controlled, and will finally be consummated by an all-powerful and all-loving Father; that the Causer behind the causality of the universe is not blind and impersonal, but is rather all-knowing, personal, and whose very nature is Love. Therefore, the serious scientist and the serious Christian agree: for presumptuous man to feel that his little will exists outside of this scheme of things, that all of his important decisions are finally made in the mysterious recesses of some kind of "cause and effect vacuum," is equivalent to one of the little characters in *Peanuts* getting the idea that both he and the artist, Schulz, produce the strip together. Who is it that finally "draws all"? The *Creator* draws all. For just as the *Peanuts* children have not the slightest existence of their own unless their creator draws them, "No one can come to me unless the Father who sent me draws him," said Jesus. "For apart from me you can do nothing" (Jn. 6:44; 15:5).

Is it I, God, or who, that lifts this arm? But if the great sun move not himself, but is an errand-boy in heaven; nor one single star can revolve, but by some invisible power; how then can this one small heart beat; this one small brain think thoughts; unless God does that thinking, does that living, and not I. (Melville)[10]

Any eight-year-old schoolboy can tell us that all life on the earth is brought forth and sustained solely by energy from the sun. Without the sun our planet would not only be cold and lifeless, but would probably have no separate existence of its own. An individual man, however, like the weather, is extremely complex making totally accurate predictions of his behavior impossible, even for himself. And because men can never see all of the forces acting on themselves to cause them to re-act in the ways they do, men will often have the illusion of finally being "free" from the order and necessity of nature. Thus man's *illusion* of "free-will"

comes from the same kind of simplistic mistake we see in the preceding cartoon, in which Charlie Brown believes that man himself is finally capable of keeping himself warm.

This is the inconsistency of which Whitehead was writing when he said:

> Western peoples exhibit on a colossal scale a peculiarity which is popularly supposed to be more especially characteristic of the Chinese. Surprise is often expressed that a Chinaman can be of two religions, a Confucian for some occasions and a Buddhist for other occasions. . . . But there can be no doubt that an analogous fact is true of the West, and that the two attitudes involved are inconsistent. A scientific realism, based on mechanism, is conjoined with an unwavering belief in the world of men and of the higher animals as being composed of self-determining organisms. This radical inconsistency at the basis of modern thought accounts for much that is half-hearted and wavering in our civilisation. It would be going too far to say that it distracts thought. It enfeebles it, by reason of the inconsistency lurking in the background.[11]

To think of "human freedom" as "self-controlled movement," said Kafka. "What a mockery of holy Mother Nature!"[12]

But the Christian is more concerned that the idea of "free-will" makes a mockery of God, than with the more symptomatic problems of its making a mockery of nature or enfeebling civilization. For to say that God is the sovereign God everywhere except in the uttermost recesses of man's heart, is to say that God is not God in the very place where it matters most for man. Thus man's stubborn insistence on his own "free-will" is actually no more than a last-ditch effort to prevent God from being God by man's remaining master of his own fate, captain of his own soul, and hence finally his own "Creator." "Free-will" is man's

most subtle attempt to get rid of God by gaining control over him. It is no accident that whenever a Christian culture becomes saturated in the heresy of "free-will" (Pelagianism), this culture will also begin toying with and living the ideas of "religious atheism." And of course from "religious atheism" it is only one more short step to a more honest and consistent position: the final deification of man and outright atheism. Any ability to "do-it-himself" that man thinks he has in the presence of God, marks the end of faith in God and the beginning of man's faith in himself. From that point on, the extent to which man increases in his supposed ability to "do-it-himself," will determine the extent to which he will have even less and less use for the idol he calls "God." No one saw more clearly than Dostoyevsky that "free-will" necessarily meant atheism. As one of his characters, Kirillov, could put it.

> I have no higher idea than disbelief in God . . . . to recognize that there is no God and not to recognize at the same instant that one is God oneself is an absurdity . . . . the attribute of my godhead is self-will![13]

If man is at all capable of "saving" himself (or of saving anyone else, for that matter), he will finally need no Savior, but will himself be "God." And this man "is the Enemy. He rises in his pride against every god, so-called . . . and even takes his seat in the temple of God claiming to be a god himself" (2 Thess. 2:4, NEB).

The justification of the sinner . . . consists in the sole righteousness of God, wherein the sinner is utterly and completely unrighteous, and has no righteousness whatever of his own side by side with the righteousness of God. Whenever we desire an independent righteousness of our own we are forfeiting our only chance for justification, which is through God alone and his righteousness. God alone is righteous. (Bonhoeffer)[14]

Thus the heresy of Pelagianism can be seen as man's worship of his own "independence," his belief in his own ability to provide for himself quite apart from the grace of Provid-ence. The Pelagian is one who simply wants to make a virtue of his own necessity. The term "Semi-Pelagianism" was coined in the sixteenth century to account for those who "presume to share God's task with him" (Kierkegaard), the "officious collaborators with God" (Barth). Pelagians worship a demigod; Semi-Pelagians worship a semigod. Pelagians say, "Don't worry about it, God, I can do it!" Semi-Pelagians say, "With my help, God, you can do it!" In order to give the reader an even better understanding of these two old heresies of the Church, we will here call in Snoopy, who in the first panel will enact the role of the Pelagian, while in the final panel will be seen as the Semi-Pelagian:

"If you and we belong to Christ, guaranteed as his and anointed, it is all God's doing," said St. Paul. "It is in full reliance upon God, through Christ, that we make such claims. There is no question of our being qualified in ourselves: we cannot claim anything as our own. Such qualification as we have comes from God" (2 Cor. 1:21; 3:4, 5, NEB). Most offensive of all to the Pelagian mentality is that "it is, remember, by grace and not by achievement that you are saved . . . . It was nothing you could or did achieve—it was God's gift which saved you. No one can pride himself in earning the love of God. The fact is that what we are we owe to the hand of God upon us" (Eph. 2:5, 8, 9, Phillips). Karl Barth, in commenting on this passage of St. Paul's, has said:

> We dislike hearing that we are saved by grace, and by grace alone. We do not appreciate that God does not owe us anything, that we are bound to live from his goodness alone, that we are left with nothing but the great humility, the thankfulness of a child presented with many gifts. For we do not like at all to look away from ourselves. We would much prefer to withdraw into our own inner circle . . . and to be with ourselves. To put it bluntly: we do not like to believe.[15]

Even the Christian has an unfortunate built-in tendency to forget who God is and to forget that God himself has already saved the world. Whenever the Christian begins to exalt himself as the worthy co-worker of God, he is immediately booted from the realm of the faithful by an unseen Power and again must go grumbling off to make his bed with the men of this world. This is why St. Paul reminded each of his fellow Christians in Rome "not to think of himself more highly than he ought to think. . . . Bless those who persecute you; bless and do not curse them . . . . do not be haughty . . . never be conceited . . . . never avenge yourselves, but leave it to the wrath of God . . . . Do not be overcome by evil, but overcome evil with good" (Rom. 12:3, 14, 16, 19, 21). The Christian must never become so impatient with evil that he becomes a Savior himself. Salvation, along with everything else, is always in the hands of God alone. "If flesh and blood take offense here, and grumble," says Luther, "well, let them grumble; they will achieve nothing; grumbling will not change God! And

however many of the ungodly stumble and depart, the elect will remain."[16]

The Christian, or anyone else, is already defeated the moment he believes he can at all take on the world singlehandedly. For it is only through Christ that "we are more than conquerors" (Rom. 8:37). This is why Kafka could say, "In the fight between you and the world back the world."

The dog is a traditional symbol for faith in the church. Black-and-white dogs in particular have been used as symbols of the Dominicans (*Domini canes*, "dogs of the Lord"), who wore black-and-white habits. This symbol originates from the fact that a canine-like Canaanite woman once literally dogged Jesus for his help. Finally, when she crawled to Jesus' feet and begged his help, he told her, " 'It is not right to take the children's bread and throw it to the dogs.' But she answered him, 'Yes, Lord; yet even the dogs under the table eat the children's crumbs.' " Apparently this was exactly the kind of follower Jesus was looking for—the person who, having been reduced to the level of a nothing, a dog, was willing to trust only in him, in him who also was a nothing, a dog. In this way Jesus was not only "the Dog God," but was also the God of the dogs, the lowly and humble. "O woman, great is your faith! Be it done for you as you desire" (Mt. 15:22–28; Mk. 7:24–30). Because Jesus alone is the righteousness of the Christian, the Christian needs constantly to be reminded of who a Christian is: one who has been chosen. Any independent righteousness or merit or virtue or "ability" of the Christian's own, will only come between him and his Lord. And thus St. Paul could say:

> My brothers, think what sort of people you are, whom God has called. Few of you are men of wisdom, by any human standard; few are powerful or highly born. Yet, to shame the wise, God has chosen what the world counts folly, and to shame what is strong, God has chosen what the world counts weakness. He has chosen things low and contemptible, mere nothings, to overthrow the existing order. And so there is no place for human pride in the presence of God. You are in Christ Jesus by God's act, for God has made him our wisdom; he is our righteousness; in him

we are consecrated and set free. And so . . . "If a man is proud, let him be proud of the Lord." (1 Cor. 1:26–31, NEB)

This is the kind of advice that all Christians—even Snoopy—need always to remember:

The fact that only Christ is the Christian's righteousness is the basis for Christ being seen as the "sun of righteousness" in the prophecy of Malachi. This, in turn, is the reason that Christ is frequently symbolized by the sun.

For behold, the day comes, burning like an oven, when all the arrogant and all evildoers will be stubble; the day that comes shall burn them up, says the Lord of hosts. . . . But for you who fear my name the sun of righteousness shall rise, with healing in its wings. (Mal. 4:1, 2)

The Christian has absolutely no grounds for self-pride or "boasting" as long as he worships God. For he will know that only God is God, and that his own relationship to God is created and sustained entirely by God himself. Man's belief in his own "free-will," his autocracy, is nothing more or less than the most common and pernicious form of self-righteousness/self-worship. As W. H. Auden has put it:

As long as the self can say "I," it is impossible not to rebel;
As long as there is an accidental virtue, there is a necessary vice:
And the garden cannot exist, the miracle cannot occur.[17]

As a Christian, "I" can never be humble; "I" can only be *humbled*. No one who seriously believes that *he* has done justly, can walk *humbly* with his God.

The self-righteousness of "free-will" should never be considered merely a minor defect of the Christian. The Christian's righteousness belongs *entirely* to Christ or he is no Christian. "I bear them witness that they have a zeal for God, but it is not enlightened. For, being ignorant of the righteousness that comes from God, and seeking to establish their own, they did not submit to God's righteousness" (Rom. 10:2–3). In speaking of one of the scribes who encountered Jesus, Barth tells us:

> "But he desired to justify himself" (Lk. 10:29). . . . This lust is human disobedience discovered at its root! For what happens when one confronted with God's claim endeavors to establish his own righteousness? Apparently he makes out of God's claim a claim of his own, namely the claim that he can and will himself satisfy God's demands. . . . From hence, on the basis of this deception of sin, comes the "unenlightenment" of our "zeal for God." Just let no one think that, because it is based on *ignorance* and because it is always a zeal for God, it is a relatively harmless and forgivable zeal, perhaps to be regretted on account of its imperfection but nevertheless to be praised on account of its good intention. No, its ignorance is *disobedience*, and it is a *lie* to call it zeal for God! *Sin* triumphs in this zeal, more, infinitely more, than in what we think we know as idolatry, blasphemy, murder, adultery, and robbery; infinitely more because here . . . God himself has been made the cause and pretext of sin.[18]

The actual *attitude* of self-righteousness is only one of a thousand ways in which the actual *belief* in self-righteousness, or "self-will," can manifest itself. But of this belief and all its manifestations, the righteousness and sovereignty of God demands that no one "be inflated with pride as you patronize one and flout the other. Who makes you, my friend, so important? What do you possess

that was not given you? If then you really received it all as a gift, why take the credit to yourself?" (1 Cor. 4:7, NEB). Who makes even you, Lucy, so important as you patronize one and flout the other?

"No one can judge a criminal, until he recognizes that he is just such a criminal as the man standing before him, and that he perhaps is more than all men to blame for that crime. When he understands that, he will be able to be a judge" (Dostoyevsky).[19] "Free-will" inevitably leads to the *intolerance* of self-righteousness: "If I can achieve good for myself, in spite of many hardships, etc., others can and should as well." But the Christian is necessarily one who loves only because God first loved him and continues to hold him in the relationship of love. "Love," says Bonhoeffer,

> is something which happens to a man, something passive, something over which he does not dispose. . . . Love means the . . . transformation of one's entire existence by God. . . . Love, therefore, is not man's choice, but it is the election of man by God. . . . The relation between the divine love and human love is wrongly understood if we say that the divine love precedes the human love, but solely for the purpose of setting human love in motion as a love which, in relation to the divine love, is an inde-

pendent, free, and autonomous activity of man . . . . there is no love which is free or independent from the love of God. In this, then, the love of man remains purely passive. Loving God is simply the other aspect of being loved by God.[20]

The Christian is a man who has been "for-given." That is, all of his life, as well as all that in any way distinguishes him from the non-Christian, has been given to him for absolutely no merit or deserving of his own. The Christian is one who has come to love God and know of God's love for him not because of, but *in spite of* everything the Christian is and has been. And for this reason the Christian is better "able to bear patiently with the ignorant and erring, since he too is beset by weakness" (Heb. 5:2, NEB). Or, as Christ put it, "he who is forgiven little, loves little" (Lk. 7:47). "Why," asks Paul Tillich,

> do children turn away from their righteous parents and husbands from their righteous wives, and vice versa? Why do Christians turn away from their righteous pastors? Why do people turn away from their righteous neighborhoods? Why do many turn away from righteous Christianity and from the Jesus it paints and the God it proclaims? Why do they turn to those who are not considered to be righteous? Often, certainly, it is because they want to escape judgment. But more often it is because they seek a love which is rooted in forgiveness; and this the righteous ones cannot give. . . . Each of us who strives for righteousness would be more Christian if more were forgiven him, if he loved more and if he could better resist the temptation to present himself as acceptable to God by his own righteousness.[21]

Thus the Christian, the true dog of faith, will "turn away from" the self-righteousness of "self-will" in others, as well as in himself:

Man lives his life from beginning to end, making his smallest and largest decisions, *totally* by the grace of God. Man's shortsighted belief in his own self-determination is the basis for what the New Testament calls "boasting," or the sin of "pride." "If Abraham was justified by anything he had done," said St. Paul, "then he has a ground for pride" (Rom. 4:2, NEB). The effectiveness of the proclamation of the Christian message is measured by the extent to which it "works"—produces results and bears fruit—by putting men actively to work from the correct "starting point"—that is, Jesus. But we are doomed from the very beginning to subvert this starting point, this foundation, if any or all of the resulting work is not understood to be Christ's righteousness and work and not our own. The heresy of "free-will" is fatal to faith because it attributes *righteousness*—which belongs to God alone—to men themselves. And "no one is good but God alone" (Mk. 10:18). Otherwise faith in God is immediately subverted by man's faith in himself. And the truth that is so simple and yet so hard for us to learn, is that God is not man, nor is He the world.

Come now, you who say, "Today or tomorrow we will go into such and such a town and spend a year there and trade and get gain"; whereas you do not know about tomorrow. What is your

life? For you are a mist that appears for a little time and then vanishes. Instead you ought to say, "If the Lord wills, we shall live and we shall do this or that." As it is, you boast in your arrogance. All such boasting is evil. (Jas. 4:13–16)

Apart from our "arrogance," another one of the more obvious manifestations of our lack of faith in God and his righteousness, is superstition—religious and otherwise. Superstition will inevitably arise whenever faith in God is undermined by faith in oneself. As Barth has put it:

> Anyone who has once allowed himself to take his life in his own hand in this or that form of "righteousness by works" should, if he is wise enough, just be sure not to forget the eternal, brazen, great laws of his fate . . . he just should not leave the calendar of his astrological possibilities for this week and for next autumn too far out of reach. It is also typical of a life . . . which has been dishonored and emptied by our autocracy that we, like bad boys waiting for the teacher, must peer around in interstellar space, keeping a lookout for something which perhaps would still overcome us and what it might mean for us.[22]

When man is reduced to the shaky little foundation of faith in only himself, which is the faith of "free-will," he will anxiously grasp for support and become enslaved to the most bizarre assortment of odd chains and loose ends.

There are two basic distinctions between the New Testament
concepts of "justification by faith" and "justification by works of
the law." First, justification by works of the law held that man's
proper relationship to God is basically brought about through
man's obedience to an abstract command ("the law"), or to a
group of commands ("works of law"); justification by faith, on
the other hand, meant worshiping a particular man—the historical
Jesus of Nazareth. As a result of this first and most fundamental
distinction, a second distinction was usually made between "righteousness by faith" and "righteousness by works of law": righteousness by law was usually understood as man's own keeping of the
God relationship (and hence this righteousness was man's own);
whereas righteousness by faith was always understood as a relationship that God *keeps man in* (and hence this righteousness,
from beginning to end, belonged only to God). "Then what be-

comes of our boasting?" asks St. Paul. "It is excluded. On what principle? On the principle of works? No, but on the principle of faith. For we hold that a man is justified by faith apart from works of law" (Rom. 3:27, 28). Thus "the terrible language of the Law is so terrifying because it seems as if it were left to man to hold fast to Christ by his own power, whereas in the language of love it is Christ that holds him fast" (Kierkegaard).[23] In the above cartoon, then, we can see how Linus has received a "letter of the law."

"But thanks be to God, who continually leads us about, captives in Christ's triumphal procession, and everywhere uses us to reveal and spread abroad the fragrance of the knowledge of himself!" (2 Cor. 2:14, NEB). The fact that he is Christ's captive, and not vice versa, has always been a "doctrine of great comfort" to the Christian. Luther put it this way:

> I frankly confess that, for myself, even if it could be, I should not want "free-will" to be given to me, nor anything to be left in my own hands to enable me to endeavor after salvation; not merely because in face of so many dangers, and adversities, and assaults of devils, I could not stand my ground and hold fast my "free-will" (for one devil is stronger than all men, and on these terms no man could be saved); but because, even were there no dangers, adversities, or devils, I should still be forced to labour with no guarantee of success, and to beat my fists in the air. If I lived and worked in all eternity, my conscience would never reach comfortable certainty as to how much it must do to satisfy God. Whatever work I had done, there would still be a nagging doubt as to whether it pleased God, or whether He required something more. The experience of all who seek righteousness by works proves that, and I learned it well enough myself over a period of many years, to my own great hurt. But now that God has taken my salvation out of the control of my own will, and put it under the control of His, and promised to save me, not according to my working or running, but according to His own grace and mercy, I have comfortable certainty that He is faithful and will not lie to me. . . .[24]

The Christian, like any other man, has many "troubles"; but the anxiety in these troubles has been conquered through obedience—by God's grace—to Jesus alone, who could say:

How little faith you have! No, do not ask anxiously, "What are we to eat? What are we to drink? What shall we wear?" All these are things for the heathen to run after, not for you, because your heavenly Father knows that you need them all. Set your mind on God's kingdom and his justice before everything else, and all the rest will come to you as well. So do not be anxious about tomorrow; tomorrow will look after itself. Each day has troubles enough of its own. (Mt. 6:31–34, NEB)

Again, what does it mean to "set our minds on God's kingdom and his justice"? It means to "Humble yourselves . . . under God's mighty hand, and he will lift you up in due time. Cast all your cares on him, for you are his charge" (1 Pet. 5:6, 7, NEB). One evening, when Jesus and his disciples were crossing the sea of Galilee by boat, "there arose a great storm on the sea, so that the boat was being swamped by the waves." The terrified disciples knew they should look to their new manager, Jesus, the Dog God, for help. Why had their new manager not already busied himself by rebuking the wind and sea, which only then became calm? Why had he not already rebuked the disciples for their anxiety and lack of faith in him? Why? "He was asleep" (Mt. 8:23–27).

"Be not anxious for the morrow." This is not to be taken as a philosophy of life or a moral law; it is the gospel of Jesus

Christ. . . . It is not care that frees the disciples of care, but their faith in Jesus. . . . It is senseless to pretend that we can . . . alter the circumstances of this world. Only God can take care, for it is he who rules the world. Since we *cannot* take care, since we are so completely powerless, we *ought* not to do it either. If we do we are dethroning God and presuming to rule the world ourselves. (Bonhoeffer)[25]

Only through Jesus, the Dog God, are we men safe in the surrounding darkness and do we find the comfort, the rest, the freedom from anxiety that we so sorely need. Only the seemingly weak Dog God has power enough to be the true "Guardian of your souls" (1 Pet. 2:25). And if for one moment the Christian forgets in whom he has trusted and once again becomes the captain of his own soul, then Chaos is come again. For "we know that no child of God is a sinner; it is the Son of God who keeps him safe, and the evil one cannot touch him" (1 Jn. 5:18, NEB):

Said Bonhoeffer, who was hanged, at thirty-nine, on a Nazi gallows for plotting to kill Hitler: "If we fall into the hands of men, and meet suffering and death from their violence, we are none the less certain that everything comes from God. The same God who sees no sparrow fall to the ground without his knowledge and will, allows nothing to happen, except it be good and profitable for his children and the cause for which they stand. We are in God's hands. Therefore, 'Fear not.'"[26]

But if the proclamation of the gospel of God's grace and sovereignty removes from us all grounds for "boasting" or "pride" or "free-will," does it not also remove from us all grounds for responsible action? For this gospel clearly tells us that man himself is finally not responsible for the smallest event that occurs in the world, but is—like the world itself—totally and completely in the hands of the sovereign and almighty God. Again, the Christian faith finds itself in complete accord with the scientist as scientist: "I do not at all believe in human freedom in the philosophical sense. Everybody acts not only under external compulsion but also in accordance with inner necessity" (Einstein).[27] But does this not undermine responsible obedience to God if we cannot act but only *must* act? "Every man is a born hypocrite," Kierkegaard reminds us;[28] and will not this hypocrite, man, attempt to avoid being held accountable by God by throwing up to God His own word that finally we are not accountable, that God Himself is finally accountable for all that happens? The answer is "Yes." Man, the hypocrite, will always avoid being held accountable in any way he can:

Must I be *held* accountable if I am not finally accountable? Must I answer for my mistakes if they are not finally mine? The answer to this question, whether we happen to like it or not, is: Yes (POW!) In the Sight of God, Thou Must!

Neither does the POWer behind Lucy's "POW!" worry about such questions. "For *thine* is the POWer":

This mysterious power—the power which limits man and is master of him even when he thinks he is his own master—is God, the controller of man's future. . . . *It is God who makes man finite,*

who makes a comedy of man's care, who allows his longing to
miscarry, who casts him into solitude, who sets a terminus to
his knowing and doing, who calls him to duty, and who gives the
guilty over to torment . . . at the same time it is God who forces
man into life and drives him into care; who puts longing and the
desire for love in his heart . . . and who places him in the eternal
struggle between self-assertion and duty. God is the enigmatic
power beyond time, yet master of the temporal; beyond being,
yet working in it. (Bultmann)[29]

When a man finally gets it through his head and heart that "the
wages of sin is death," that "the results of disobedience is POW!"
he will no longer worry about the questions of his self-assertion:
Am I really responsible? Must I answer for my mistakes? Is God
really being fair? Who is responsible? Who is accountable? How
can I turn to God? Why does he allow evil? Is there a God?
How can I prove it?—all of these questions will become mere
child's play. When a man finally learns what "must" means, he
then becomes a Christian. For in "must" there are no grounds for
"boasting" and no grounds for disobedience. When God finally
reveals himself as "Yes (POW!) Thou Must!" only one response
is then possible: truly humble obedience and—finally—gratitude.
For "who has given a gift to [God] that he might be repaid?"
(Rom. 11:35). One thing is sure: Christians "do not *wish* to be
what they are; they *have* to be. And therefore they *are*" (Barth).[30]
St. Paul was not referring simply to the office of an apostle, but
to the experience of every Christian, when he wrote:

> Even if I preach the Gospel, I can claim no credit for it; I can-
> not help myself; it would be misery for me not to preach. If
> I did it of my own choice, I should be earning my pay; but since
> I do it apart from my own choice, I am simply discharging a
> trust. (1 Cor. 9:16, 17, NEB)

When two other apostles, Peter and John, were called into court
and ordered "to refrain from all public speaking and teaching
in the name of Jesus," their reply was, "Is it right in God's eyes
for us to obey you rather than God? . . . We cannot possibly give
up speaking of things we have seen and heard" (Acts 4:18-20,
NEB). Einstein is no doubt right: "Everybody acts not only
under external compulsion but in accordance with inner neces-

sity." But the inner necessity that rules the Christian is none
other than Christ himself. The Christian proclamation involves
many forceful commands: Come! Follow! Obey! Go! But the fact
that it gives commands does not mean that it believes man to
be—even for one moment—a "free agent." It is, rather, from
the very fact that the Church knows man is *not* free, that the
force of these commands is increased. "A man is the slave of whatever has mastered him" (2 Pet. 2:19, NEB). And the Church
knows well enough that there are other forces in the world "con-
tending" against God for the mastery of man. Luther was being
completely true to the New Testament (cf. 2 Tim. 2:25, 26)
when he said, "The human will is, as it were, a beast between
[God and Satan]. If God sit thereon, it wills and goes where
God will . . . . If Satan sit thereon, it wills and goes as Satan
will. Nor is it in the power of its own will to choose, to which
rider it will run, nor which it will seek; but the riders themselves
contend, which shall have and hold it."[31] It is for this very reason
that whenever the New Testament's command for obedience is
made, there immediately follows—in the proper order and often
in the same breath—the reminder of *whose* power and *whose*
righteousness is behind *all* obedience: "Seek ye first the kingdom
of God . . . . and *his* righteousness." "You must work out your
own salvation in fear and trembling . . . . for it is God who works
in you, inspiring both the will and the deed, for his own chosen
purpose" (Phil. 2:12, 13, NEB). "I live; yet not I, but Christ
liveth in me" (Gal. 2:20, KJV). This "reminder" is always a part
of the New Testament's message. For it knows that just as soon
as the Christian begins thinking of himself as a self-made "new
man," as a great do-it-yourself power, another POWer will immediately reduce him once again to status of "the old man."

True freedom is not a choice between alternatives; our one freedom is obedience to the will of God. What we call freedom as "free will" is not freedom. We are free if we agree with God, otherwise we are prisoners . . . . The liberty of free will is sin! It is the shame of humanity that we live as if we could choose. (Barth)[32]

The fact that the Christian knows his life to be completely determined does not make him any less "determined" in his will. "It is an interesting fact of history that people who have held strongly to the doctrine of divine predestination have never been apathetic or irresponsible."[33] As a matter of fact, studies have been made showing that these people are, if anything, uncommonly responsible.[34] For who will turn to God first? The man who believes that repentance is always easily within his own power, and hence "tomorrow" will turn to the demigod on the periphery of his "free-will"; or the man who fears the God who is the Lord, and thus turns to him now? "Therefore, knowing the fear of the Lord, we persuade men" (2 Cor. 5:11). The Christian knows that he has been brought to obey only by the Influence behind the influence of influence. Only in this way is human pride excluded, thus allowing God to be God:

"When all is said and done," said Bonhoeffer, who knew what it was to say and do much, "the sovereign power belongs to God."[35] Indeed, the words and works of such theological giants as Paul, Augustine, Luther, Calvin, Bonhoeffer, and Barth, all clearly teach us that it is not in the least necessary to be a Pelagian in order to be a Pioneer. But God's sovereignty over his creation leads us up against one more very hard problem: if God himself is entirely answerable for the universe, then God has some answering to do. If God is going to be the Lord, then he should know better than to have "mercy upon whomever he wills, and . . . harden the heart of whomever he wills" (Rom. 9:18). What right has God to give and to take away? (Job 1:21). Who does God think he is to "form the light, and create darkness," to "make peace, and create evil"? (Is. 45:7, KJV). Last but not least, he should never have put that snake in the Garden in the first place. This God has apparently got completely out of control and needs some good democratic rules to follow! Otherwise, we will light no more candles in his behalf, we will withdraw from the universe!

In the next chapter, with all of the courage of Lucy as our guide, we shall attack God! (Happily, he needs no defense.)

12 Slip-ups, Doghouses, and Free Psychiatric Help

There is only a spiritual world; what we call the physical world is the evil in the spiritual one, and what we call evil is only a necessary moment in our endless development. —KAFKA[1]

It seems to me that many people attend church on Sunday with the same feeling that they attend a theatre. They just sit there and enjoy what is going on. —SCHULZ[2]

This preaching in churches has become an almost heathenish and theatrical thing. . . . In paganism the theatre was the church —in Christendom the churches have practically become theatres. Why so? Why, in this way. It is agreeable, and not devoid of a certain pleasure, to commune with the highest thoughts through the imagination once a week. Nothing more than that. And this has actually become the norm for the sermons. . . .—KIERKEGAARD[3]

And my ending is despair
Unless I be relieved by prayer
Which pierces so that it assaults
Mercy itself, and frees all faults.
                    —SHAKESPEARE, The Tempest, Epilogue

"THE WORLD TONIGHT" IS THE TITLE of a popular radio news program. At the end of each broadcast, the announcer makes a statement that sounds as if it might have been taken straight from the Bible: "The World Tonight was prerecorded for presentation at this time." The announcer just as easily could have said with "the Preacher" of the Old Testament: "That which is, already

has been" (Eccles. 3:15). This is also the same kind of statement the New Testament is making when it says: "In Christ [God] chose us before the world was founded, to be dedicated, to be without blemish in his sight. In his love he destined us—such was his will and pleasure—to be accepted as his sons through Jesus Christ" (Eph. 1:4, 5, NEB). This kind of statement tends to rankle us men. For one thing, we feel that if the job of programming the world had been left to us it would not have turned out to be the depressing "world tonight" that it invariably is, with its wars and rumors of wars, its poor that we seem to have with us always, its "evil thoughts, fornication, theft, murder, adultery, coveting, wickedness, deceit, licentiousness, envy, slander, pride, foolishness," to use the terms Jesus used in describing the contents of "the heart of man" (Mk. 7:21–22). As a matter of fact, we would have created a universe in which men would bypass the hellish world altogether and would go to heaven—go *directly* to heaven; they would not pass the world; they would not collect the thousand natural shocks that flesh is heir to in this jail-like world. Unfortunately, however, none of us was consulted as to the way things should be, not even as to the way we should be:

> For those whom [God] foreknew he also predestined to be conformed to the image of his Son, in order that he might be the first-born among many brethren. And those whom he predestined he also called; and those whom he called he also justified. (Rom. 8:29–30)

In any case, we can hardly deny the countless, seemingly unfair, inequalities—spiritual or otherwise—that exist in the world. Or, as Linus has said, "So much in this world depends on who gets born first."

The Christian doctrine of God's election ("God has mercy on whomever he wills"), invariably raises the problem of God's non-election ("God hardens the hearts of whomever he wills"); this, in turn, raises "the problem of evil," or the question of why an all-powerful, all-knowing, all-loving God permits evil and suffering and sin to exist within his creation. As we saw in the last chapter, to attribute the fact of sin finally to man, does no more than to deify man and pull God down to the level of a helpless second-rate deity. "In the presence of God there is less a problem of freedom than a problem of evil," said Camus. "You know the alternative: either we are not free and God the all-powerful is responsible for evil. Or we are free and responsible but God is not all-powerful."[4] And Camus is right. As long as God—and not man—is God, the Church would do well to refrain from being wishy-washy at this point and to "tell it like it is": God is God; and therefore we must frankly confess that God is responsible for all that is and has been and will be—including what men experience as sin and evil and suffering. This of course is the very problem that Job faced with all of the passionate intensity of his life. With furious honesty he carefully catalogued all the sufferings and sins of the world—and then hurled them into God's face, blaming him for them! Then Job asked a question about God's responsibility for evil that could be asked only by a man who knew "that the Lord is God": "—if it is not he, who then is it?" (Job 9:24).

We have already considered Schroeder's idea that, from the Christian perspective, suffering is an essential element in growth and maturity; and we have touched on the suggestion by "5" that "pain is a part of life." But "the problem of evil" still remains: Why does suffering, or "the cross," have to be *the* route to becoming a Christian and to Christian maturity? Why does pain *have* to be part of life? And what of the *unredemptive* suffering in life—suffering that would seem to be totally senseless and good for nothing and of no possible help to anyone? From the human point of view, evil is *the* inexplicable slip-up of the universe; the slip-up that tends to eclipse belief in any God who really knew what he was doing; a slip-up of far more painful consequences to men than the slip-up mentioned below:

As John Henry Newman put it, "The real mystery is, not that evil should never have an end, but that it should ever have had a beginning."[5] The so-called "Deuteronomic" view of suffering, championed by Lucy ("If a person has bad luck, it's because he's done something wrong . . ."), was firmly rejected not only by Job and Jesus, but is often pooh-poohed in *Peanuts* as well. For Jesus himself suffered far more than a "sliver in his finger." And yet, the New Testament tells us, "Christ was innocent of sin" (2 Cor. 5:21, NEB).

It is quite obviously the case for both the New and Old Testaments that God, and God alone, is completely in charge of the entire universe. "Even sin, death, the devil and hell—works of God's permissive will which are negative in their effects—even these works do not constitute any exception to the general rule. For even in these God's knowing and willing are gracious, even though they take effect as negation (and in that sense are permissive). Even the enemies of God are the servants of God and the servants of His grace" (Barth).[6] Who gives and takes away? God. Who brings the rain upon the just and the unjust? God. Who makes weal and creates woe? God. Who is both "great and terrible"? Who made the entire "created universe . . . the victim of frustration, not by its own choice, but because of him who made it so" (Rom. 8:20, NEB)? Who is the creator of a "design whose purpose is everywhere at work" (Eph. 1:11, NEB)? Who says "to the snow . . . , 'Fall on the earth'; and to the shower and the rain, 'Be strong' "? God, always God: "Whether for correction, or for his land, or for love, he causes it to happen" (Job 37:6, 13):

It is easy enough perhaps for men to say that "God is God" and that "God is love" when things go well and when the skies are clear and blue, furnishing a soft background for the birds to

fly and sing in. But the real test of the Christian's faith comes only in the face of the utmost darkness, the most senseless and apparently meaningless tragedies, the bitterest and most insupportable losses of our lives. Then especially is it important that the Christian be able to say, "God is God" and "God is love"; and thus also be able to say with Job: "The Lord gave, and the Lord has taken away; blessed be the name of the Lord" (1:21). "By believing Him just when to us He seems unjust," was the acme of faith for Luther.[7] Unfortunately, we are not given the choice of accepting God on our terms; if we accept him at all, it must be on *his* terms. Otherwise our faith will be the faith of so many Pollyannas. When Carlyle was told of the Pollyanna who had said, "I accept the universe," his famous comment was: "By God! she'd better."[8]

Ultimately, Christianity has no explanation for the existence of evil. "I guess there are some things we will never know in this lifetime!" says "Pig-Pen"; and this is certainly one of them. If we "know" here, we are presuming to know where the Bible remains stubbornly silent. The problem of evil, said Luther, is "by far the most awesome secret of Divine Majesty."[9] All of our attempts to get God off this hook do him a great disservice; they do no

more than make him look like a tedious old fool who somehow
managed to botch the entire universe, and is now completely at
the mercy of man to bail him out. Take for example the following conversation from *A Day in the Death of Joe Egg*, in which
a clergyman attempts to "console" the mother of a spastic child:

Vicar: My dear, your child's sickness doesn't please God. In fact,
        it completely brings Him down.
Sheila: Why does He allow it then?
Vicar: How can we know?
Sheila: Then how can you know it doesn't please Him?
Vicar: We can't know. Only guess. It may be disease and in-
        firmity are due to the misuse of the freedom He gave us.
        Perhaps they exist as a stimulus to research.
Sheila: Research?
Vicar: Against infirmity and disease.
Sheila: But if He didn't permit disease, we shouldn't need re-
        search.
Vicar: But He does so we do. . . . My dear, the Devil is busy
        day and night. God does His best but we don't Help
        Him much. . . . He's only human. No, He's not, how silly
        of me![10]

Christianity, which works for God's *special* will that exists inside
his *general* will, comes no closer to an "explanation" for evil than
simply pointing to the end of history and saying with Paul: "I
consider that the sufferings of this present time are not worth
comparing with the glory that is to be revealed to us" (Rom.
8:18). We have no other "answer" than this. And this answer is
difficult, *crushingly* difficult, to believe. But this is why Kafka
could say, in what we feel to be a magnificent declaration of faith:

How much more crushing than the most pitiless conviction of
our present sinful state is even the feeblest conviction that there
will be eternal justification for our temporal existence. Only our
strength in supporting this second conviction, which in its purity
completely subsumes the first, is the measure of faith.[11]

And this means the "eternal justification," "the glory that is to
be revealed," for *all* men! Dostoyevsky is another great writer who
has expressed faith in such a final justification for all mankind:

I am convinced that the hurt will form a scar and then become

smooth, that the whole sorrowful comedy of human contradictions
will disappear like a miserable phantom, like a . . . weak, human,
Euclidean understanding the size of an atom, and that finally at
the end of the world, in the moment of eternal harmony, something so precious will appear that it will be adequate for all
hearts, for the stilling of all dissent, for the atonement of all
blood that has been spilt, that will be adequate not only for the
forgiveness, but also for the justification of all that has happened
to man.[12]

For writers such as Golding and Updike, children have often
been used to personify man's original and basic estrangement
from God. In these cases, the children are drawn to resemble
the same mean and vicious little savage we frequently see in our
own back yards, as well as in *Peanuts*. Dostoyevsky and Camus, on
the other hand, are writers who have used children to personify
the problem of evil. For them, the finally innocent suffering of
all mankind becomes excruciatingly clear in the suffering of very
young children, who obviously are completely innocent of the
knowledge of good and evil: "For the hundredth time I repeat,"
pleaded Dostoyevsky, ". . . I've only taken the children, because
in their case what I mean is so unanswerably clear. Listen! If all
must suffer to pay for the eternal harmony, what have children
to do with it, tell me, please? It's beyond all comprehension why
they should suffer, and why they should pay for the harmony."[13]
And we would be foolish to think that the children of *Peanuts*
are not also frequently used as symbols of innocent suffering:

"I'll be glad when I grow up, and can move out of this neighborhood!" says Patty to Charlie Brown. "Everyone around here bores me!" "*Everyone?*" he asks hopefully. "Especially 'everyone'!!!" she answers, glaring at the withered Charlie Brown. Charlie Brown, whose globe-like head the other kids enjoy ridiculing, is a zero, a sort of walking cipher, "a no one" (as he says). He is also "everyone"—the very world itself. For in this suffering little child of the world, we can also see the rest of the world, made "the victim of frustration" by the Creator. But he is even something more than this; because a circle is also a symbol for eternity. Charlie Brown's perfectly round head is also a built-in halo with the face of all mankind on it. In Charlie Brown, Schulz has done in cartoon form exactly what van Gogh wanted to do in his paintings: "In a picture I want to say something comforting, as music is comforting. I want to paint men and women with that something of the eternal which the halo used to symbolize, and which we seek to convey by the actual radiance and vibration of our coloring."[14] God loves you, Charlie Brown! God loves you, Mankind!

The love of God for all mankind is a certainty obtained only through Christ; and "the self-attestation of Jesus Christ is none other than that which is handed down to us by Scripture, and it comes to us in no other way than by the Word of Scripture" (Bonhoeffer).[15] The Church calls the Bible "Holy" because it is, as Luther could say, the cradle in which Christ is laid. "Take Christ from the Scriptures—and what more will you find in them?" asked Luther.[16] The Church points to the Bible not because the Bible itself is God, but because it is the holy ground

one must pass *through* in order to make contact with the single historical "point" that was God—Jesus of Nazareth. For it is only *through* the Bible that we know of Jesus, who alone is the Word behind the Bible's many words.

> And behold, a woman who had suffered from a hemorrhage for twelve years came up behind him and touched the fringe of his garment; for she said to herself, "If I only touch his garment, I shall be made well." Jesus turned, and seeing her he said, "Take heart, daughter; your faith has made you well." And instantly the woman was made well. (Mt. 9:20–22)

The Bible is like the garments worn by Christ. The woman who was healed by touching those garments was not made well by her faith in the garments as such, but only by her faith in the man who wore them. "I do believe that the scriptures are holy," says Schulz, "but I do not believe that the Bible itself is a holy instrument to be worshipped."[17] Schulz knows his Bible. For years he has been the leader of a small group of adult Bible students who have simply made it their practice to carefully go through the Bible from beginning to end, verse by verse, and then to start all over. I happen to know, from embarrassing personal experiences, that confronting Schulz with some bit of biblical wisdom, is about like Violet's confrontation of Linus in the following cartoon:

Schulz has probably best summed up his approach to the Bible by saying, "Let the Bible speak to you!"[18] By this, we are sure that he does not mean to minimize the importance of historical criticism and biblical research, but that he does feel "that intelligent and fruitful discussion of the Bible begins when the judgment as to its human, its historical and psychological character has been made and *put behind* us" (Barth).[19] Kierkegaard was another champion of this more direct approach to the Bible: "Above all things," he said, "read the New Testament without a commentary. Would a lover dream of reading a letter from his beloved with a commentary!"[20]

> Suppose that it was said in the New Testament—we can surely suppose it—that it is God's will that every man should have 100,000 dollars: do you think there would be any question of a commentary? Or would not everyone rather say: "It's easy enough to understand, there's no need of a commentary, let us for heaven's sake keep clear of commentaries—they could perhaps make it doubtful whether it is really as it is written. . . . But what is found in the New Testament (about the narrow way, dying to the world, and so on) is not at all more difficult to understand than this matter of the 100,000 dollars. The difficulty lies elsewhere, in that it does not please us—and so we must have commentaries and professors and commentaries . . . for we really wish it to be doubtful, and we have a tiny hope that the commentaries may make it so.
>
> Then is learning not evil? Is it not an invention of us men because we have no desire to understand what is only too easy to understand—an invention by means of which we are strengthened in . . . shirking and hypocritical evasion?
>
> We have invented learning in order to escape from doing God's will. For we certainly understand this much, that in face of God and his clearly understood will no one dares to say "I do not wish it." . . . So we defend ourselves by having recourse to the pretense that his will is so difficult to understand, and so (and he will surely be flattered and consider it praiseworthy on our part) we study and research and so on: that is to say, we defend ourselves by hiding behind folios. (Kierkegaard)[21]

In studying the Bible, then, a little learning can apparently be a very dangerous thing:

Schulz is traditionally Protestant in his view of the Bible as furnishing a sufficient link with the one historical event of the past that is absolutely crucial to faith—the man Jesus. As Bonhoeffer could say of the writers of the New Testament: "Our forefathers are witnesses of the entry of God into history. It is the fact of the appearance of Jesus Christ nineteen hundred years ago, a fact for which no further proof is to be sought, that directs our gaze back to the ancients."[22] It is for this reason that Schulz's view of *the church* tends to be Bible-centered rather than tradition or church-centered. The church should be as simple as possible, constantly avoiding the temptation to insert itself between the witness of scripture and the individual believer. And because the Bible is *the* sufficient connecting-link with the past, the

church's tendency to cling to all of its ancient and revered traditions and ecclesiastical trappings, only clouds the church's more effective witness to a modern world. For this reason, we can often read "church" for "Pig-pen" in *Peanuts*, and expect the cartoon to make complete theological sense:

Schulz, like Bonhoeffer, apparently believes that "religion is no more than a garment for Christianity"; and therefore, like Bonhoeffer, he would very much like to see a more "religionless Christianity"—that is, a Christianity "interpreted in such a way as not to make religion a pre-condition for faith," as Bonhoeffer put it. Or, as Schulz has said:

> I think our theology right now is so clouded that we are more confused now than the Scribes and the Pharisees ever were . . . . the picking of a certain day as being more holy than another day or saying a certain food is more holy, arguing about whether or not we should speak in tongues, or about whether or not prayer should be in one language or another, or whether something is a sacrament or an ordinance, or whether Jesus is coming or not coming again. We can list them by the dozens. It's frightening isn't it? What have we done to this marvelous faith?[22a]

In his famous treatise entitled *The Babylonian Captivity of the Church*, Martin Luther struck out against the captivity of the church to traditions that only obscured the biblical meaning of faith. Today, the church still largely exists within this captivity—its desire to cling to "religious" incrustations that make it seem to be little more than an interesting cultural fossil, an object of ridicule bogged down in its own ecclesiastical mudhole, a curiosity to be quickly passed by and scarcely to be taken seriously.

"Pig-pen, why are you always so dirty?" Charlie Brown asks him. "When in the world are you going to clean up?" "I have affixed to me the dirt and dust of countless ages," replies Pig-pen. "Who am I to disturb history?" The task of the organized church is always to point beyond herself to her Lord. Whenever the self-important church begins pointing to herself as master rather than servant, she will also begin exercising a kind of spiritual "rebirth control." In such cases, the gospel that points only to Jesus, who is "the bread of life," will be closely controlled by the church in order that the church herself can gain mastery over men. But when the church's brothers are given bread in this manner, fewer and fewer of them will feel like eating:

We are not advocating here the kind of "cheap grace" in which the bread of life is freely distributed to all without cost. This bread will always cost a person no less than his entire life. But this means a life given in obedience to Christ, rather than given to the Church as such. The Church itself is never Christ; but it is that *body* of men and women in whom Christ actually dwells. Thus it is a "mystical body," a body that is finally only known to God. It costs everything to belong to Christ. Unfortunately, it costs next to nothing to belong to a church. On a given Sunday in any large, metropolitan area in America, it would be possible for a person to begin a one-man ecumenical movement by becoming a member in good standing of a dozen churches, all

of different ecclesiastical backgrounds. They all want members, and discriminating questions are seldom asked. Says Bonhoeffer:

> The price we are having to pay to-day in the shape of the collapse of the organized Church is only the inevitable consequence of our policy of making grace available to all at too low a cost. We gave away the word and sacraments wholesale, we baptized, confirmed, and absolved a whole nation unasked and without condition. Our humanitarian sentiment made us give that which was holy to the scornful and unbelieving. We poured forth unending streams of grace. But the call to follow Jesus the narrow way was hardly ever heard.[23]

And what could Bonhoeffer possibly mean by "the collapse of the organized Church"? Perhaps the following cartoon can serve as an example:

Whenever grace becomes cheap or whenever Christianity is understood only as "churchianity," what passes for Christian faith will involve nothing but the most shallow externals. And today, nothing is more common in "Christendom." Here are two examples: the first taken from Denmark in 1850; the second a scene from the United States in 1968:

How a man can receive a particular impression of religion at a certain date and at a certain time is to me an inexplicable form of shallowness: to be full of Christmas joy at Christmas time and not to think of Good Friday, to be profoundly sorrowful on Good Friday and not to think of anything else. That is the best proof that religion is something entirely external to one. (Kierkegaard)[24]

Schulz has described his "ideal" church in this way:

I tend to lean toward the primitive church, toward a basic church which is merely a gathering together of believers. I do not like a highly-organized church. I think that as soon as the congregation reaches a level of one hundred or so people, it is time to build a new church. As soon as the congregation gets to the point where you are not on fairly intimate terms with every other person in that church, then you have become too big, you are no longer a gathering of believers, but have become a theatre where people can attend services. I do not think you can attend a church service. Service is not something which is there to be viewed as if it were a play or movie. You should be part of this because you are part of the people who have gathered together because you belong to God. I certainly believe that a church has to grow and has to be organized in its works to accomplish things, but I am fearful of an overly organized church.[25]

It *would* seem that any organized church should have at least "more than ordinary love" for its own members (2 Cor. 2:4, NEB), as well as more than ordinary love for others. Perhaps, then, Charlie Schulz was also describing his ideal church—and how difficult it is to find—in the following cartoon:

"And I am very fearful," continues Schulz, "of a church which equates itself with Americanism. This is a frightening trend: people who regard Christianity and Americanism as being virtually the same thing."

Occasionally Snoopy's doghouse takes on many of the aspects Schulz likes to look for in a church. The church-as-doghouse was strongly suggested in one series of cartoons when Snoopy let the birds use his doghouse for their meetings—birds that are often seen carrying political placards around Snoopy's doghouse. All of this bore many of the earmarks of the "frightening trend" that Schulz mentioned above.

At first, Snoopy saw nothing wrong in the birds using his doghouse for their meetings: "I think that's rather nice," he said, while listening in from on top. "They always open their meetings with a song!" But later, after he began listening more closely, he became horrified of "their terrible plans" and ran them off with a loud "Rarf!" "Let them find someplace else to hold their

meetings," he said. However, like all of the characters in *Peanuts*, the birds are used to play a variety of roles; and in the following cartoon, their role would seem to be more becoming to the image of the church-as-doghouse:

> Even the sparrow finds a home, and the swallow a nest for herself, where she may lay her young, at thy altars, O Lord of hosts, my King and my God. Blessed are those who dwell in thy house, ever singing thy praise! (Ps. 84:3, 4)

Then of course there was the famous episode when Snoopy's doghouse (Holy Smoke!) burned down. But Snoopy seemed to take the loss in his stride, and a new doghouse was soon built, the second just as amazing as the first. (There was a van Gogh in the first doghouse; in the second there is an Andrew Wyeth.) And, from what Schulz has said about the constant need for the church to renew itself in new little churches, perhaps this is the way it *should* be:

> The church of the Bible is significantly the tabernacle, the portable tent. The moment it becomes a temple it becomes essentially only an object of attack. . . . Undeniably the central interest of both Testaments is not in the building of the church but in its destruction, which is always threatening and even beginning.

In the heavenly Jerusalem of Revelation nothing is more finally significant than the church's complete absence: "And I saw no temple therein." (Barth)[26]

The chief end of dogs is to bite people on the leg, and to sleep in the sun! And "what is the chief end of man?" asks the old catechism: it is "to glorify God, and to enjoy him forever." It is easy enough to see how Snoopy *enjoys* God—he logs a lot of sleep on top of that doghouse. But how does he glorify God—apart from "biting a few appropriate legs"? Do you not see what his nose does, even as he *enjoys?* (Actually, Snoopy is more of a *pointer* than a beagle.) The tabernacle is an old symbol for the church taken over from the Old Testament. And throughout the history of the church's art, the tabernacle has usually been represented as looking very much like the traditional doghouse. (Some of the earliest tabernacles were even drawn with birds perched on their roofs.)[27] And the church-tabernacle *is* a doghouse, actually. It is a gathering of nobodies who at one time or another have found themselves "in the doghouse" with God, only to discover later that they have really found a home, be it ever so humble. "The real Church is the lowliest, the poorest, the meanest, weakest thing that can possibly exist under God's

heaven, gathered as it is around a manger and a cross. . . . And the real Church is also the highest, richest, most radiant and mighty thing under God's heaven" (Barth).[28] But the Church is no refuge from the world. It is rather that ark of safety upon which the Christian is enabled to face the vicissitudes of life:

Unless the Lord builds the house, those who build it labor in vain.

Unless the Lord watches over the city, the watchman stays awake in vain. It is in vain that you rise up early and go late to rest,

eating the bread of anxious toil; for he gives to his beloved sleep. (Ps. 127:1, 2)

All Snoopy's doghouse needs in order to be a first-rate little church is a steeple. But then there is that nose of his. (Or should we call it a "snoople"?)

A great part of the need for an organized church lies in the Christian's need for organization and discipline in his own life—especially in his spiritual life. Man lives not by bread alone, but also needs "every word that proceeds from the mouth of God" (Mt. 4:4). And just as the body must have regular exercise and nourishment and discipline, so must man's spirit. Being largely a "creature of habit," man's evil habits can only be overcome by stronger good habits. "Emotions are not expelled by reason, but only by stronger emotions," said Bonhoeffer.[29] And thus the questions of spiritual discipline—prayer, study, Bible reading, church attendance, etc.—will always be taken seriously by the Christian. Or, as Tillich has said, "It is not unimportant to know the right hour for praying and the right hour for not praying."[30]

"Therefore it is meet that noble minds keep ever with their likes," said Shakespeare. "For who [is] so firm that cannot be seduced?"[31] Throughout the New Testament there is the same recognition for the necessity of community and fellowship in order to withstand the constant temptation to follow other gods. Only Jesus is strong enough to face the devil alone in the wilderness; the disciples are always sent in groups of two or more. The weak will need the strong; the strong will need each other;

and all will need Christ, the source of all strength. "We exhort you, brethren, admonish the idle, encourage the fainthearted, help the weak, be patient with them all" (1 Thess. 5:14). And when a new disciple asks his right-hand man to help him "disciple-ine" his left hand, he needs a right-hand man who is stronger than he is:

Mutual strengthening and support from man-to-man relationships will always be a necessary and important element within the Christian faith. But this relationship should never be expected to have the strength that is available in the direct man-to-God relationship. And the attitude of this relationship is always the attitude of prayer, of total submission and obedience, of being bowed before God in thought, word, and deed. And thus the entire Christian life is one of "praying constantly" (1 Thess. 5:17). Prayer itself, the act of addressing God, is also an act of obedience, and should never be thought of as a means of manipulating God's will into conformity with ours. "Manipulate" means to control with one's hands. And this is exactly the control over God that many would attempt to exercise through "prayer." But God is never in the palm of anyone's hands, even if those hands are folded.

"Prayer does not change God," said Kierkegaard, "but it changes the one who offers it."[32] The childish idea that prayer is a handle by which we can take hold of God and obtain whatever we desire, leads to easy disillusionment with both what we had thought to be God and what we had thought to be prayer.

Prayer is a means by which God takes more direct control over us. It is the act "in which confidence in self gives way before confidence in God" (Barth).[33] The first request of confidence in God is: "*Thy* kingdom come, *Thy* will be done"; the final request of this confidence is: "Nevertheless not my will, but thine, be done" (Lk. 22:42). Still, we are quite free to boldly request anything from God in our prayers: "Have no anxiety, but in everything make your requests known to God in prayer and petition with thanksgiving" (Phil. 4:6, NEB). Thanksgiving comes in knowing that it is God himself who prays in us and through us; and that God is always true to his promise to grant even now life, joy, inward peace to those who are even now true to him. Obedience to God always *immediately* results in this inward gift. Just as soon as our lives are given to him, the burden of these lives is taken from us. It is that simple, and there is no "waiting period." Quite often, the gift of this joy will result in surprising "fringe benefits"; but these secondary benefits are never promised and should never be expected. One should never "hope to make some profit out of the Christian religion. There is real profit, of course, but it comes only to those who live contentedly as God would have them live" (1 Tim. 6:5–6, Phillips). Only "rest," joy, life is promised: "Come to me . . . and I will give you rest." Hence there is only one valid "reason" for loving God: we love the joy that we experience in simply loving him. But is this not to love joy rather than God? Not at all! For this joy *is* God in the person of his Spirit. Therefore to love God primarily for any fringe benefits or for any "presents" that we may receive, is not to love him at all.

It is wrong to think of prayer as an activity to be distinguished from "work." "Prayer is no substitute for work," as the saying goes. But because prayer is also an activity of Christian obedience, it is also an activity of the Christian's "work." This is borne out by the fact that often we do not want to pray as we know we should. Then how is one to know when to stop "praising the Lord" and to start "passing the ammunition"? Again, the answer to this question is a matter for our critical intelligence: "All . . . must aim at one thing: to build up the church." Whatever would seem to do this most effectively, this we should do. Apparently Erasmus knew what he was talking about when he could look at the Christians of his time and say, "Your brother needs your help, but you meanwhile mumble your little prayers to God, pretending not to see your brother's need."[34]

Just as the Christian life is a life lived exclusively "in the name of Jesus," so also is all Christian prayer prayed in the name of Jesus. "To pray 'in the name of Jesus,'" said Kierkegaard, "may perhaps be explained most simply . . . in this way":

> In the first place it means: I myself am nothing, I have no power, nothing to say from myself—but it is the name of the King. . . . I dare not approach God without a mediator; if my prayer is to be heard then it will be in the name of Jesus, what gives it strength is that name. Next . . . [it is] . . . to pray in such a way that it is conformity with the will of Jesus. I cannot pray in the name of Jesus to have my own will; the name of Jesus is not a signature of no importance, but the decisive factor . . . it means to pray in such manner that I dare name Jesus in it, that is to say think of him, think his holy will together with whatever I am praying for. Finally . . . . with prayer in the name of Jesus, Jesus assumes the responsibility and all the consequences, he steps forward for us, steps into the place of the person praying.[35]

From the Christian perspective, prayer in any *other* name—even "in the name of all the gods at once," as pagan Rome used to pray—is of no use. It is like howling words to the wind, or being plugged into the wrong power source.

The psychiatrist is one of the great high priests of modern civilization. "The Doctor is IN" largely because our troubled age knows of nowhere else to go. But what is a psychiatrist? Often he can be little more than a professional friend: he will patiently listen to all our problems, give us encouragement, and try his best to understand—all for a fee. But even in doing this the psychiatrist meets a basic human need—the simple need we all have to *talk* to someone who we feel will understand our problems and will have our best interests at heart. Prayer also meets this need; and finally it is *only* prayer that can meet it adequately. "The counselor and psychiatrist can *help*," says Tillich,

> he can liberate us, but can he make us whole? . . . They cannot because they themselves need wholeness and are longing for salvation. Who heals the healer? There is no answer to this in the old reality. Everybody and every institution are infected, the healer and the healed. Only a new reality can make us whole, breaking into the old one, reconciling it with itself. It is the humanly incredible, ecstatic, often defeated, but never conquered faith of Christianity that this new reality . . . has appeared in fullness and power in Jesus, the Christ, the Healer and Savior. This is said of Him because He alone . . . is the reality of reconciliation, because in Him a new reality has come upon us in which we and our whole existence are accepted and reunited.[36]

Meanwhile, the old reality does the best it can:

The world of *Peanuts* is a world of sighs, "sighs too deep for words"—which is another way of saying that *Peanuts* is a world of prayer. In a college Commencement Day address that Schulz delivered,[37] he began by quoting the following New Testament text from Paul's letter to the Romans: "Likewise the Spirit helps us in our weakness; for we do not know how to pray as we ought, but the Spirit himself intercedes for us with sighs too deep for words" (Rom. 8:26). Schulz concluded his remarks by saying:

No matter what I consider to say, I come back to a passage in the New Testament that contains a truth in which I firmly believe. In the last chapter of the Gospel of John we find Peter and Thomas, Nathaniel, the sons of Zebedee and two others who are unnamed turning back to their old profession of fishing. . . .

And so as we move over the shore of the Sea of Tiberias we find Peter and his friends returning at dawn from fishing. A figure is standing on shore by a small charcoal fire. They gather round this fire, none daring to speak even though they know it is Jesus who has been waiting for them. Jesus turns to Peter, and asks, "Simon, son of John, do you love me more than these?" "Yes, Lord; you know that I love you." Jesus said to him, "Feed my lambs." Then a second time Jesus asks, "Simon, son of John,

do you love me?" and Peter answers, "Yes, Lord; you know that I love you." Jesus said, "Tend my sheep." Then a third time Jesus turns to Peter and asks, "Simon, son of John, do you love me?"

Imagine the flood of words that could have sprung from Peter's mouth at this time. The explanations, the apologies, the tears of anguish, but Peter has a better answer. It is the answer of supreme faith. "Lord, you know everything; you know that I love you."

When the excitement of these days passes away, and when some of the visions begin to grow a little dim; when it becomes impossible to put into words the prayer you want to speak, then we must be able to lift our heads up, and say with all faith as Peter did, "Lord, you know that I love you."

AMEN.

Notes

PREFACE

1. Søren Kierkegaard, *For Self-Examination and Judge for Yourselves!*, tr. Walter Lowrie (Princeton: Princeton University Press, 1944), p. 116.
2. Albert Camus, *Resistance, Rebellion, and Death*, tr. Justin O'Brien (New York: Alfred A. Knopf, 1961), p. 239.

1. OF PARABLES AND PEANUTS

1. Dietrich Bonhoeffer, *Letters and Papers from Prison*, rev. ed. Eberhard Bethge, tr. Reginald Fuller (New York: The Macmillan Co., 1967), p. 153.
2. Pierre Berton, *The Comfortable Pew* (Philadelphia: J. B. Lippincott Co., 1965), p. 99.
3. Charles Schulz, "Happiness Is Lots of Assignments," *Writers Yearbook*, 1965 ed., p. 46.
4. Marshall McLuhan and Quentin Fiore, *The Medium Is the Massage* (New York: Bantam Books, 1967), p. 10.
5. Lewis Carroll, *Alice's Adventures in Wonderland and Through the Looking-Glass* (New York: Collier Books, 1962), p. 21.
6. *Karl Barth's Table Talk*, ed. John D. Godsey (Richmond, Va.: John Knox Press, 1962), p. 19.
7. Herman Melville, *Moby Dick* (New York: The Modern Library, 1950), p. 29.
8. Quoted in *The World Treasure of Religious Quotations*, ed. Ralph L. Woods (New York: Hawthorn Books, 1966), p. 385.
9. Edward Albee, *The American Dream and the Zoo Story* (New York: Signet Books, 1963), p. 30.
10. Nikos Kazantzakis, *Zorba the Greek* (New York: Ballantine Books, 1952), p. 119.
11. Kierkegaard, *The Point of View* (London: Oxford University Press, 1950), p. 25.
12. Dietrich Bonhoeffer, *The Cost of Discipleship*, rev. ed. (New York: The Macmillan Co., 1963), pp. 206 ff.
13. C. H. Dodd, *The Parables of the Kingdom* (New York: Charles Scribner's Sons, 1961), p. 1.

14. "Religion and the Mission of the Artist," in *The New Orpheus*, ed. Nathan A. Scott, Jr. (New York: Sheed and Ward, 1964), p. 63.

15. Quoted in Roger Hazelton, *A Theological Approach to Art* (Nashville: Abingdon Press, 1967), p. 16.

16. Cf. Eta Linnemann, *Jesus of the Parables* (New York: Harper & Row, 1966), p. 47; Joachim Jeremias, *Rediscovering the Parables* (New York: Charles Scribner's Sons, 1966), p. 115.

17. Kierkegaard, *The Point of View*, op. cit., pp. 24–25.

18. *The Journals of Søren Kierkegaard*, ed. and tr. Alexander Dru (London: Oxford University Press, 1938), p. 259.

19. "Ingenue Visits Peanuts," *Ingenue* (Aug. 1965), p. 82.

20. "It's Your Life Charlie Schulz" by Jaroslav Vajda, *This Day* (Oct. 1964), p. 12.

21. "A Conversation with Charles Schulz," *Psychology Today*, Vol. 1, No. 8 (Jan. 1968), p. 21.

22. Arthur Miller, *Death of a Salesman* (New York: Viking Compass Edition, 1958), p. 56.

23. "Knowing You Are Not Alone," *Decision*, Vol. IV (Sept. 1963), p. 9.

24. Karl Barth, *The Word of God and the Word of Man* (New York: Harper & Brothers, 1957), p. 306.

25. *Pascal's Pensées*, tr. W. F. Trotter (New York: E. P. Dutton & Co., 1958), Fragment 295, p. 85.

26. Quoted in *Karl Barth: How I Changed My Mind*, ed. John D. Godsey (Richmond, Va.: John Knox Press, 1966), p. 12.

27. Kierkegaard, *Attack upon Christendom*, tr. Walter Lowrie (Boston: The Beacon Press, 1956), p. 2.

28. "Knowing You Are Not Alone," op. cit., p. 8.

29. Charles Schulz, "A Visit with Charles Schulz," *Christian Herald*, Vol. 90, No. 9 (Sept. 1967), p. 62.

30. Charles Schulz, "Happiness Is to Dance with Snoopy and Talk with His Creator," *Youth*, Vol. 19, No. 6 (Mar. 1968), p. 10.

31. "Knowing You Are Not Alone," op. cit., p. 9.

32. Karl Barth, *The Humanity of God*, tr. J. N. Thomas and Thomas Wieser (Richmond, Va: John Knox Press, 1960), p. 92.

33. Theodore A. Gill, "From the President's Desk," *The San Francisco Theological Seminary Chimes*, Vol. XI, No. 1 (Spring 1964), p. 2.

34. *Rediscovering the Parables*, op. cit., p. 89.

35. *The Comfortable Pew*, op. cit., p. 99.

36. Charles Schulz, "Meet the Creator of Peanuts," *Christian Business Men's Committee Contact*, Vol. 25, No. 2 (Feb. 1967), p. 5.

2. INTERPRETING THE SIGNS OF THE TIMES

1. Dorothy Sayers, *Introductory Papers on Dante* (New York: Harper & Brothers, 1954), p. 19.

2. Albert Camus, *The Myth of Sisyphus*, tr. Justin O'Brien (New York: Vintage Books, 1955), pp. 89, 8.

3. Kierkegaard, *Purity of Heart*, rev. ed., tr. Douglas V. Steere (New York: Harper & Brothers, 1948), pp. 27–28.
4. Nathaniel Hawthorne, *The Marble Faun* (New York: The New American Library, 1961), p. 273.
5. "Religion and Literature," in *Selected Essays of T. S. Eliot* (New York: Harcourt, Brace and Company, 1950), p. 354.
6. Charles Schulz, "It's Your Life, Charlie Schulz," *This Day*, Oct. 1964, p. 12.
7. Ingmar Bergman, "Sex and the Swedish Master," *Time*, Nov. 15, 1963, p. 72.
8. Denis De Rougemont, *The Christian Opportunity*, tr. Donald Lehmkuhl (New York: Holt, Rinehart and Winston, 1963), p. 75.
9. Charles Schulz, "Who Is Charlie Brown?" *School Briefs*, Vol. 31, No. 2 (Glenview, Ill.: Scott, Foresman and Co., 1966), p. 1.
10. "Religion and Literature," *op. cit.*, p. 350.
11. Kazantzakis, *op. cit.*, p. 155.
12. *Hamlet*, III, iv.
13. "Knowing You Are Not Alone," *op. cit.*, p. 9.
14. Kenneth Hamilton, *In Search of Contemporary Man* (Grand Rapids: William B. Eerdman's Publishing Co., 1967), p. 15.
15. Melville, *op. cit.*, p. 162.
16. John Dillenberger and Claude Welch, *Protestant Christianity* (New York: Charles Scribner's Sons, 1954), p. 48.
17. Karl Barth, *The Epistle to the Romans*, tr. Edwyn C. Hoskyns (London: Oxford University Press, 1933), p. 96.
18. *The Complete Poetry and Selected Prose of John Donne*, ed. Charles M. Coffin (New York: Modern Library, 1952), p. 559.
19. Quoted in W. K. Wimsatt, *The Verbal Icon* (Lexington: University of Kentucky Press, 1967), p. 7.
20. Charles Schulz, "Good Grief," *Time*, Vol. 85, No. 15 (Apr. 9, 1965), p. 81.
21. Charles Schulz, "A Redbook Dialogue: Jack Lemmon and Charles Schulz," *Redbook*, Vol. 130, No. 2 (Dec. 1967), p. 50.
22. *The Journals*, *op. cit.*, p. 80.
23. *Introductory Papers on Dante*, *op. cit.*, p. 19.
24. W. K. Wimsatt, *op. cit.*, p. 5.
25. Friedrich Nietzsche, *The Use and Abuse of History*, tr. Adrian Collins (New York: The Liberal Arts Press, 1957), p. 33.
26. Karl Barth, *The Humanity of God*, *op. cit.*, p. 18.
27. Walter R. Bowie, *Interpreter's Bible* (Nashville: Abingdon Press, 1951), p. 173.
28. "Good Grief," *op. cit.*, p. 80.
29. "Happiness Is Lots of Assignments," *op. cit.*, p. 46.
30. Charles Schulz, "Cartooning," unpublished mimeographed article, 1967, pp. 1, 2.
31. "A Visit with Charles Schulz," *op. cit.*, pp. 59, 61.

3. SAVIOR?!—WHO NEEDS A SAVIOR?

1. Charles Schulz, tape-recorded conversation at University of the Pacific, Stockton, Calif., May 16, 1967.
2. *The Book of Common Prayer* (New York: The Church Pension Fund of the Protestant Episcopal Church in the United States of America, 1945), p. 604.
3. Dorothy Sayers, *Creed or Chaos* (New York: Harcourt, Brace and Company, 1949), p. 38.
4. *Einstein on Peace*, ed. Otto Nathan and Heinz Norden (New York: Simon and Schuster, 1960), 562.
5. *Mark Twain Tonight!* ed. Hal Holbrook (New York: Pyramid Books, 1959), p. 181.
6. Quoted in *The World Treasury of Religious Quotations, op. cit.*, p. 588.
7. *Martin Luther: Selections from His Writings*, ed. John Dillenberger (New York: Garden City, 1961), p. 203.
8. *Karl Barth's Table Talk, op. cit.*, p. 39.
9. Dietrich Bonhoeffer, *Ethics*, tr. Neville Horton Smith (New York: The Macmillan Co., 1965; London: Collins, 1964), p. 20 (Collins ed. cited).
10. Quoted in *Existentialism from Dostoevsky to Sartre*, ed. Walter Kaufmann (New York: Meridian Books, 1957), p. 74.
11. Kazantzakis, *op. cit.*, pp. 173–174.
12. W. J. McGucken, *Catholic Education* (New York: American Press, 1953), p. 19.
13. Taylor Caldwell, "The Novelist and the Problem of Evil," 1965 *Writer's Yearbook, op. cit.*, p. 74.
14. Kierkegaard, *Concluding Unscientific Postscript*, tr. D. F. Swenson and Walter Lowrie (Princeton: Princeton University Press, 1944), p. 523.
15. Quoted in *Decision, op. cit.*, p. 13.
16. *Pascal's Pensées, op. cit.*, Fragment 533, p. 144.
17. Karl Barth, *The Word of God and the Word of Man, op. cit.*, p. 54.
18. Quoted in "A Leaf, a Lemon Drop, a Cartoon Is Born," *Life*, Vol. 62, No. 11 (Mar. 17, 1967), p. 80.
19. *Basic Writings of Saint Augustine*, ed. W. H. Oates (New York: Random House, 1948), Vol. I, p. 3.
20. Camus, *The Myth of Sisyphus, op. cit.*, p. 4.
21. *Pascal's Pensées, op. cit.*, Fragment 194, p. 55.
22. "Good Grief," *op. cit.*, p. 81.
23. William Golding, *Lord of the Flies* (New York: Capricorn Books, 1959), p. 133.
24. "A Redbook Dialogue: Jack Lemmon and Charles Schulz," *op. cit.*, p. 135.
25. Karl Barth, *Deliverance to the Captives*, tr. Marguerite Wieser (New York: Harper & Brothers, 1961), p. 146.
26. Dietrich Bonhoeffer, *Letters and Papers from Prison, op. cit.* (1st ed.), p. 17.

27. Dillenberger and Welch, *Protestant Christianity,* op. cit., p. 29.

28. Donne, op. cit., p. 477.

29. Karl Barth, *Against the Stream,* tr. Ronald Gregor Smith (New York: Philosophical Library, 1954), p. 57.

30. *Pascal's Pensées,* op. cit., Fragment 453, p. 127.

31. C. S. Lewis, *The Four Loves* (New York: Harcourt, Brace & World, Inc., 1960), p. 180.

32. Bonhoeffer, *Ethics,* op. cit., pp. 73–74.

33. "America's Four Conspiracies," in *Religion in America,* ed. John Cogley (New York: Meridian Books, Inc., 1958), p. 24.

34. T. S. Eliot, *The Complete Poems and Plays* (New York: Harcourt, Brace & Co., 1952), p. 184.

35. "Classical Protestantism," in *Patterns of Faith in America Today* (New York: Harper & Brothers, 1957), p. 31.

36. Harry Emerson Fosdick, *Christianity and Progress* (New York: Fleming H. Revell Co., 1922), p. 175.

37. Bonhoeffer, *Cost of Discipleship,* op. cit., p. 189.

38. *Pascal's Pensées,* op. cit., Fragment 441, p. 124.

39. Bonhoeffer, *Letters and Papers from Prison,* op. cit., p. 103.

40. Bonhoeffer, *The Cost of Discipleship,* op. cit., p. 324.

41. Quoted in *The World Treasury of Religious Quotations,* op. cit., p. 296.

42. Kierkegaard, *The Last Years,* ed. and tr. Ronald Gregor Smith (New York: Harper & Row, 1965), p. 101.

4. WHERE YOUR BLANKET IS, THERE WILL YOUR HEART BE ALSO

1. Bonhoeffer, *Ethics,* op. cit., p. 113.

2. C. S. Lewis, *Mere Christianity* (New York: The Macmillan Co., 1960), p. 54.

3. *Pascal's Pensées,* op. cit., Fragment 425, p. 113.

4. Barth, *Deliverance to the Captives,* op. cit., p. 90.

5. T. S. Eliot, *The Complete Poems and Plays,* op. cit., p. 365.

6. Kierkegaard, *Works of Love,* tr. Howard and Edna Hong (New York: Harper & Brothers, 1962), p. 39.

7. *Pascal's Pensées,* op. cit., Fragment 81, p. 24.

8. Bonhoeffer, *The Cost of Discipleship,* op. cit., p. 193.

9. *Decision,* op. cit., p. 9.

10. Bonhoeffer, *The Cost of Discipleship,* op. cit., p. 196.

11. Melville, *Moby Dick,* op. cit., p. 4.

12. Franz Kafka, *The Great Wall of China* (New York: Schocken Books, 1948), p. 283.

13. Barth, *The Epistle to the Romans,* op. cit., p. 52.

14. "A Conversation with Charles Schulz," op. cit., p. 66.

15. Francis Thompson, "The Hound of Heaven," *Modern American Poetry—Modern British Poetry* (New York: Harcourt, Brace and Co., 1950), p. 88.

16. Kierkegaard, *The Journals,* op. cit., p. 51.

17. T. S. Eliot, *The Complete Poems and Plays*, op. cit, p. 363.

5. THE HEART IS A SLAVE

1. *Einstein on Peace*, op. cit., p. 556.
2. Barth, *The Word of God and the Word of Man*, op. cit., p. 58.
3. Nathaniel Hawthorne, *The House of Seven Gables* (New York: Washington Square Press, Inc., 1940), p. 191.
4. Bonhoeffer, *The Cost of Discipleship*, op. cit., p. 193.
5. Kazantzakis, op. cit., p. 334.
6. Quoted in *The Climate of Faith in Modern Literature*, ed. Nathan A. Scott, Jr. (New York: The Seabury Press, 1964), p. 77.
7. Albert Camus, *The Myth of Sisyphus*, op. cit., p. 4.
8. *Einstein on Peace*, op. cit., p. 568
9. Quoted in Antonina Vallentin, *The Drama of Albert Einstein*, tr. Moura Budberg (New York: Doubleday & Co., 1954), pp. 290, 291.
10. Herbert Butterfield, *Christianity and History* (New York: Charles Scribner's Sons, 1950), p. 47.
11. "A Conversation with Charles Schulz," op. cit., p. 13.
12. Donne, op. cit., p. 562
13. Kierkegaard, *The Sickness unto Death* (Princeton: Princeton University Press, 1951), p. 92.
14. T. S. Eliot, *The Complete Poems and Plays*, op. cit., p. 237.
15. David E. Roberts, *Psychotherapy and a Christian View of Man* (New York: Charles Scribner's Sons, 1950), p. 108.
16. *Hamlet*, IV, iv.
17. Albert Camus, *The Fall*, tr. Justin O'Brien (New York: Alfred A. Knopf, 1958), p. 144.
18. Bonhoeffer, *The Cost of Discipleship*, op. cit., p. 214.
19. Karl Barth, *Deliverance to the Captives*, op. cit., p. 138.
20. Reginald H. Fuller, *The New Testament in Current Study* (New York: Charles Scribner's Sons, 1962), p. 9.
21. Karl Barth, *Community, State and Church*, ed. Will Herberg (New York: Anchor Books, 1960), p. 76.
22. *The Book of Common Prayer*, op. cit., p. 580.
23. *Pascal's Pensées*, op. cit., Fragment 508, p. 139.
24. Paul Tillich, *The New Being* (New York: Charles Scribner's Sons, 1955), p. 38.
25. T. S. Eliot, *Selected Essays*, op. cit., p. 443.

6. THE BROKEN HEART

1. Bonhoeffer, *The Cost of Discipleship*, op. cit., p. 99.
2. Kierkegaard, *The Journals*, op. cit., p. 413
3. *Pascal's Pensées*, op. cit., Fragment 546, p. 146.
4. Donne, op. cit., p. 252.
5. Fyodor Dostoyevsky, *The Brothers Karamazov*, tr. Constance Garnett (New York: The Modern Library, 1950), p. 315.

6. Kafka, *The Great Wall of China*, op. cit., p. 286.
7. Kierkegaard, *The Journals*, op. cit., p. 21
8. Oscar Wilde, "The Ballad of Reading Gaol," quoted in *The Literature of England* (Chicago: Scott, Foresman & Co., 1948), p. 891.
9. Kierkegaard, *The Last Years*, op. cit., p. 166.
10. Barth, *The Word of God and the Word of Man*, op. cit., p. 80.
11. "A Conversation with Charles Schulz," op. cit., p. 19.
12. Kierkegaard, *The Last Years*, op. cit., p. 357.
13. Kierkegaard, *The Sickness unto Death*, op. cit., p. 56.
14. Barth, *Deliverance to the Captives*, op. cit., p. 91.
15. Quoted in *The Modern Tradition: Backgrounds of Modern Literature* (New York: Oxford University Press, 1965), p. 838.
16. Lewis Mumford, *Saturday Review of Literature*, vol. xxxi, No. 26 (June 26, 1948), p. 29.
17. Camus, *The Myth of Sisyphus*, op. cit., p. 39.
18. J. B. Phillips, *New Testament Christianity* (New York: The Macmillan Co., 1956), p. 103.
19. William Barrett, *Irrational Man* (New York: Garden City, 1958), p. 226.
20. *Macbeth*, V, i.
21. Kafka, *The Great Wall of China*, op. cit., p. 287.
22. *The Martin Luther Christmas Book*, tr. Roland H. Bainton (Philadelphia: Muhlenberg Press, 1956), p. 47.
23. T. S. Eliot, *The Complete Poems and Plays*, op. cit., p. 342.
24. "A Visit with Charles Schulz," op. cit., p. 66.
25. "A Conversation with Charles Schulz," op. cit., p. 66.
26. Julian N. Hartt, *Toward a Theology of Evangelism* (Nashville: Abingdon Press, 1955), p. 15.
27. Samuel Beckett, *Endgame* (New York: Grove Press, Inc., 1958), p. 18.
28. "Good Grief," op. cit., p. 19.
29. *Pascal's Pensées*, op. cit.
30. Kazantzakis, op. cit., p. 258.
31. "Who Is Charlie Brown?" op. cit., p. 2.
32. Quoted in *Dostoevsky*, Edward Thurneysen, tr. Keith R. Crim (Richmond, Va.: John Knox Press, 1964), p. 13.
33. Kierkegaard, *The Sickness unto Death*, op. cit., pp. 13–14.
34. Kafka, *The Great Wall of China*, op. cit., p. 283.

7. GOOD NEWS OF A GREAT JOY WHICH WILL COME TO ALL THE PEOPLE

1. *Karl Barth's Table Talk*, op. cit., p. 15.
2. Bonhoeffer, *Ethics*, op. cit., p. 206.
3. Dostoyevsky, *The Brothers Karamazov*, op. cit., p. 940.
4. Kierkegaard, *Concluding Unscientific Postscript*, op. cit., p. 323.

5. Karl Barth, *Church Dogmatics*, Vol. II/2, Authorised Translation (Edinburgh: T. & T. Clark, 1957), p. 13.

6. Barth, *Deliverance to the Captives*, op. cit., p. 87.

7. Melville, *Moby Dick*, op. cit., p. 513.

8. Dostoyevsky, *The Brothers Karamazov*, op. cit., pp. 57–58.

9. John Updike, *Pigeon Feathers and Other Stories* (Greenwich, Conn.: Fawcett Publications, Inc., 1963), pp. 94–105.

10. *Martin Luther: Selections from His Writings*, op. cit., p. 170.

11. Emil Brunner, *The Christian Doctrine of God*, tr. Olive Wyon (London: Lutterworth Press, 1949), p. 351.

12. Emil Brunner, *Our Faith*, tr. J. W. Rilling (London: SCM Press, 1949), p. 121.

13. Bonhoeffer, *Letters and Papers from Prison*, op. cit., p. 103.

14. *Hamlet*, III, i.

15. *Macbeth*, V, v.

16. Nicolas Berdyaev, *The Destiny of Man*, tr. Natalie Duddington (London: Geoffrey Bles, 1954), p. 268.

17. *What Luther Says: An Anthology*, ed. Ewald M. Plass, Vol. III (St. Louis: Concordia Publishing House, 1959), p. 4074.

18. *Ibid.*, p. 4263.

19. Quoted in Georges Casalis, *Portrait of Karl Barth*, tr. Robert McAfee Brown (New York: Doubleday & Co., 1964), p. xxx.

20. *Mark Twain Tonight!*, op. cit., p. 118.

21. Camus, *The Myth of Sisyphus*, op. cit., p. 91.

22. Donne, op. cit., p. 481.

23. Barth, *The Humanity of God*, op. cit., pp. 58–59.

24. "A Visit with Charles Schulz," op. cit., p. 60.

25. Barth, *Church Dogmatics*, Vol. II/2, op. cit., p. 315.

26. Karl Barth, *Evangelical Theology*, tr. Grover Foley (New York: Holt, Rinehart and Winston, 1963), p. 136.

27. Karl Barth, *Call for God*, tr. A. T. Mackay (New York: Harper & Row, 1967), p. 92.

28. Barth, *Deliverance to the Captives*, op. cit., p. 150.

29. Bonhoeffer, *Ethics*, op. cit., p. 198.

30. Casalis, *Portrait of Karl Barth*, op. cit., pp. xxx–xxxi.

8. JESUS—THE DOG GOD

1. *The Prayers of Kierkegaard*, ed. Perry D. LeFevre (Chicago: University of Chicago Press, 1956), p. 100.

2. "Happiness Is to Dance with Snoopy and Talk with His Creator," op. cit., p. 10.

3. "Conversations with Kafka," Gustav Janouch, *The Partisan Review Anthology*, ed. William Phillips and Phillip Rahu (New York: Holt, Rinehart and Winston, 1962), p. 131.

4. Robert McAfee Brown, "Laughter's Not a Sin," *The New York Times Book Review*, Vol. LXX, No. 6 (Feb. 7, 1965), p. 6.
5. Bonhoeffer, *Ethics*, op. cit., pp. 108–109.
6. *A Compend of Luther's Theology*, ed. Hugh Thomson Kerr, Jr. (Philadelphia: The Westminster Press, 1943), p. 49.
7. Harvey Cox, *The Secular City* (New York: The Macmillan Co., 1965), p. 131.
8. Bonhoeffer, *Ethics*, op. cit., p. 71.
9. Dietrich Bonhoeffer, *Christ the Center*, tr. John Bowden (New York: Harper & Row, Publishers, 1966), p. 36.
10. Kafka, *The Great Wall of China*, op. cit., p. 298.
11. Kierkegaard, *Training in Christianity*, tr. Walter Lowrie (Princeton: Princeton University Press, 1944), p. 25.
12. *Ibid.*, p. 41.
13. Bonhoeffer, *Christ the Center*, op. cit., p. 36.
14. Kierkegaard, *Training in Christianity*, op. cit., p. 136.
15. Bonhoeffer, *Letters and Papers from Prison*, op. cit., p. 219.
16. Donne, op. cit., p. 478.
17. Kierkegaard, *Training in Christianity*, op. cit., p. 52.
18. "Foreword," tr. from the German by Dietlef Schwanke, from Robert L. Short, *Ein Kleines Volk Gottes Die Peanuts* (Basel: Friedrich Reinhardt Verlag, 1965), p. 10.
19. Kierkegaard, *Training in Christianity*, op. cit., pp. 46, 47.
20. *Ibid.*, pp. 53–54.
21. "Lord of the Dance" by S. Carter, quoted in *Risk*, Vol. II, No. 3, 1966.
22. Quoted in Bonhoeffer, *The Cost of Discipleship*, op. cit., p. 277.
23. Kierkegaard, *Training in Christianity*, op. cit., p. 127.
24. Kierkegaard, *Attack on Christendom*, op. cit., p. 197.
25. Kierkegaard, *Training in Christianity*, op. cit., p. 14.
26. "The Backlash from Q-29BW," *Time*, Vol. 86, No. 22 (Nov. 26, 1965), p. 28.
27. "Knowing You Are Not Alone," op. cit., p. 9.
28. *Pascal's Pensées*, op. cit., Fragment 547, p. 147.
29. *Interpreter's Bible*, op. cit., Vol. VII, p. 451.
30. Quoted in *The Christian Century*, Vol. LXXXII, No. 6 (Feb. 10, 1965), p. 177.
31. Barth, *Church Dogmatics*, Vol. I, Part 1, op. cit., p. 134.
32. Bonhoeffer, *Letters and Papers from Prison*, op. cit., p. 95.
33. Donne, op. cit., p. 478.
34. Quoted in "Faith in Search of Understanding," John Updike, *The New Yorker*, Vol. XXXIX, No. 34 (Oct. 12, 1963), p. 203.
35. T. S. Eliot, *The Complete Poems and Plays*, op. cit., p. 119.
36. Barth, *The Epistle to the Romans*, op. cit., p. 26.
37. Bonhoeffer, *Ethics*, op. cit., p. 69.
38. Bonhoeffer, *Christ the Center*, op. cit., p. 83–84.

39. Barth, *Evangelical Theology*, op. cit., p. 23.
40. Kierkegaard, *The Last Years*, op. cit., p. 154.
41. Karl Barth, "No!" in *Natural Theology*, with Emil Brunner, tr. Peter Fraenkel (London: The Centenary Press, 1946), p. 67.
42. "Happiness Is to Dance with Snoopy and Talk with His Creator," op. cit., p. 6.
43. Dorothy Sayers, *Creed or Chaos*, op. cit., pp. 3–4.
44. Bonhoeffer, *Christ the Center*, op. cit., p. 75.
45. *Pascal's Pensées*, op. cit., Fragments 277, 278, p. 78.
46. Bonhoeffer, *The Cost of Discipleship*, op. cit., p. 266.
47. Kierkegaard, *Philosophical Fragments*, tr. David F. Swenson (Princeton: Princeton University Press, 1936), p. 87.
48. Quoted in Philip S. Watson, *Let God Be God* (Philadelphia: Fortress Press, 1947), p. 102.
49. *Ibid.*, p. 103.
50. *Van Gogh: A Self-Portrait*, ed. W. H. Auden (Greenwich, Conn.: New York Graphic Society, 1961), p. 302.
51. Kierkegaard, *Training in Christianity*, op. cit., p. 136.
52. *The Basic Writings of Saint Augustine*, op. cit., Vol. I, pp. 105–106.

9. YOU SHALL GOD YOUR NEIGHBOR AS YOURSELF

1. Dostoyevsky, *The Brothers Karamazov*, op. cit., p. 721.
2. Dietrich Bonhoeffer, *No Rusty Swords*, tr. Edwin H. Robertson and John Bowden (New York: Harper & Row, 1965), p. 166.
3. Kierkegaard, *The Journals*, op. cit., p. 317.
4. Butterfield, *Christianity and History*, op. cit., p. 146.
5. Bonhoeffer, *Ethics*, op. cit., p. 194.
6. Dostoyevsky, *The Brothers Karamazov*, op. cit., p. 62.
7. Bonhoeffer, *Ethics*, op. cit., pp. 50–52.
8. Bonhoeffer, *The Cost of Discipleship*, op. cit., p. 290.
9. Bonhoeffer, *Ethics*, op. cit., p. 205.
10. Barth, *Evangelical Theology*, op. cit., p. 111.
11. J. D. Salinger, *Franny and Zooey* (New York: Bantam Books, 1955), p. 198.
12. *The Martin Luther Christmas Book*, op. cit., p. 38.
13. Quoted in *The Encyclopedia of Religious Quotations* (Westwood, N.J.: Fleming H. Revell Co., 1965), p. 227.
14. "Love Me with All Your Heart," Peer International Corp. (BMI).
15. Bonhoeffer, *Letters and Papers from Prison*, op. cit., p. 103.
16. Barth, *The Humanity of God*, op. cit., p. 82.
17. Barth, *Community, State and Church*, op. cit., pp. 82–84.
18. Bonhoeffer, *Ethics*, op. cit., p. 82.
19. Bonhoeffer, *The Cost of Discipleship*, op. cit., p. 109.
20. G. K. Chesterton, *Tremendous Trifles* (New York: Dodd, Mead & Co., 1909), p. 168.

21. Barth, *The Faith of the Church*, tr. Gabriel Vahanian (New York: Meridian Books, Inc., 1958), p. 32.
22. Kierkegaard, *Training in Christianity*, op. cit., p. 271.
23. Bonhoeffer, *Letters and Papers from Prison*, op. cit., p. 196.
24. Barth, "No!", op. cit., p. 118.
25. Bonhoeffer, *Ethics*, op. cit., p. 137.
26. Bonhoeffer, *The Cost of Discipleship*, op. cit., p. 158.
27. Kierkegaard, *The Journals*, op. cit., p. 213.
28. "Happiness Is to Dance with Snoopy and Talk with His Creator," op. cit., p. 8.
29. Henry David Thoreau, *Walden* (New York: The New American Library, 1953), p. 56.
30. Eliot, *Selected Essays*, op. cit., p. 378.
31. Kierkegaard, *Training in Christianity*, op. cit., p. 249.

10. BLESSED ARE THE POOR IN SPIRIT

1. Bonhoeffer, *The Cost of Discipleship*, op. cit., p. 33.
2. "A Visit with Charles Schulz," op. cit., p. 66.
3. Melville, op. cit., p. 48.
4. Barth, *The Word of God and the Word of Man*, op. cit., p. 273.
5. Kierkegaard, *The Journals*, op. cit., p. 355.
6. *Ibid.*, p. 200.
7. Fuller, op. cit., p. 10.
8. *Ibid.*, p. 21.
9. Bonhoeffer, *Ethics*, op. cit., p. 136.
10. Martin Luther, *Commentary on Galatians*, tr. Erasmus Middleton (London: William Teggo Co., 1850), p. 244.
11. *The Martin Luther Christmas Book*, op. cit., p. 53.
12. Quoted in *The World Treasury of Religious Quotations*, op. cit., p. 561.
13. Kierkegaard, *The Last Years*, op. cit., p. 246.
14. "Knowing You Are Not Alone," op. cit., p. 9.
15. Tillich, *The New Being*, op. cit., p. 149.
16. "Choose Something Like a Star" from *Complete Poems of Robert Frost* (New York: Holt, Rinehart and Winston, Inc., 1945), p. 575.
17. Barth, *Evangelical Theology*, op. cit., p. 49.
18. Rudolf Bultmann, quoted in *The Honest to God Debate*, ed. D. L. Edwards (Philadelphia: The Westminster Press, 1963), p. 138.
19. *Van Gogh: A Self-Portrait*, op. cit., p. 184.
20. Bonhoeffer, *Christ the Center*, op. cit., p. 115.
21. Kierkegaard, *The Journals*, op. cit., p. 314.

11. JUST WHO'S IN CHARGE HERE?

1. Bonhoeffer, *The Cost of Discipleship*, op. cit., p. 93.
2. "A Visit with Charles Schulz," op. cit., p. 65.
3. Barth, *Church Dogmatics*, IV/1, p. 41.
4. *Pascal's Pensées*, op. cit., Fragment 518, p. 141.

5. *A Compend of Luther's Theology,* op. cit., p. 90.

6. "Happiness Is to Dance with Snoopy and Talk with His Creator," op. cit., p. 14.

7. Albert Einstein, *Ideas and Opinions* (New York: Crown Publishers, 1954), p. 8.

8. J. D. Salinger, *The Catcher in the Rye* (New York: Signet Books, 1953), p. 14.

9. Einstein, *Ideas and Opinions,* op. cit., p. 39.

10. Melville, op. cit., p. 535.

11. Alfred North Whitehead, *Science and the Modern World* (New York: The Macmillan Co., 1925), p. 73.

12. *Selected Short Stories of Franz Kafka,* tr. Willa and Edwin Muir (New York: The Modern Library, 1952), p. 173.

13. Fyodor Dostoyevsky, *The Possessed,* tr. Constance Garnett (New York: Modern Library, 1936), pp. 629–630.

14. Bonhoeffer, *The Cost of Discipleship,* op. cit., p. 308.

15. Barth, *Deliverance to the Captives,* op. cit., p. 40.

16. *Martin Luther: Selections from His Writings,* op. cit., p. 195.

17. *The Collected Poetry of W. H. Auden* (New York: Random House, 1945), p. 412.

18. Barth, *Community, State and Church,* op. cit., p. 87.

19. Dostoyevsky, *The Brothers Karamazov,* op. cit., p. 385.

20. Bonhoeffer, *Ethics,* op. cit., pp. 52–53.

21. Tillich, *The New Being,* op. cit., pp. 13–14.

22. Barth, *Community, State and Church,* op. cit., p. 92.

23. Kierkegaard, *Training in Christianity,* op. cit., p. 71.

24. *Martin Luther: Selections from His Writings,* op. cit., p. 199.

25. Bonhoeffer, *The Cost of Discipleship,* op. cit., p. 198.

26. *Ibid.,* p. 243.

27. Einstein, *Ideas and Opinions,* op. cit., p. 8.

28. Kierkegaard, *The Last Years,* op. cit., p. 357.

29. Rudolf Bultmann, *Essays,* tr. J. C. G. Greig (New York: The Macmillan Co., 1955), pp. 3, 5.

30. Barth, *The Word of God and the Word of Man,* op. cit., p. 69.

31. *A Compend of Luther's Theology,* op. cit., p. 90.

32. *Karl Barth's Table Talk,* op. cit., p. 99.

33. Randall Stewart, *American Literature and Christian Doctrine* (Baton Rouge: Louisiana State University Press, 1958), p. 13.

34. E.g., Max Weber, *The Protestant Ethic and the Spirit of Capitalism,* and R. H. Tawney, *Religion and the Rise of Capitalism.*

35. Bonhoeffer, *The Cost of Discipleship,* op. cit., p. 295.

12. SLIP-UPS, DOGHOUSES, AND FREE PSYCHIATRIC HELP

1. Kafka, *The Great Wall of China,* op. cit., p. 290.

2. "Knowing You Are Not Alone," op. cit., p. 8.

3. Kierkegaard, *The Journals,* op. cit., p. 243.

4. Camus, *The Myth of Sisyphus*, op. cit., p. 42.

5. John Henry Newman, *Parochial and Plain Sermons* (Westminster, Md.: Christian Classics, Inc., 1966), Vol. VI, p. 139.

6. Barth, *Church Dogmatics*, Vol. II/2, op. cit., p. 92.

7. *Martin Luther: Selections from His Writings*, op. cit., p. 200.

8. John Bartlett, *Familiar Quotations*, Centennial Ed. (Boston: Little, Brown and Co., 1955), p. 560.

9. *Martin Luther: Selections from His Writings*, op. cit., p. 190.

10. Peter Nichols, *A Day in the Death of Joe Egg* (London: Faber and Faber, 1967; New York: Grove Press, 1967), pp. 40–41.

11. Kafka, *The Great Wall of China*, op. cit., p. 303.

12. Thurneysen, *Dostoevsky*, op. cit., p. 60.

13. Dostoyevsky, *The Brothers Karamazov*, op. cit., p. 290.

14. *Van Gogh: A Self-Portrait*, op. cit., p. 319.

15. Bonhoeffer, *Christ the Center*, op. cit., p. 75.

16. *Martin Luther: Selections from His Writings*, op. cit., p. 172.

17. "Happiness Is to Dance with Snoopy and Talk to His Creator," op. cit., p. 10.

18. "Meet the Creator of Peanuts," op. cit., p. 6.

19. Barth, *The Word of God and the Word of Man*, op. cit., pp. 60–61.

20. Kierkegaard, *The Journals*, op. cit., p. 384.

21. Kierkegaard, *The Last Years*, op. cit., p. 334.

22. Bonhoeffer, *Ethics*, op. cit., p. 89.

22a. "Happiness Is to Dance with Snoopy and Talk with His Creator," op. cit., p. 11.

23. Bonhoeffer, *The Cost of Discipleship*, op. cit., p. 58.

24. Kierkegaard, *The Journals*, op. cit., p. 363.

25. "A Visit with Charles Schulz," op. cit., p. 66.

26. Barth, *The Word of God and the Word of Man*, op. cit., p. 72.

27. Eric Newton and William Neil, *2000 Years of Christian Art* (New York: Harper & Row, 1966), p. 22.

28. Barth, *Against the Stream*, op. cit., p. 65.

29. Bonhoeffer, *Letters and Papers from Prison*, rev. ed., tr. Reginald Fuller (New York: The Macmillan Co., 1967), p. 206.

30. Tillich, *The New Being*, op. cit., p. 135.

31. *Julius Caesar*, I, ii.

32. Kierkegaard, *Purity of Heart*, op. cit., p. 51.

33. Barth, *Church Dogmatics*, Vol. II/2, op. cit., p. 180.

34. "The Enchiridion," ed. and tr. F. L. Battles, *The Library of Christian Classics*, Vol. XIV (Philadelphia: Westminster Press, 1953), p. 320.

35. Kierkegaard, *The Journals*, op. cit., p. 336.

36. Tillich, *The New Being*, op. cit., pp. 40–41.

37. Stockton and Santa Rosa, California *Monitor*, June 16, 1966, p. 5.

.in. Man's wholeness is restored by the King himself or not at all. Or, as Christ could put it, "With men this is impossible, but with God all things are possible" (Mt. 19:26). Zorba, of Kazantzakis' *Zorba the Greek*, in spinning an imaginative parable of the origin of man's sinfulness, at the same time gives us a good idea of why Dostoyevsky could say, "The best definition of man is the ungrateful biped":[10]

> "D'you know," he said, "how God made man? Do you know the first words this animal, man, addressed to God?"
>
> "No. How should I know? I wasn't there."
>
> "I was!" cried Zorba, his eyes sparkling.
>
> "Well, tell me."
>
> Half in ecstasy, half in mockery, he began inventing the fabulous story of the creation of man.
>
> "Well, listen boss! One morning God woke up feeling down in the dumps. 'What a devil of a God I am! I haven't even any men to burn incense to me and swear by my name to help pass the time away! I've had enough of living alone like an old screech-owl. Ftt!' He spat on his hands, pulled up his sleeves, put on his glasses, took a piece of earth, spat on it, made mud of it, kneaded it well and made it into a little man which he stuck in the sun.
>
> "Seven days later he pulled it out of the sun. It was baked. God looked at it and began to split his sides with laughter.
>
> "'Devil take me,' he says, 'it's a pig standing on its hind legs! That's not what I wanted at all! There's no mistake, I've made a mess of things!'
>
> "So he picks him up by the scruff of his neck and kicks his backside.
>
> "'Go on, clear off! All you've got to do now is to make other little pigs; the earth's yours! Now, jump to it. Left, right, left, right. . . . Quick march! . . .'
>
> "But, you see, it wasn't a pig at all! It was wearing a felt hat, a jacket thrown carelessly across its shoulders, well-creased trousers, and Turkish slippers with red tassels. And in its belt—it must have been the devil who'd given it that—was a pointed dagger with the words: 'I'll get you!' engraved on it.
>
> "It was man! God held out his hand for the other to kiss, but man twirled up his moustache and said:
>
> "'Come on, old 'un, out of the way! Let me pass!' "[11]

In the Garden of Eden story, God gives "Adam" (the Hebrew

deed the Savior of the world" (Jn. 4:42) assumes that the wo
indeed needs a savior. Or, as Luther could put it, "if we believe
that Christ redeemed men . . . we are forced to confess that all
of man was lost; otherwise, we make Christ either wholly super-
fluous, or else the redeemer of the least valuable part of man
only; which is blasphemy, and sacrilege."[7] And Luther was here
only echoing St. Paul, who could say: "We have reached the
conclusion that one man died for all and therefore all mankind
has died" (2 Cor. 5:14, NEB).

The New Testament, then, introduces a radically new solution
to the radical, or "root," predicament of man, the same old predicament also described at the outset of the Old Testament.
The Genesis story of Adam and Eve in the Garden of Eden is
a parable designed to tell us what the spiritual predicament of
mankind is and always has been, rather than how this situation
actually came into being. And what is our situation? Simply this:
all of us "originate" or come into life lacking the one thing we
really do need, as it finally turns out—faith in our creator. This
originally none of us has. None of us shows up in the world
with God built-in or even with a built-in devotion to God, but
only with a built-in devotion to the world itself. Man was
"created in the image of God," and hence it is still possible for
him to be re-created into a man of faith. But this image was
drastically shattered in man's "Fall" and subsequent expulsion
from the paradise of Eden. "What man has lost in the Fall is
his faith. . . . He has lost his relation as an obedient child of
God . . ." (Barth).[8] Faith, then, is unnatural to us; it is not
inherent in us to have this trust.

In addition to the Garden of Eden story, there can be countless parabolic ways of making the same point about man. In
one cartoon, Lucy is reading a well-known nursery rhyme:
"Humpty Dumpty sat on a wall,/ Humpty Dumpty had a great
fall./ All the King's horses and all the King's men/ Couldn't
put Humpty Dumpty together again." Concludes Lucy: "That's
the way it goes!" This is indeed the way it goes with man. Man
comes into life not a whole man but in "disunion with God,
with men, with things, and with himself" (Bonhoeffer).[9] All
the King's horses and all the King's men cannot put him together